"Broadcast is dying. Viewer choic
and Simpson, two industry insiders,
business trends that will be mainstream before you know it."
Patrick Barry, VP Connected TV, Yahoo!

"Greenfield and Simpson's new version of *IPTV and Internet Video* is a must-read for
anyone working in online video services to get an understanding of the subject from
Viewer, Advertiser & Publisher perspectives."
Keval Desai, Director, Product Management, Google TV

"Every television executive needs to have a strategy for dealing with the growth of
the Internet for media delivery. Greenfield and Simpson will not only help you get
your plan started, they will help you truly understand the seismic shifts that are
going on today."
Shelly Palmer, President, National Academy of Television Arts & Sciences, NY

"This book is an outstanding resource for convergence professionals who are racing
to further monetize the ever-expanding world of broadband internet media."
**Greg Douglass, Accenture Global Managing Director, Media and
Entertainment Practice**

"Taking your content to the Web? It's Broadcasting, but not as we know it. If you're
having trouble keeping up with the changing world, relax! In this book, Howard and
Wes take us through all we need to know, plainly and simply."
John Varney, former BBC CTO

"This is the right book at the right time. Greenfield and Simpson offer a clear and
compelling overview of the emerging IPTV space that is at once an accessible introduction to the basics and a guide to thinking through issues of implementation and
strategy."
**Paul Saffo, Silicon Valley Forecaster and Consulting Associate Professor of
Engineering, Stanford University**

"Like DBS before it, IPTV is coming, like it or not. It's proliferating globally, thus
broadcasters must understand the impact of this technology. *IPTV & Internet Video*
provides a comprehensive view to this critical, emerging industry development in a
single, well-conceived volume. Technology and media professionals beware: this
will change your business. Authors Greenfield and Simpson get it done here, from
micro to macro."
**Jimmy Schaeffler, Chairman, Senior Research Analyst,
The Carmel Group**

"From video content creators, aggregators, and distributors to IT professionals and
media executives, everyone can take something from this book. The straightforward yet detailed approach arms you with the information you need to make
highly informed technology and business decisions on IPTV and Internet video.
A valuable tool for making sense of this rapidly evolving industry."
Sandy Malcolm, Executive Producer, CNN.com

IPTV and Internet Video

IPTV and Internet Video:
Expanding the Reach of Television Broadcasting

2nd edition

Wes Simpson and Howard Greenfield

AMSTERDAM • BOSTON • HEIDELBERG • LONDON
NEW YORK • OXFORD • PARIS • SAN DIEGO
SAN FRANCISCO • SINGAPORE • SYDNEY • TOKYO

Focal Press is an imprint of Elsevier

Focal Press is an imprint of Elsevier
30 Corporate Drive, Suite 400, Burlington, MA 01803, USA
Linacre House, Jordan Hill, Oxford OX2 8DP, UK

Library of Congress Cataloging-in-Publication Data
Greenfield, Howard (Howard Alan)
  IPTV and Internet video : expanding the reach of television broadcasting / Howard
Greenfield and Wes Simpson. — 2nd ed.
    p. cm.
  Rev. ed. of IPTV and Internet video : new markets in television broadcasting / Wes Simpson &
Howard Greenfield. 2007.
  ISBN 978-0-240-81245-8
  1. Internet television. 2. Television broadcasting. 3. Digital video. I. Simpson,
Wes. II. Title.
  TK5105.887.S56 2009
  384.550285'4678—dc22

                                                                    2009020032

British Library Cataloguing in Publication Data
A catalogue record for this book is available from the British Library

ISBN: 978-0-240-81245-8

For information on all Focal Press publications
visit our website at www.elsevierdirect.com

Printed in the United States of America
09   10   11   5   4   3   2   1

Contents

Dedication

Thanks to my loving wife, Laurie, and our fantastic children, Taylor and Cameron, for giving me your support and gentle encouragement to embark on this fascinating journey.

—Wes Simpson

Dedicated to my parents, Sam and Rose Greenfield, for lifting me on their shoulders and keeping me in their great hearts.

—Howard Greenfield

Acknowledgments

The authors acknowledge the many industry experts and thought leaders whose open, generous dialogues—and vision—have provided insights that contribute so significantly to our work. This book benefits from their ideas and from the influence of their efforts upon tomorrow's technology, business, and culture.

We also salute a great many other kind individuals close to our work and dreams for their help and support in pulling it all together to accomplish this awesome task: Angelina Ward, Beth Millett, Joanne Tracy, Mark Weiss, Olaf Nielsen, Keith Galitz, Gene de Vore, Justin Radke, Pierre Costa, John Trimper, Paul Atwell, Graeme Packman, Cesar Bachelet, Jon Haass, Dan Gillmor, John Markoff, Françoise Groben, Barbara Bouchet, Ephraim Schwartz, Susan Daffron, Jean Anderson, Bill Veltrop, Steve Schneider, Clare Henjum, Keval Desai, Mark Valahovic, and Dan Oakey.

About the Authors

Wes Simpson is president and founder of Telecom Product Consulting, an independent consulting firm that focuses on helping companies develop and market video and telecommunications products. He is a frequent speaker and analyst for the video transport marketplace. In the past five years he has spoken at IBC, NAB, BroadcastAsia, SMPTE, VidTrans, and a number of other conferences. Wes is author of the well-received book "Video Over IP: A Practical User's Guide to Technologies and Applications," 2nd edition published by Focal Press in 2008.

Wes has more than 28 years experience in the design, development, and marketing of products for telecommunication applications. Before founding Telecom Product Consulting, he was COO of VBrick Systems, Inc., a manufacturer of MPEG video equipment. Earlier, at ADC Telecommunications, Wes was the director of product management for the DV6000, a market leading video transport system. He previously held a variety of marketing and engineering positions in the telecommunications industry. Wes was a founding member of the Video Services Forum and a member of its board of directors from 1997 to 2001. He holds a BSEE from Clarkson University and an MBA from the University of Rochester.

Howard Greenfield is president of Go Associates, a global consulting firm that helps companies bring technology to the marketplace. He is a digital media and business development strategist, as well as an accomplished columnist published around the world. Howard has held senior management and consulting positions with Sun Microsystems, Informix Software, British Telecom, and Apple, Inc. and was responsible for creating and leading Sun's first Media Lab.

For the last twenty-five years, Howard has been a successful technology developer, manager, educator, and writer. In addition to front-line collaborative development engagements with large organizations like Xerox PARC, Ericsson, and the American Film Institute, he has held leadership roles in numerous early stage companies. These include positions with start-ups in online video editing, streaming, content management, and ad insertion. Three of these were subsequently acquired by Ariba, IBM, and Microsoft.

Howard has presented and moderated at conferences throughout Silicon Valley, Europe, and Asia. He has served on government and cultural advisory boards that include the State of California, UK Trade & Invest, CNET, and others. His writing covers the convergence of the Internet, Broadcast, and Telecommunications industries. Howard holds a graduate degree in Interactive Technology from Stanford University.

The authors welcome any comments, questions, or insights from readers. Please feel free to send e-mail to Wes at wes.simpson@gmail.com and to Howard at howard@go-associates.com.

Introduction

The world is changing very fast. Big will not beat small anymore. It will be the fast beating the slow.

Rupert Murdoch

The traditional business model for broadcasters, which has worked reasonably well for the past few decades, is starting to break down. Increasingly, consumers are demanding (and starting to receive) their video content in ways that were impractical even a few years ago. Today, billions of videos are streamed every month and millions of subscribers have signed up for IPTV services around the world. Consider the following.

- **Television Has Moved to the Web.** Viewers around the world tuned in to watch the 2008 Olympics in record numbers using their PCs and other Internet-connected devices (There were 2.3 million views for Michael Phelps's second gold medal win.) In the United States, the number of stream views and clip downloads increased by a huge factor between 2002 and 2009. YouTube served 5.4 billion streams to 89 million unique viewers in March 2009 while Hulu delivered 348 million prime-time and movie programming streams.[1]
- **DVR Time Shifting and Ad-Zapping.** The use of digital video recorders in the United States has skyrocketed over the past few years, with a variety of stand-alone solutions as well as those integrated into set top boxes from satellite and cable television providers. In 2008, 20 million DVRs were expected to be added to homes around the world. The 56 million DVR homes total that year are forecast to grow to over 208 million by 2013.[2] Broadcast advertisers have grown increasingly upset by the practice of commercial skipping and the loss of their ability to control the timing when viewers watch ads for specific events, such as movie openings or store sales.
- **Media Has Gone Mobile.** With more than a billion mobile phones sold each year, they are becoming ever more video capable. So-called smart phones will, in fact, comprise more than half the mobile phones sold in the next few years. The iPhone 3G is in 70 countries, outselling the Blackberry Q3 2008 with 200 million mobile App Store application purchases/downloads through the same period. Also, new standards for mobile file and stream delivery are often based on IP technology, indicating an increase in market penetration in coming years.

[1]Nielsen Online, April 2009.
[2]Informa Telecoms and Media, http://www.storagenewsletter.com/news/consumer/informa-telecoms-media-dvr-pvr-sales

- **Everyone Wants to Be a Producer.** Meanwhile, a wide range of user-generated video content continues to drive viewers to sites like youtube.com, which generated more than 176 million stream views per day in March 2009. Increasingly, various audiences are perfectly happy to watch certain types of video content on normal PC displays.
- **Podcasting Is Official.** When Adam Carolla left mainstream radio in early 2009 for a podcast-only presence, his podcast was downloaded over 1 million times in the first week it was available, which greatly exceeded original expectations.[3] By 2013 there is expected to be a podcast audience of nearly 38 million in the United States alone.[4]
- **You Are Now Free to Placeshift.** Devices from Sling Media, Apple, Vudu, Roku, and many others are now allowing consumers to move content among several different viewing devices, such as PCs, home television sets, and portable media players.

What had been only whisperings about the promise of new digital media networks for the last 25 years has become an audible roar and a commercial revolution is building. How will traditional broadcasters compete with the surge of disruptive technology ahead? One way is by understanding and harnessing some of the key technologies that support these competitive video outlets. Both IPTV and Internet video depend on IP technology, something not completely foreign to the broadcasting industry.

Television broadcasters have long been intensive IP technology users. A walk around any modern video production facility will reveal all types of devices that use IP technology, from digital editing stations to file servers to playout control systems. It is also highly unusual nowadays to find a broadcast executive who doesn't use some type of IP-enabled device, such as a laptop computer, portable e-mail device, or voice over IP telephone.

However, until recently, it has not been feasible to deliver broadcast-quality video to consumers over IP networks. Today, with the growth of high-speed networks and the adoption of IP technology by carriers around the world, video delivery over IP networks is not only feasible, it is becoming the only way to reach some categories of viewers. The key for both established and aspiring video content distributors will be to understand how IP technology will affect the ways viewers watch and pay for video content.

This book explores both the technologies of video delivery and the business aspects, as IP increasingly permeates through production, delivery, and business practices. IP technology creates a wide array of new ways to deliver content to consumers, particularly when compared to traditional linear broadcasting supported by advertising. From a business perspective, IP video opens up many avenues for generating revenue, including customer payments in many forms and opportunities for sponsorships and advertising. The ease of implementing new technologies on an IP platform means that different business models can be supported. It's a combined creative challenge and window of opportunity.

---

[3]http://www.podcastingnews.com/2009/03/01/adam-carolla-podcast-makes-radio-irrelevant
[4]http://www.ovrdrv.com/stats/2009/03/podcasting-goes-mainstream.asp

Who Should Read This Book

This book is focused on providing readers a solid understanding of the technologies and business issues surrounding IPTV and Internet video. Care is taken to present major concepts clearly while staying above the specific details of individual implementations. Case studies are used to provide real-world examples of this technology being used to deliver actual services to paying customers.

Executives, managers, and technologists will benefit from the information in this book. Executives will find a guide to many different technology and business options that can be used to attain strategic goals for many kinds of organizations, ranging from large established media and telecommunications providers to small start-ups.

Managers will find a variety of technologies and business models that can be used to achieve their organizations' strategic video delivery business goals. Technologists will find overviews of a number of different tools and techniques that can be used to construct video delivery systems, allowing them to quickly identify areas for further research and paths to implementation.

Many different industry segments are being substantially affected by the current wave of IPTV and Internet video delivery systems.

- Existing broadcasters will be introduced to a variety of techniques that can be used to deliver content and new ways to enhance viewer experiences.
- Telecommunications network operators will discover a range of services and delivery models that will enable their companies to benefit from existing plant and infrastructure investments, as well as providing a guide to new possibilities for network migration.
- Media providers and content owners will see a range of choices that can be used to deliver content to viewers in both local markets and around the globe and will see different business models for maximizing the value of their assets.
- IT architects and software developers will get a high-level view of ways that applications, middleware, and server systems are being integrated into media delivery, creating new, hybrid network operations.
- Investors will gain a deeper understanding of the technologies and business practices that impact this wildly diverse marketplace and generate new investment models. The increased ability to identify specific sectors that warrant their support will drive clearer investment decisions.

Features of This Book

This book has been designed to make it easy for readers to find a wide variety of information quickly and efficiently. The following three features complement the main focus of each chapter to provide even more insight for decision makers.

The Corner Office View

Placed near the beginning of each chapter is a brief "Corner Office View" section. Each of these sidebars offers direct quotations from influential industry executives pioneering the future who offer meaningful perspective on the industry and its current direction.

Reality Checks

Because this book is aimed at decision makers who need to understand both the benefits and the drawbacks of this new technology, we have added a section at the end of each chapter to serve as a Reality Check. Sometimes, this section is devoted to application studies or market data that pertain to the subject of the chapter. Other times it is focused on issues or concerns that may serve to limit the widespread deployment of a technology. Either way, we hope to highlight issues that will help readers get a better understanding of the wild and wonderful world of IP video.

Glossary

Understanding the jargon used in this industry is essential to gaining a good appreciation of the important issues facing executives. This book includes an extended glossary, with more than 180 technical terms defined in crisp, clear language.

Chapter Topics (Organization of This Book)

Twelve chapters cover key IPTV and Internet video technical deployment and business monetization topics. Each chapter is designed to address an important issue for broadcasters and service providers. Readers are encouraged to choose whatever chapters interest them in any order, with the caveat that some of the more fundamental topics are described in the early chapters. In some cases, the latter chapters will refer to information presented in early chapters.

Chapter 1: What Is Internet Protocol, and Why Use It for Video?

This chapter analyzes the basic motivations for using IP networks to deliver video services. We also take a look at the market trends driving the rapid growth in this market.

Chapter 2: Types of IP Video

This chapter focuses on four types of video service that are commonly delivered over IP networks: IPTV (Internet Protocol Television), IPVoD (Internet Protocol Video on Demand), Internet TV (Internet Television), and Internet video. Each category is explained, and various system attributes are compared across the various delivery methods.

Chapter 3: Business Models

Many different business models are being tried for both IPTV and Internet video. We cover equipment costs, programming costs, and viewer payment methods. The chapter concludes with an in-depth look at a real IPTV system that met its financial goals ahead of plan.

Chapter 4: Network Overviews

This chapter covers the basic architecture of both IPTV and Internet video systems. All of the key elements of both types of systems are described, including hardware and software functions.

Chapter 5: IP—The Internet Protocol

IP is essential for IPTV and Internet video. We provide a good introduction to IP and some popular types of devices that support it. Multicasting, a key concept for IPTV, is also explained.

Chapter 6: Video Compression

Video compression is a requirement for essentially all IPTV and Internet video systems. We begin with a discussion of the basics and then describe the most popular compression systems—the MPEG family, Microsoft Windows Media, and others.

Chapter 7: Maintaining Video Quality and Security

This chapter focuses on video quality and security. Video and network impairments are described, along with the techniques system designers have used to minimize or compensate for those errors. Several techniques for both conditional access and digital rights management are described.

Chapter 8: Sizing up Servers

Servers are widely used for IPTV and Internet video systems. Several technologies are described, including a focus on servers used for VOD, advertising, and live streaming, which are all key for IPTV and Internet video systems.

Chapter 9: The Importance of Bandwidth

Many different services compete for a limited amount of IP bandwidth. We examine the ecosystem of DSL technology and home networks and give an example of network bandwidth calculation.

Chapter 10: Set-Top Boxes

The set top box is a crucial component of any IPTV network. It must receive video packets, decompress them, and display images in real time. The STB and middleware systems must also handle all of the user interaction for an IPTV system.

Chapter 11: Internet Video Technologies

A variety of different technologies can be used for Internet video services, including true streaming, download, and progressive download and play. We look at each of these technologies and the associated protocols and media players.

Chapter 12: The Future of IP Video

This chapter looks at a range of possible futures for both IPTV and Internet video. Business drivers, advanced technology, and mobile media devices are all discussed. We wrap up with a look through the eyes of business leaders, soothsayers, and technical wizards as they try to discern the future from a variety of perspectives.

Summary

Throughout this book, you will find discussions about the future and about some of the forces reshaping video as a medium. Including this perspective has been intentional. IP has nearly unlimited creative potential for reinventing the way common tasks are accomplished and how entire global architectures are implemented. Without a constantly improving Internet functionality, this book could never have been written.

It's clear that the future is going to be different from the broadcast and communications environment of today. It is hoped that the reader will enjoy the insights and benefit from the expertise we've strived to provide. Moreover, we trust this book will provide a key to understanding the vast range of opportunities that will involve us all as technology and business developers and as an audience in a new world of media.

Foreword

In 1999, my objective at Broadcast.com was to turn the Internet into a medium that would perform much like DirecTV of the Web. We were on a mission to reinvent broadcast communications.

Today, a decade later looking ahead to 2010 and beyond, the industry mission still seems to be the same: finish the bridge between on-air and online programming. I've always believed that the evolution of video would create opportunity, but the playing field has changed and the stakes have gone way up. Broadcast-quality SD and HD video, combined with the reach of the Internet, are beginning to offer remarkable new interactivity, personalization, and on-demand access for the viewer.

As an industry, we've worked part way through the basic challenges of IP networks, bandwidth, compression, three-screen access, and a series of devices from set top box, PC, and smart phone to new business, ad, and service models. What we're going to see in the next phase is break-away performance in new features, service offerings, and resulting revenues.

In this book, Greenfield and Simpson explore both the technologies of IP video delivery and the business impacts of these new developments. IP video presents a wide range of new ways to deliver content to consumers. From a business perspective, it opens up many avenues for generating ROI, including customer payments in many forms, and opportunities for sponsorships and advertising. The ease of implementing new technologies on an IP platform will spawn a combined creative challenge and window of opportunity.

We are witnessing breathtaking change in the way that video is delivered. A medium that once primarily provided one-size-fits-all entertainment for the masses has become a versatile data type easily integrated over your set top box or browser for news, sports, and entertainment, as well as within-text documents, email, social networking, commercial transactions, and IT enterprise applications. But any potential delivery system needs to make scale and make good business sense to content providers if it is to monetize to its full potential.

The seismic shift in the market is driving the search for clear, concise information that can be used to make better-informed decisions. This market transformation and new direction is exactly where *IPTV and Internet Video* focuses its attention for the reader. As one chapter header begins: "In five years," says Bill Gates, "people will laugh at the TV we've had up to now." But how will traditional broadcasters compete with the surge of disruptive technology ahead? Changes that pose an upheaval for many content producers, advertisers, and business managers will provide a once-in-a-lifetime opportunity for others to gain advantage and benefits in the media world on the horizon.

What will make the new TV great are more viewer choices and more content available wherever the viewers are—at home or away, fixed or mobile, local or remote. More content diversity, affordable, and often free to the viewer will be supported by new ways to find content and new social aspects of watching content. We are now just scratching the surface. *IPTV and Internet Video* is a thorough executive briefing that provides solid descriptions of the key technologies from a manufacturer-independent view. The authors, Howard Greenfield and Wes Simpson, interpret the state of the play with the help of front-line industry leaders delivering valuable insights and trend analyses.

The bottom line is consumers want the biggest selection of TV networks and on-demand content that we can get. We watch it alone. We watch it with friends. We watch it on our schedule from our DVR, our IPTV program guide, or our PC. We watch it when scheduled so we can talk about it with our friends while we watch or after we watch. Why? Because we know they are watching too. We want to watch while we are on the couch and surf the entire universe of hundreds of channels offering thousands of hours of programming.

TV is enmeshed in our lives. As John Varney, former BBC CTO, says in this book: "We are starting to see the first signs of a coming together of social networks, user creation and video distribution. If this is sustained, then the democratizing effects will make this the most fascinating phase in broadcasting history."

Being chief Maverick cheerleader is exciting and fulfilling. But my roots in today's TV revolution have provided a perspective on a new era of interactive visual communication. The momentum is reshaping our lives and deeply affecting global business sectors. Broadcasting, entertainment, Internet, and telecommunications will never be the same as video becomes ubiquitous.

As we move ahead into a new decade, the time has never been better to explore the forces at work in the growth of this new industry. The best is yet to come, and this is the message provided and backed up by the authors of *IPTV and Internet Video*. We've come a long way since 1999, and video delivery innovation is only continuing to accelerate. The adventure ahead will help us all learn and grow—and hopefully, prosper—as our imagination is challenged.

Mark Cuban
Founder Broadcast.com,
HDNet, owner Dallas Mavericks

1 What Is Internet Protocol, and Why Use It for Video?

Nothing is really real unless it happens on television.
Daniel J. Boorstin, American social historian and educator

Before we try to define *Internet Protocol* (IP) and why it is a good solution for video, it's appropriate to consider what may be obvious—that video transport over IP networks is not only here today, but is poised to further dominate video service delivery for many years to come. As this occurs, new media communications services that can only be imagined will continue to arise along with it. We are at the dawn of what may be the most fascinating phase in broadcasting history.

We will discuss the reasons more in this chapter, and the spread of IP will form a subtext throughout the rest of this book. However, there is little doubt that a large and vigorous market continues to develop though a confluence of improved compression, faster data links, more sophisticated software, and evolving viewer habits. So, let's explore these trends then see how they impact network, technology, and business decisions today. Later, in the final chapter, we'll look at where these trends are likely to lead us in the decades ahead.

Digital video is a precisely timed, continuous stream of constant bit rate information, which commonly works on networks where each signal is carried over a channel that is purpose-built for video. In contrast, IP networks carry many different kinds of data from a huge variety of sources on a common channel, including e-mail, Web pages, instant messaging, *voice over IP* (VoIP), and many other types of data. With all of these data flowing together, the Internet is, at best, a loosely timed collection of information that is broken up into discrete packets. Clearly, IP and video don't make an ideal marriage of technologies.

Despite this fundamental incompatibility, the market for IPTV and Internet video is exploding. Why? Well, the answer to that question boils down to five basic arguments.

- Because broadband IP networks reach so many households in developed countries, video service providers can use these networks to deliver video services without having to build their own networks.
- IP can simplify the task of launching new video services, such as interactive programming, *video on demand* (VOD), and targeted, viewer-specific advertising.
- The cost of IP networking continues to decline due to the massive volume of equipment produced each year and the existence of worldwide standards.
- IP networks can be found in every country in the world, and the number of users with high-speed Internet connections continues to grow at a rapid pace.

- IP is a perfect technology for many other applications, including data transactions (such as e-mail or banking), local area networking, file sharing, Web surfing, and many others.

The Corner Office View

"IPTV is a huge growth initiative. It's huge for us, it's huge for our partners. Count the number of TVs, and you don't have to get a lot of money per TV per year to start feeling kind of excited about the size of the opportunity."
— *Steve Ballmer, CEO, Microsoft*[1]

This chapter begins with a brief summary of the market trends for IPTV and Internet video. It then discusses in greater depth the five forces mentioned earlier that are driving the migration of video into IP, followed by a look at some issues that need to be addressed by any system or organization trying to send video over an IP network. The chapter concludes with a case study of a successful IPTV network installation.

The Internet Protocol

Internet Protocol provides a mechanism for directing packet flows between devices connected on a network. IP is a common protocol used throughout the Internet and any of the millions of other networks that use IP. Without IP, chaos would reign because there would be no way for one device to send data specifically to another.

At its heart, IP is a standard method for formatting and addressing data packets in a large, multifunction network such as the Internet. A packet is a unit of information (a collection of bytes) in a well-defined format that can be sent across an IP network. Typically, a message such as e-mail or a video signal will be broken up into multiple IP packets. IP can be used on many different network technologies, such as Ethernet LANs, long-haul fiber optic and telephony networks, and wireless Wi-Fi links.

A number of different video services operate on IP networks. Applications range all the way from low-resolution, low frame rate applications such as Web cams to high-definition (HD) television and medical images. IP technology is incredibly widespread, and a huge variety of video technologies can use IP networks.

The Market for IP Video

Because so many different video applications can be implemented over IP networks, it can be hard to quantify them, and any attempt to do so will be outdated quickly. Nevertheless, a few facts and figures may be interesting:

---

[1]IPTV International, Volume 2, Issue 2.

- AT&T originally rolled out its U-verse[SM] IPTV offering in 2004 under the code name Project Lightspeed with the intention of making it available to 19 million homes in the company's service area by the end of 2008.[2] After planning an investment of $4.6 billion to make this a reality, they reached a million customers by the beginning of 2009.
- In November 2008, China's IPTV systems reached a million viewers. China Telecom is investing 100 million yuan per year to implement the IPTV network and will set up a national IPTV business operating center to develop and innovate new products and content offerings. Of the 1 million Chinese IPTV customers, 700,000 are in Shanghai, where China Telecom plans to focus their development efforts before bringing them to other parts of the country.[3]
- By September 2006, France Telecom already had 421,000 ADSL Digital Television (IPTV) subscribers (an increase of 38% over the 306,000 IPTV subscribers reported June 30, 2006).[4] By the end of 2008, this number had increased dramatically to 1,899,000. Figure 1.1 shows the subscriber growth over four years, with a cumulative annual growth rate of 120%.
- In October, 2006, Google agreed to acquire YouTube, a leading Web site that allows users to view and upload original videos, for $1.65 billion. At the time, YouTube was delivering more than 100 million video views every day and receiving 65,000 video uploads daily.[5] By 2008, in September alone, 12.6 billion online videos were

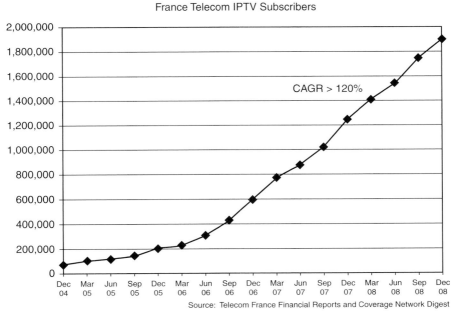

Figure 1.1 *France Telecom's IPTV subscriber growth, 2004–2008.*

[2]AT&T Corporate press release, May 8, 2006.
[3]http://www.tmcnet.com/usubmit/2008/12/25/3877895.htm
[4]France Telecom press releases, July 27 and October 26, 2006.
[5]Google/YouTube joint press release, October 9, 2006.

streamed over U.S. broadband connections. Hulu.com, an Internet video portal developed and supported by NBC and Fox and launched in 2007, hosted more than 145 million of those views.

- The 2008 Beijing Olympics were a global online video success story. NBC offered 2200 live hours to Internet users with 75.5 million streams served, doubling the streams offered and unique users for the 2004 Athens and 2006 Torino games combined. The 1.24 billion page views for the Beijing games were also up over 100% from the 561.1 million views for Athens and Torino combined.[6]
- Market research firm MRG predicts that the number of global IPTV subscribers will grow from 24.4 million in 2008 to 92.8 million by 2012 (with service revenue totaling over $37 billion by that time).[7] See the Reality Check section at the end of this chapter for more detailed IPTV and broadband subscriber growth trends.

The number of applications for video transport over IP networks is large and constantly growing. This book focuses on IPTV and Internet video, which are defined in detail in Chapter 2. However, a number of other applications that use video transport over IP networks deserve to be mentioned.

- Videoconferencing has moved out of the realm of dedicated rooms with specialized telecom data circuits into the world of desktop PCs interfacing with IP networks. New initiatives by HP, Cisco, and others are delivering high-performance *telepresence* functionality, giving users the illusion of being in the same room, whereas systems only a few years ago were characterized by low bit-rate deployments suitable for low-resolution "talking head" video but not much else.
- Web cams have become widespread, particularly for low-cost, real-time communication. Applications include everything from security surveillance and business teleconferencing, to weather watching to social networking. These systems previously ran at low frame rates (10 or fewer frames per second) but now have very impressive 30 frames per second specifications that make Internet communications very effective.
- Most video surveillance devices intended for use in security applications have migrated to IP technology. There are a number of reasons for this transition, but one of the most compelling is the ability to use existing or easy-to-install Ethernet data cabling in place of coaxial video cables. In these networks, IP protocols and Ethernet cabling are simply used as means to provide point-to-point connectivity between cameras, video recorders, and displays.
- In the world of professional video production, IP networks are used for a variety of purposes (as is the case in many other modern businesses). IP networks are used to provide connections between video editing workstations and file servers in a production studio. IP networks are used to transmit high-quality video files and live feeds from remote venues back to production facilities. They are also used to move video files containing raw footage, finished programming, and advertisements to and from virtually every studio, posthouse, and broadcaster in business today. Limelight Networks alone, for example, store over 4 petabytes of content on their network.

---

[6]http://www.nytimes.com/2008/08/25/sports/olympics/25online.html?bl&ex=1219896000&en
=262a7f83cc5b8c72&ei=5087
[7]IPTV Global Forecast—2008 to 2012, Bi-Annual Global IPTV Forecast, April 2008. Published by Multimedia Research Group, Inc., www.mrgco.com6. A list of these ports was located at www.iana .org/assignments/port-numbers in August 2006.

Not all of the aforementioned applications relate directly to the broadband focus of this book, but all of them contribute to a multibillion-dollar market momentum with IP as the video network protocol of choice.

Arguments in Favor of IP Video

There are a number of reasons companies and individuals decide to transport video signals over IP networks. Three of the most popular revolve around the flexibility of IP networks, their low cost, and the incredible coverage that IP networks provide within an organization and around the world. Let's examine each of these arguments in more detail.

Internet Protocol Network Flexibility

The number of applications of IP networks is truly staggering. One way to estimate this is to look at the number of applications that have been assigned IP port numbers managed by the Internet Assigned Numbers Authority (IANA). Among the several thousand registered ports are port 80 for the HyperText Transfer Protocol (http), port 25 for the Simple Mail Transfer Protocol (smtp), and port 110 for the Post Office Protocol–Version 3 (pop3), which are used for e-mail.

Counting the number of IP ports is just measuring the tip of the iceberg of IP applications, as many other programs use the protocols that have these port assignments. For example, there are literally dozens of e-mail programs that work on a variety of operating systems (Windows, Mac-OS, Linux, etc.), which all communicate by means of the ports defined for smtp and pop3.

Many different devices support IP. In addition to desktop and laptop PCs, servers and mainframes with a variety of different software operating systems can be configured to use IP. In addition, many other devices in the video world have Ethernet ports to enable all sorts of functions, ranging from simple status monitoring and control all the way up to HD video transport.

Internet Protocol is also very flexible because it is not tied to a specific physical communication technology. IP links have been successfully established over a wide variety of different physical links. One very popular technology for IP transport is Ethernet, which is the dominant network technology in local area networks. Many other technologies can support IP, including wireless links (such as Wi-Fi) and SONET and ATM telecom links. IP will even work across connections where several network technologies are combined, such as a wireless home access link that connects to a cable TV system offering cable modem services, which in turn sends customer data to the Internet by means of a fiber optic backbone.

For broadcasters, this flexibility is important, but it is also a challenge. It is important because it gives broadcasters a choice among a large number of technologies and business models that can be used to deliver content in new formats. It is a challenge because it is impossible to choose a single solution for delivering video over IP networks that will suit all potential viewers.

Internet Protocol Cost Advantages

Economics is where things start to get interesting, as IP technology has a very low hardware cost. Virtually all new PCs and laptops come equipped with Ethernet ports. A quick scan of the Web shows that Gigabit Ethernet interface cards (which operate at 1000 Mbps) can be purchased for as little as $15. Other infrastructure, such as Ethernet switches, can be purchased for as little as $10 per port. For other networking technologies, such as ATM, SONET, or even SDI video routers, costs are typically 5 to 20 times more expensive.

Basic IP software is also very inexpensive or often free. All major computer operating systems include built-in IP software "stacks" that support many different IP services without added cost to the user. This is important not only in commercial applications, but also for home users who might want to access Internet video services while retrieving their e-mail. This is not to say that all IP video software is inexpensive—far from it. The software necessary to put together a functioning IPTV delivery platform that is scalable to hundreds of video channels and thousands of viewers can easily cost millions of dollars.

The low costs of IP networks are of great benefit to broadcasters for two reasons. First, low cost means that much of the network infrastructure needed to connect a video source to a viewer has already been purchased and installed by potential viewers; that which hasn't can be purchased affordably by the broadcaster. Second, as viewer expectations for quality and availability of content grow, putting upward pressure on network bandwidths, broadcasters can safely assume that the IP networks will continue to expand in capacity (which has proven to be a safe assumption for every year over the past three decades).

Internet Protocol Ubiquity

Internet Protocol networks are truly pervasive in the postmillennial world. Both Antarctica and Greenland have more than 7500 Internet hosts each; the United States has 315 million.[8] Private IP networks exist in hundreds of millions of homes and businesses around the world—IP is the default technology today when people want to connect two computers together in order to share a printer or an Internet connection. For the traveler, wireless Internet connectivity is increasingly available in hotels, airports, coffee shops, and via *3G* mobile phone data networks in towns and cities around the globe.

High-speed data access lines are continuing to be installed at a rapid rate in most developed countries. In the United States, data collected by the Federal Communications Commission's Wireline Competition Bureau show that by the end of

---

[8]http://www.nationmaster.com/graph/int_hos-internet-hosts

U.S. Residential High Speed Lines

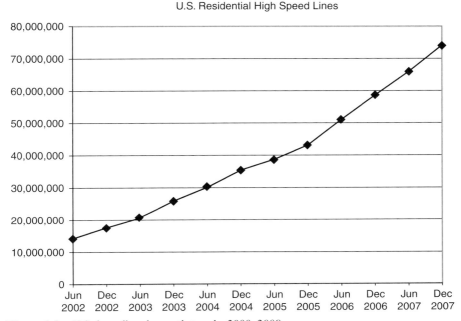

Figure 1.2   *U.S. broadband growth trends, 2000–2008.*
Source: Data provided for the Broadband Forum by Point Topic.

2007, 74 million households had high-speed lines, which is an increase of more than 50% from the end of 2005. The United States is adding nearly 1 million broadband subscribers per month, and subscribers are expected to grow worldwide from 452 million in 2008 to 876 million by 2012.[9] Figure 1.2 shows the trend in the United States for the past five years.

For broadcasters, the global reach of the Internet is both good and bad. It's good in the sense that anyone in the world with a suitable network connection is part of the potential audience for the broadcaster. (For example, it is perfectly possible to see the local weather radar for Connecticut from a hotel room in Tokyo.) It's bad in the sense that the role of the local broadcaster can be fiscally undermined by the disintermediation capability of the Internet. (Viewers in a locality have no need to watch a Hollywood movie by way of their local broadcaster's Web site when they can just as easily get the content directly from the studio's film library.)

Most television studios also now offer their most popular programs on their own and syndicated Web sites such as Hulu, Veoh, and the Roku platform used by both Netflix and Amazon. The BBC iPlayer is another example of this phenomenon. If you miss the original broadcast, you can always watch it later. Appointment-based viewing is dead. Moreover, many content providers are inventing new ways

[9]In-Stat, http://www.instat.com/press.asp?Sku=IN0804057MBS&ID=2398, October 16, 2008.

to monetize their media assets with various online advertising formats, which is discussed later.

For many, the easiest way to get into a competitive U.S. or global market is online. "The broadcast era is over, content is not king anymore ... distribution is king," says MMAX Enterprises sports channel executive Chuck Vaughn. "Maybe that's a temporary situation," says Vaughn, "but the fragmentation has shifted everything on its head which is why everyone in Hollywood is nervous."

Is Roku Really IPTV?

Purists formally consider IPTV a fully managed broadband network service delivered through a set-top box. By that definition, the Roku box is not officially IPTV, but after you've used one for a month, it definitely provides a great TV experience. "My understanding of IPTV," says Roku VP of Consumer Products Timothy Twerdahl, "is that they are managed and therefore limited to what they can monetize. But our box is about an open platform and getting whatever you want to."

"We don't believe in disk drives," Twerdahl told me this month. "They fail, they're noisy, and people don't want them in their living room." Weighing less than a pound, the Roku supports composite, S-Video, component, and HDMI, as well as standard and high-definition modes at 16:9 720p and 480p (anamorphic). Providers digitize four different bit rates for each piece of content and Roku selects which to deliver based on the customer's broadband speed rate, ensuring no delays from rebuffering. A 1 Mbps Internet connection is all that's needed to watch over the Roku, which looked to us the same as if it were a regular broadcast being delivered over the television. The requirement for HD, however, is a minimum of 4 Mbps.[10]

Arguments against IP Video

While there are powerful forces driving the use of IP networks for video transport, it is important to understand some of the potential drawbacks of this new technology. The first argument is primarily economic and revolves around the history of many things on the Internet being free of charge. The second is technical and centers on the difficulty of taking smooth, constant bit rate video signals and adapting them for transmission over IP networks. The third argument focuses on the dilemma of combining video signals that have very high demands for network resources on links that must carry other traffic and determining which uses will get priority. Let's look at each one of these in more detail.

---

[10]"Meet the Roku," Howard Greenfield, IPTVi magazine, April 2009.

The Difficulty of Competing with Free

In some ways, the Internet is still dealing with some bad habits that were established in the early days, when content was available for free to anyone who was able to connect. This spirit lives on today in a variety of ways, particularly in the widespread use of illegal file sharing for valuable music and video content.

Any broadcaster hoping to sell content over the Internet needs to be aware of these traditions and expectations and develop a policy to deal with them. One popular method is to deliver the content for free, but to include advertising on the Web site or inserted into the content itself. Another method is to charge fees on a subscription or pay-per-view basis. Both of these options are discussed more in Chapter 3.

Obtaining legal access to content can also be a challenge. Many content owners have separate licensing terms for different forms of distribution. For example, a movie studio will have different terms and different licensees for each type of release: theatrical, pay-per-view, subscription television, DVD, commercial television, and others. Creating a functional team inside a network-based carrier's organization to obtain these licenses can be an expensive and time-consuming process.

The difficulty of competing with free is no better represented than in the demise of recording industry revenues. One anecdote about the early days of Napster conveys this well.[11] The conversation was with a father who had just surprised his teenage daughter with three music CDs that, through close family research, he knew she would love to have. Her response on receiving the gift was, "Dad! You bought these for me? Why didn't you tell me? We could have just downloaded them off the Internet!"

The power of free seems to have prevailed over the rush to litigate when content stakeholders such as RIAA and Viacom sought and sometimes won high-profile convictions against illegal file sharing. Theft of services has not become less of an issue, but inevitably some content will be stolen by some users some of the time. Also, as technology advances, the skills of encryption crackers will increase, forcing improvements to be made to encryption algorithms that modern *digital rights management* (DRM) is based on. It is incumbent upon content owners to ensure that all of their valuable content is protected with the latest available DRM technology.

Accommodating Viewing Preferences

Introducing new viewing habits into large populations of viewers can be difficult and time-consuming. Basic IPTV services closely mirror broadcast television and cable TV, but so do viewer expectations about these services. Viewers will expect (and rightly so) that these basic services on IPTV offer a similar level of video quality and system performance to pre-existing forms of delivery. More advanced services, such as video-on-demand and interactive programming, may require viewers to develop new patterns.

---

[11]From www.go-associates.com/files/DigitalPiracy.pdf

These habits aren't impossible to change. For example, viewers have learned new habits and embraced digital video recorders where the 56 million DVRs installed globally are expected to nearly quadruple to 208 million by 2013.[12] However, introducing new interactive services can be a long and expensive learning curve. Plus, IP system operators must be conscious about competitors who create services that can work over their existing broadcast and cable TV facilities. New service providers need to take these factors into account, particularly when creating business plans for exciting new services that may be highly profitable but also require a change in viewing habits. In other words, for IPTV to succeed, many feel that "it either has to be a perfect but less expensive TV option to what people have now," as Broadcasting & Cable Online says, to offer the same variety of programming delivered by Comcast or DirecTV. It must either be offered "for less or it has to be a perfect complement to what people have now. It can't just offer an alternative way of delivering content that people already have."[13]

Network Jitters

Whenever continuous signals such as video are sliced into packets for transport over an IP network, difficulties can arise. These mainly stem from the need for the packets to arrive in a timely manner, and in the same order they were sent. When this doesn't happen, it places a tremendous burden on the receiving device to realign the packets properly, while at the same time doing all of the processing necessary to produce the decoded video output. Some of these variations can be accommodated through the use of memory buffers in the receiving device, but these add a delay to the end-to-end video connection and lengthen the time required to change channels.

Broadcasters need to realize that these potential impairments exist and that there are methods for dealing with problems as they occur. Some of these solutions (such as increasing network bandwidth or replacing network routers) may not only be expensive but also impractical for networks that rely on the Internet.

A Matter of Priority

One of the great benefits of IP networks is the number of different applications that are supported. However, one of the burdens this flexibility places on network administrators is the need to prioritize the applications. Without a priority system, time-critical packets can run into delays caused by the congestion of packets from many different flows, which can happen surprisingly often on IP networks.

Unfortunately, the existing mechanisms for handling priority packets on private networks are limited at best. These schemes are also useless on the public Internet, as priority routing is not implemented there. To understand why, consider the dilemma of deciding which packets in the public Internet should receive priority.

---

[12]Informa Telecoms & Media Global DVR Forecasts report, 10/08, http://www.storagenewsletter.com/news/consumer/informa-telecoms-media-dvr-pvr-sales

[13]*Broadcasting & Cable,* This link seems to not work though it appears the same as the one that *does* work which is: http://www.broadcastingcable.com/blog/Beyond_the_Box/11469-one_zillion_reasons_why_I_m_skeptical_about_Zillion_TV.php March 4, 2009.

Each user will naturally consider their packets to be more important than those of other users. Without some type of global prioritizing or pricing scheme for different classes of packet services, efforts to add priority filtering to the Internet will be impossible.

Inside private networks, priority systems can be used, but difficulties still exist. Again, the problem arises from determining which types of signals will get priority. The argument for giving video signals priority over other signals is clear, as video signals do not perform well if their packets are delayed or dropped. However, video signals are one of the largest users of bandwidth on most networks and can take up a significant portion of the available capacity. Hence, the dilemma about choosing suitable priority levels can occur on almost any type of IP network.

Reality Check

For this chapter's Reality Checks, we first explore an impressively large forecast that has been published for this market. While the amount of growth projected in this forecast is quite extensive it certainly isn't the highest growth projection that we have seen. In the second Reality Check, we take a look at the IPTV market in France, which must be called a success by any measure.

Market Forecast

By any standard, the market for IPTV services has grown rapidly for the past few years, and industry observers generally expect that trend to continue. As can be clearly seen on the following charts, the pace of IPTV subscriber growth continues to accelerate. It is projected that there will be 93 million IPTV subscribers worldwide by 2011 and revenues will approach $14B by 2012. Growth in 2008 broadband subscribers for the top 10 countries (Figure 1.3) and IPTV subscribers (Figure 1.4) reflect this forecast.[14]

IPTV in France

At industry conferences everywhere, IPTV is a hot topic, and for good reason: service providers are rapidly rolling out IPTV services to consumers all over the planet. Not every venture produces a winner, but there have been a number of successful deployments, and more are on the way.[15]

---

[14]http://www.tvover.net/2009/03/25/IPTV+Growth+Doubles+In+North+America+In+2008.aspx

[15]From a presentation entitled "IPTV—Overview and Keys to Success," September 10, 2006, at IBC, Amsterdam, and subsequent interviews. For more information, please visit www.uands.com. Graeme Packman, of Understanding & Solutions, a U.K.-based consulting firm, gave a very interesting presentation on IPTV during IBC and provided additional data used here.

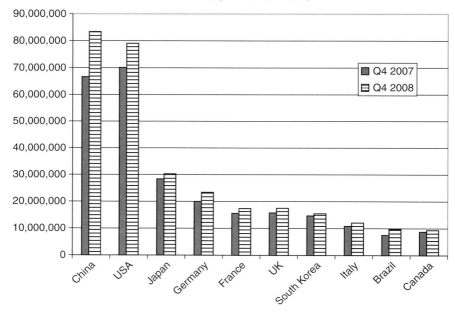

Figure 1.3 *Top 10 broadband countries, by subscribers, Q4 2007–Q4 2008.*
Source: Data provided for the Broadband Forum by Point Topic.

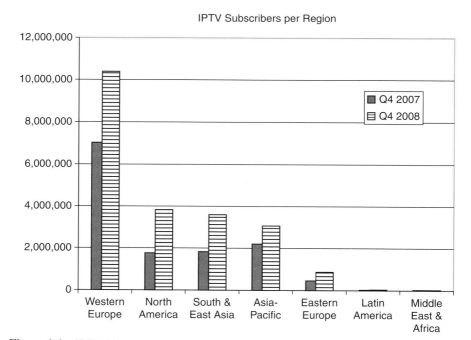

Figure 1.4 *IPTV Subscribers, Q4 2007–Q4 2008.*
Source: Data provided for the Broadband Forum by Point Topic.

One country where IPTV took hold early was France. Between 2004 and 2006, more than 400,000 subscribers signed up for IPTV service from Orange (France Telecom). Alternative ISP Free provided an IPTV service with more than 80 channels in a package that included Internet access and telephony. About two-thirds of Free's 1.9 million broadband subscribers were eligible for this package. Other IPTV providers in France included alternative operator Neuf Cegetel, which had recently acquired AOL France, Telecom Italia subsidiary Alice, and T-Online (Deutsche Telekom) subsidiary Club Internet.

The success of IPTV in France occurred for a number of reasons, some of which were specific to the French market and some that may also have been true for other locations.

- **Pricing.** Due to a competitive market, the prices for IPTV services were very low. Orange/France Telecom's basic IPTV service with more than 40 channels cost 16 Euros per month. Free's basic triple-play package, which included high-speed ADSL2+ Internet access and free voice calls to fixed lines in more than 20 countries and IPTV, cost 30 Euros per month. At this low price, many Free customers were happy purchasing the package just to get Internet and telephone service and didn't utilize the television services. Incumbent Orange started to bundle its basic IPTV service, which includes more than 30 channels, free of charge with some of its broadband access offerings.

- **Weak competition.** As mentioned earlier, the main alternatives to IPTV were cable TV and satellite, both of which achieved penetration far below levels in other countries. In the case of cable TV, up until 2005 there were several cable operators who had not converted the analog base to digital as rapidly as in the United Kingdom, and most of these systems were without VOD capability. In the case of satellite TV, penetration was hurt by strict local planning rules that make it impossible for many potential subscribers to mount antennas on their homes. As a result, for many potential viewers, IPTV was possibly the only way to get digital TV services.

- **Wide range of content.** The channel offerings of the two largest IPTV suppliers were quite extensive. In addition to channels from all over France, both services offered basic-tier international programming from a number of other countries in Europe and the Middle East. In addition, Orange/France Telecom offered more than 200 premium channels. Both operators also partnered with media group Canal+ to offer premium content.

- **New services (HD and VOD).** While not as important as the reasons mentioned previously, both HD content and VOD services may have acted to drive subscribers to IPTV. The HD broadcast market in France was much less developed than the U.S. market at the time. IPTV service providers were positioning themselves to capture HD business by deploying HD-capable *set, top boxes* (STBs) early on. In France, VOD services were also not common, and IPTV providers were, in practicality, the first providers to offer VOD.

Other countries in Europe presented a different picture for IPTV. For example, the United Kingdom, a country with roughly the same number of television households as France, had twice as many digital satellite subscribers (more than 7 million). NTL/Telewest operated digital cable TV systems that passed half the homes in the United Kingdom and had 3.3 million subscribers. Overall, the penetration of digital TV services in the United Kingdom was almost 70% of viewers, a much higher ratio than in France or many other countries in Europe. As a result of these and other factors, the penetration of IPTV in the United Kingdom has been lower. However, recent services, such as BT Vision's IPTV service, which had 376,000 subscribers by the end of 2008, have somewhat altered this trend.[16]

Summary

IPTV remains a force to be reckoned with today and for the foreseeable future, as powerful market drivers push companies and consumers to adopt this technology. Even though a number of issues must be addressed before IPTV can reach its full potential, these issues are surmountable and are not very different in scope or magnitude from the difficulties that face any new technology.

This chapter covered the basic motivations for using IP networks to deliver video services, including the flexibility, ubiquity, and cost advantages that have persuaded many carriers to begin offering these services. It took a look at the market trends that are driving the rapid growth in this market. It then examined several factors pushing the spread of this technology. The chapter concluded with a look at some issues that work against IPTV—although none of these appears to be anything more than the teething pains of a new technology.

---

[16]TelecomView, http://telcotv-view.blogspot.com/2009/02/bt-adds-56k-iptv-subscribers-in-4q08.html, February 12, 2009.

2 Types of IP Video

This is definitely the Wild West in some ways; it's in the very early stages, and people are still learning.

Adam Berrey, vice-president of marketing and strategy, Brightcove

There are many different ways that IP networks are currently being used to deliver video programming, ranging from professional "contribution" networks connected between sports stadiums and broadcasters all the way to Web cameras that enable people to have face-to-face video chats across continents. This chapter focuses on four of the major types of networks being used to deliver video content to (home) viewers.

When someone uses the term "IPTV" it can be very difficult to understand the intended meaning. Did the speaker mean to indicate the highly structured television delivery systems being built by telephone companies around the world, or was the discussion about the wild and wooly world of user-generated video content portals on the Internet? With the present terminology, it's hard to tell.

In any rapidly changing technology, the terms used to define the field will tend to change over time. Witness the rapid evolution of personal computing and communication devices—laptops used to be quite distinct from mobile phones, but these categories are starting to blur with the introduction of smart phones and netbooks. This transformation is also happening in the world of IP video, where the boundaries between IPTV and Internet video are starting to break down.

Originally, two categories appeared to be enough, when there seemed to be a clear difference between the terms "*IPTV*" and "*Internet video*." This difference still exists, but there have been a large number of new services introduced since 2006 that don't really fit into either category. For example, how do you classify a service that is delivered as a continuous stream over the Internet, is funded by advertising, and plays on a computer screen or a mobile device? How about a subscription-based service that enables viewers to watch movies and network programs on a television connected to a set-top box that plays content on-demand from the Internet? Neither of these examples can easily be placed into either of the two original categories.

The Corner Office View

Let's start with what IPTV is not. Specifically, it is not TV that is broadcast over the Internet. While the "IP" in its name stands for Internet Protocol, that doesn't mean people will log onto their favorite Web page to access television programming. The IP refers to a method of sending information over a secure, tightly managed network that results in a superior entertainment experience.

In particular, IPTV allows the service provider to deliver only those channels that the consumer wants at any given time—unlike traditional television broadcasting, where every channel is delivered to every home on the network. For the first time, it will be economical to deliver a college basketball game to everyone who wants to see it, for example, rather than just a particular local community.

—Mike Quigley, president and chief operating officer of Alcatel[1]

Two New Categories

To help clear up some of this confusion, it makes sense to come up with two new categories that fit in between "IPTV" and "Internet video." The first, "Internet TV," is similar in many respects to Internet video, with a significant difference: viewers watch "channels" of streamed content rather than selecting from a collection of video files that can be played on-demand. A good example of this is NASA TV,[2] which provides hours of live and prerecorded programming each day (including live coverage of all the space shuttle launches and landings); viewers can simply "tune in" whenever they want. Similarly, with CNN.com Live (http://www.cnn.com/live/) and Bloomberg Live TV (http://www.bloomberg.com), when viewers "tune in" they are simply connected to the real-time stream at whatever point it happens to be; perhaps midsong or midsentence. To watch different content than what is currently playing, viewers need to switch to another channel.

The second new category is "IPVOD" for professionally produced video-on-demand content that can be played over a PC or an appliance (STB) connected to a television and the Internet. Many of these services are branded by a provider and carry advertising or are available through a subscription program. Some popular examples include Hulu.com and the "Watch Instantly" feature of Netflix.com, which can be viewed online with a PC/Web browser or on a television using a Roku STB. To protect this valuable content from unauthorized use, it is often transmitted using strong digital rights management (DRM) protection, which is not the case for much of the available Internet video content.

[1]*Business Week*, May 20, 2005.
[2]http://www.nasa.gov/multimedia/nasatv/schedule.html

The bulk of this chapter is devoted to comparing these four delivery classifications using a variety of criteria. For this chapter's Reality Check, we take a look at MobiTV, a service that offers programming using several of these video delivery approaches.

Comparing the Networks

Each video delivery system can be compared using a variety of characteristics, as shown in Table 2.2. Each of these characteristics is explained in the sections that follow.

Network Type

Networks for IP video transport can be categorized into two types: public and private as shown in Table 2.1. The most important public network is the Internet, where viewers from many different locations can get access to a range of video sources. These sources may have public or private URLs, but they all share the same delivery network. The three delivery mechanisms used over public networks (IPVOD, Internet TV, and Internet video) must be capable of working in a "best-effort" environment, meaning that video sources and receivers must accommodate packet losses and delays.

Private networks exist in many different configurations, ranging from small point-to-point links to large systems covering millions of viewers. Each viewer must be connected directly to the network in order to have visibility of the sources and to receive services. IPTV is unique in requiring private networks, as that is the only way to give carriers the ability to control the critical network parameters that affect how video is delivered. Also, from a practical standpoint, a private network is the only economically viable way to deliver the 60 or so hours of television consumed by an average U.S. household each week; most ISPs would be unwilling or incapable of delivering that much content to all or most of their subscriber base.

Quality of Service

In IP networking, the term *quality of service* (QoS) is typically used to describe a mechanism where different services are assigned different priorities. This can be indicated right inside the standard IP packet header, allowing routers to give priority to specific packets. This mechanism can, for example, be used to give video traffic a high priority

Table 2.1 Network Type

Service Attributes	Network Type
IPTV	Private Network
IPVOD	Public Network
Internet TV	Public Network
Internet Video	Public Network

Table 2.2 Classifications of IP Video Delivery Systems

Service Attributes	IPTV	IPVOD	Internet TV	Internet Video
Network Type	Private Network	Public Network	Public Network	Public Network
Quality of Service	Managed QoS	Unmanaged QoS	Unmanaged QoS	Unmanaged QoS
Multipoint Method	True Multicasting	Unicasting	Replicated Unicasting	Unicasting
Key Protocols	True Streaming RTP over UDP	Progressive Download+Play	HTTP Streaming; Progressive D+P	HTTP Streaming; Progressive D+P
Viewing Devices	STB with Television	STB with Television or PC	PC, Mobile or Network Appliance	PC, Mobile or Network Appliance
Program Choices	Hundreds of Channels of Continuous TV	Thousands of Discrete Video Files	Thousands of Channels of Continuous TV	Millions of Discrete Video Files
User Experience	Similar to Broadcast or Cable TV	Similar to DVR or VoD	Similar to Web Surfing	Similar to Web Surfing
Channel Change Time	Quick: 1-2 seconds	Reasonable: 5-10 seconds	Slow: 10-20 seconds	Slow: 10-20 seconds (including search time)
Rewind/Fast Forward	No	Yes	No	Yes
Production Values	Professionally Produced	Professionally Produced	Professionally Produced	User Generated
Content Types	Live or Prerecorded	Prerecorded Only	Live or Prerecorded	Prerecorded Only
Program Library	Walled Content Garden	Walled Content Garden	Worldwide Reach; Quality Varies	Viewer Beware
Ownership Rights	Strong, with Digital Rights Management	Strong, Often with DRM	Fairly Strong	Weak or Nonexistent; Frequent Copyright Violations
Revenue Models	Paid by Subscription	Subscription, Fee per Episode or Ads	Often Free or with Advertising	Often Free or with Advertising
Example Providers	Local Telcos, AT&T Ui-Verse	Netflix, Hulu, CBS.com, ABC.com, Cartoon Network	NASA.tv, Local TV Broadcasters, Mogulus, mobiTV	YouTube, FaceBook

Table 2.3 Quality of Service

Service Attributes	Quality of Service
IPTV	Managed QoS
IPVOD	Unmanaged QoS
Internet TV	Unmanaged QoS
Internet Video	Unmanaged QoS

to ensure that packets are not discarded and experience minimal delays instead of waiting for lower priority, nonvideo traffic to pass through an overcrowded link.

Quality of service is relatively easy to implement on a private network, assuming that there are some consistent rules that can be applied to all of the devices, whether or not they are transporting video signals. This function is essentially useless on the public Internet because there is no mechanism to enforce a policy consistently across all of the different sources of video and other content. Without suitable priority enforcement, all users would be able to set high priorities for their traffic, rendering the prioritization scheme meaningless.

As shown in Table 2.3, IPTV services are virtually always implemented over QoS-controlled networks, whether these are carrier-based networks connected to homes or corporate in-house networks. QoS control helps ensure that a continuous, good-quality stream is delivered to each viewer, which is essential for high-quality video with real-time delivery. IPVOD, Internet TV, and Internet video don't require as much of a focus on QoS and can be configured to work on a non-QoS-controlled network.

Multipoint Method

Internet Protocol video delivery is all about transmitting video content from a source to multiple destinations. Depending on the type of service being delivered, the methods used for achieving this point-to-multipoint arrangement can vary considerably. A simple definition of unicasting is that each packet is transmitted from a single source to a single destination. Multicasting uses special processing controlled by specialized protocols to make copies of streams in real time as they flow through the network.

As shown in Table 2.4, for both IPVOD and Internet video, unicasting is the only practical approach, as it is the only way to allow viewers to have random access to

Table 2.4 Multipoint Method

Service Attributes	Multipoint Method
IPTV	True Multicasting
IPVOD	Unicasting
Internet TV	Replicated Unicasting
Internet Video	Unicasting

content (fast-forward, rewind, etc.) and to allow them to select whatever content they want and begin immediate playback.

For Internet TV, replicated unicasting is used, where each viewer gets a dedicated unicast stream (because multicasting is not supported on the Internet). Because all these streams are roughly synchronized, they can either be replicated at the video source or be replicated by specialized servers (called *reflecting servers*) that are provided by a number of service providers at locations around the Internet.

For IPTV, true multicasting can be used, as most modern networking equipment can be configured to support multicasting when installed on a private network. As explained in Chapter 4, multicasting uses a special protocol called an *Internet group management protocol* (IGMP) to make copies of packet streams when they are close to their destination, which helps improve bandwidth efficiency throughout the network.

Key Protocols

Many different protocols can be used for delivering video over IP circuits, as illustrated in Table 2.5. The most common ones, such as HTTP, which is used every day in standard Web surfing, can be used, as well as protocols that are designed specifically for delivering real-time information. The main differences between the protocols relate to the way that controls are applied to the packet streams as they flow across the various networks.

Progressive download and play can be used for IPVOD, Internet TV, and Internet video. This protocol divides the video information up into blocks of data that may represent anything from a few seconds to a few minutes of video or audio data (typically 30 to 60 seconds). The viewer's Web browser downloads each block of data before it is needed and makes data available to a media-specific browser plug-in. One advantage of this approach is the ability to work with a variety of firewall architectures, as each block of downloaded data has most of the same attributes as a normal Web page that would be downloaded by any browser. One downside to progressive D+P is that the client typically waits for the first block of data (which may consist of numerous IP packets) to be downloaded before playout begins; this buffering can occur each time the viewer uses fast-forward or rewind or whenever a new video program is selected.

HTTP streaming is often used by Internet TV and Internet video distribution and can sometimes be used for IPVOD applications. It uses the standard HyperText

Table 2.5 Key Protocols

Service Attributes	Key Protocols
IPTV	True Streaming RTP over UDP
IPVOD	Progressive Download+Play
Internet TV	HTTP Streaming; Progressive D+P
Internet Video	HTTP Streaming; Progressive D+P

Transfer Protocol familiar to Web surfers everywhere with a slight twist: instead of waiting for the browser to request successive packets of video data, the server continues to push data packets to the browser whether or not a request has been received. This helps improve Web video operation, as it allows video packets to be sent at a rate that is determined by the video and audio content, not by the viewer's browser, allowing for more natural timing.

True streaming real-time protocol (RTP) over user datagram protocol (UDP) is normally used for IPTV and can also be used for other types of video delivery. It is a one-way protocol, which means that the source controls all of the packet flow, whether or not a specific client device is receiving it. This means that RTP/UDP can be used over one-way networks such as a satellite or an over-the-air broadcast, and it also means that the stream can be replicated in the network, making it suitable for multicasting. The big benefit of RTP/UDP for high-quality video delivery is timing control—it allows high bandwidth streams to be delivered with very small receiver buffers, allowing video streams to start playback very quickly after they have been requested. RTP/UDP is not used commonly for video signals delivered over the Internet because of the difficulties in maintaining consistent end-to-end timing and because of difficulties that may be encountered in traversing some firewalls.

Viewing Devices

A variety of viewing devices are available for IP video applications as listed in Table 2.6, and the range is constantly increasing. Nevertheless, certain tendencies are apparent.

IPTV systems for home viewers are almost always based on STBs, due to the goal of many IPTV providers to directly replace cable TV, satellite, and broadcast services that are also available to viewers in most markets and so that televisions can be used for display. When IPTV is delivered in a corporate environment, PCs are often used for desktop viewing; however, STBs can also be used in these networks for nondesktop displays.

IPVOD is often delivered over STBs when these services are offered alongside IPTV services for home viewers. IPVOD can also be delivered to special-purpose STBs, such as the Roku player, which is designed to connect directly to both a home data network and a television. Another choice for IPVOD viewing is a standard PC, equipped with a suitable browser/plug-in software combination.

Internet TV and Internet video are designed primarily for PC-based viewing, although some providers also make allowances for viewing video on mobile

Table 2.6 Viewing Devices

Service Attributes	Viewing Devices
IPTV	STB with Television
IPVOD	STB with Television or PC
Internet TV	PC, Mobile or Network Appliance
Internet Video	PC, Mobile or Network Appliance

devices. Increasingly, specialized network appliances are also being developed; these units can take video streams that have been received by PCs and play them on a television or, in some cases, connect directly to the Internet (see, for example, the Apple TV product at www.apple.com/appletv).

Program Choices

Across the board, content providers are increasing the range of program choices available to viewers. However, certain common trends are apparent, as shown in Table 2.7.

IPTV systems typically offer hundreds of channels to subscribers, many of which are supported by the subscription fees that viewers pay. As a practical matter, adding too many channels is not expedient, as viewership for some of the obscure channels is very low, provider costs per channel are not insignificant, and program guide tables can become unwieldy for providers and viewers alike when too many channels are provided.

The number of Internet TV channels available at any time is a moving target, as these channels can come and go with little fanfare. As of this writing, there appear to be a few thousand channels available on the Internet, many of them copies of broadcasts provided through other mediums. Because of the costs associated with acquiring, producing, and distributing the content required for a 24/7 operation, there is a limit to the number of companies willing to make the investment to produce a channel. In some cases, Internet TV channels are being replaced with Internet video download sites as a way to give viewers flexibility.

IPVOD content choices depend on the amount of content that can be obtained from content owners; this varies widely by company and by the type of content. Sites that sell or rent video content, either for downloading or for VoD typically have thousands of choices available. There simply isn't enough professional content produced to fill a library with a million choices.

With user-produced Internet video, there are literally hundreds of millions of videos available online, with new selections being uploaded constantly (and other ones removed). In fact, every minute, twenty hours of new video content is uploaded to YouTube according to the site's blog. That's enough to equal 60,000 feature films a week. The difficulty with this quantity, of course, is finding something worth watching.

Table 2.7 Program Choices

Service Attributes	Program Choices
IPTV	Hundreds of Channels of Continuous TV
IPVOD	Thousands of Discrete Video Files
Internet TV	Thousands of Channels of Continuous TV
Internet Video	Millions of Discrete Video Files

User Experience

The best way to describe the user experience of these four categories listed in Table 2.8 is by analogy to existing services. IPTV is designed to be a direct replacement for cable TV and satellite TV and offers an identical user experience when used with an STB, including an interactive program guide used to select channels. IPVOD offers a similar experience that viewers would have when viewing an on-demand movie ordered from cable TV or when playing back an item recorded on their personal digital video recorder (DVR). Both Internet TV and Internet video offer a similar experience to Web surfing, due both to the viewing device (typically a PC) and to the method used to select content (Web searching and clicking on hot links and preview graphics).

Channel Change Time

Channel change time is the amount of time required for an IP video system to begin playback of a new channel or file of content after the user has made a request (by pressing a button on a remote control or by clicking on a Web page). The amount of time required is a major difference between the various IP video delivery technologies, as shown in Table 2.9. Because all of the major IP video delivery methods are oriented around sending a single stream to each viewer, when the viewer changes channels, the delivery network must react by sending new data to that viewer. This is different from the methods used for channel changing in multichannel delivery systems such as satellite, cable TV, and over-the-air broadcasts, where the viewer's device is constantly receiving multiple streams and simply needs to tune from one stream to another.

Table 2.8 User Experience

Service Attributes	User Experience
IPTV	Similar to Broadcast or Cable TV
IPVOD	Similar to DVR or VoD
Internet TV	Similar to Web Surfing
Internet Video	Similar to Web Surfing

Table 2.9 Channel Change Time

Service Attributes	Channel Change Time
IPTV	Quick: 1–2 seconds
IPVOD	Reasonable: 5–10 seconds
Internet TV	Slow: 10–20 seconds
Internet Video	Slow: 10–20 seconds (including search time)

IPTV systems are designed specifically to mimic the behavior of multichannel systems by keeping the channel change time very low, on the order of 1 to 2 seconds. This takes careful system design and requires technologies such as RTP/UDP to implement. IPTV delivery platforms are specially adapted to achieve this by, for example, transmitting extra frames of video to a viewer immediately after a channel change request has been made.

IPVOD systems have a slower channel change time, due in part to the greater number of content choices provided to viewers. Also, because many of these systems use progressive download and play, the channel change time is increased by the amount of time required for the first block of data to be downloaded. The use of STBs and remote controls in many IPVOD systems helps speed up channel change time, as viewer actions are easy to process.

Internet TV and Internet video systems can require even longer channel change times, due in part to the reaction time of the browser-based user interface and also in part to the larger buffers used in many applications. These buffers need to be emptied and then reloaded with new data each time the viewer changes from one content selection to another.

Rewind/Fast-Forward

Neither of the linear programming options (IPTV and Internet TV) described in Table 2.10 offers viewer control over playback users simply joins whatever program is playing at the time that they join. (Some viewing devices offer the ability to record the video as it is being played so that viewers can rewind to something that has already been delivered, but this functionality has limitations and will not work after a channel change.) Because the content is prerecorded and delivered individually to each viewer, both IPVOD and Internet video are able to offer rewind and fast-forward.

Production Values

Production values are closely related to the costs of preparing video content—higher costs are typically correlated with higher production values. As a result, paid services offer more professionally produced content than free services. In general,

Table 2.10 Rewind/Fast-Forward

Service Attributes	Rewind/Fast-Forward
IPTV	No
IPVOD	Yes
Internet TV	No
Internet Video	Yes

Table 2.11 Production Values

Service Attributes	Production Values
IPTV	Professionally Produced
IPVOD	Professionally Produced
Internet TV	Professionally Produced
Internet Video	User Generated

some trends are apparent in Table 2.11. IPTV and IPVOD almost exclusively provide professionally produced content; viewers will not be happy if they end up paying for poor-quality video. Internet TV production values tend to be more variable—the meaning of "professionally produced" is different in the United States than in other countries around the world. In general, providers of Internet TV channels supply a reasonably high grade of production; although the content may not always be compelling, at least the video is in focus and the sound is reasonably well-recorded. For Internet video, production values are up to the individual user who uploads their video—as a result, the variation in quality is enormous.

Content Types

Prerecorded content is available from all forms of IP video delivery systems—it is by far the dominant type of video available, as shown in Table 2.12. Even though many of the streams delivered by IPTV and Internet TV are streamed in real time, the vast majority of this programming is made up of prerecorded content.

Only IPTV and Internet TV are capable of delivering actual live coverage, such as a sporting event or a live news program. Of course, the term "live" is related to the total amount of delay across the delivery system—delays of up to 30 seconds are common in many Internet TV applications and in some IPTV systems; delays of a few minutes are not unheard of.

Program Library

The term *walled garden* refers to a collection of content that has been preselected by a service provider and indicates that choices outside of this collection are not available to viewers. This is virtually always the case for IPTV providers, as shown in Table 2.13, because each channel made available to viewers needs to be under the

Table 2.12 Content Types

Service Attributes	Content Types
IPTV	Live or Prerecorded
IPVOD	Prerecorded Only
Internet TV	Live or Prerecorded
Internet Video	Prerecorded Only

Table 2.13 Program Library

Service Attributes	Program Library
IPTV	Walled Content Garden
IPVOD	Walled Content Garden
Internet TV	Worldwide Reach; Quality Varies
Internet Video	Viewer Beware

control of the service provider, for both functional and financial reasons. Similarly, IPVOD services tend to be limited to the content selections that the service provider has been able to obtain from owners.

For both Internet TV and Internet video, content can be obtained from anywhere in the world, with wide variations in quality. In particular, Internet video sites that offer user-contributed content have every type of video conceivable, from the sublime to the ridiculous... (Let the viewer beware).

Ownership Rights

Ownership rights need to be enforced as a prerequisite for obtaining content from many suppliers. Enforcement often takes two forms: scrambling or encryption of content before it is delivered to viewers and DRM technologies that help control what viewers are allowed to do with the content once they have received it as listed in Table 2.14. Both IPTV and IPVOD tend to have strong ownership rights—both systems will normally use encryption (at least for certain types of content) and both will frequently use DRM. Internet TV varies widely in the amount of encryption and DRM that is used; for example, viewer-paid channels tend to use both technologies, whereas free channels may use neither. Internet video is even less controlled, with relatively little encryption or DRM employed on most sites, especially on sites that primarily offer viewer-generated content.

Revenue Models

Of course, because any revenue model can apply to any type of network, any general classification like this one is subject to exceptions and revisions. Nevertheless, it is illustrative to look at the predominant revenue models used by each of the network types, as listed in Table 2.15.

Table 2.14 Ownership Rights

Service Attributes	Ownership Rights
IPTV	Strong, with Digital Rights Management
IPVOD	Strong, Often with DRM
Internet TV	Fairly Strong
Internet Video	Weak or Nonexistent; Frequent Copyright Violations

Table 2.15 Revenue Models

Service Attributes	Revenue Models
IPTV	Paid by Subscription
IPVOD	Subscription, Fee per Episode or Ads
Internet TV	Often Free or with Advertising
Internet Video	Often Free or with Advertising

For IPTV, subscription models are the rule, both for the private network used to deliver the video and for the content flowing over that network. Many IPTV providers offer a low-cost (but not completely free) subscription option for free over-the-air channels—in part to cover the costs of building and operating the network. In corporate applications, the costs are borne by the company rather than by each individual viewer.

For IPVOD, several different revenue models are used. Subscription is one popular choice, particularly when these services accompany IPTV services or when they are offered as "all-you-can-eat" rental options. Per-episode fees, either for rental or for purchase, are often used for recent Hollywood releases. Advertising support is also commonly used for television episodes, particularly for "catch-up" TV.

Many Internet TV channels are offered for free, particularly ones that are simple repeats of television broadcasts or are sponsored through government funding. Others are subscription based, mainly those intended for mobile television viewers. A few Internet TV channels are sponsored with advertising, but with relatively few advertisements.

The largest sources of Internet video offer free viewing, particularly for viewer-created content. Advertising is often used for revenue generation, although this tends to gravitate toward content that is produced professionally. Many different forms of advertising are possible, including pre-roll (full-screen ads that play before the content plays) mid-roll (during the content), graphics that overlie the bottom of the portion of the video that appear and then disappear part way through playout, and banner or other advertising on the Web site that contains the video.

Example Providers

For each of the four listed delivery methods, some example providers are listed in Table 2.2. This is certainly not by any means an exhaustive list; it is merely an attempt to further illustrate the different categories by providing some tangible examples. More information about each of these can be found easily through a simple Web search.

Reality Check

For this chapter's Reality Check, we discuss a service that combines aspects of all the categories defined earlier.

MobiTV—Blurring the Lines

Since its formation in 1999, MobiTV has launched a variety of real-time and on-demand programming to viewers via several different user devices, including both PCs and mobile phones. The service is named MobiTV because of the substantial deployment for mobile telephone users, with more than 6 million reported users in February 2009.[3]

It is impossible to classify MobiTV into any single category listed previously. Here are some of the services currently being offered.

- Continuous, live broadcast channels delivered to mobile subscribers using a variety of smart phones, with downloaded applications. Available content includes a number of news channels, sports channels, entertainment, and specialty programming such as music videos.
- A version of MobiTV is also available to PC users and is marketed in conjunction with AT&T Broadband.
- On-demand programming, delivered over carrier's data networks. As of this writing, the content library includes a variety of television series episodes, which are typically made available the day after they are broadcast by major networks.
- For a demonstration at the NAB 2009 show, MobiTV featured mobile DTV service from PBS (KLVX) and the CW (KVCW), which is free, over-the-air television delivered using IP technology from a portion of each television station's DTV channel bandwidth.[4] In addition, the demonstration included a service called MixTV that offers a seven-day library of all previously broadcast content available on-demand over Mobile WiMAX. Interestingly, the PBS DTV broadcasts will be free to any viewer with a properly equipped mobile phone and suitable software (which may or may not be free), whereas the video-on-demand component will require a subscription.

The mobile/smart telephone versions require a monthly subscription fee for the programming on the order of $10 per month as of this writing in addition to a wireless data plan. The PC version has a fee on the order of $20 per month; PC users must supply their own broadband network connections to the Internet.

As this example shows, there is no single, universal definition for IPTV. What's important is to remember that whenever IPTV comes up in a conversation, one should be careful to qualify what the speaker is talking about before making any conclusions.

Summary

This chapter focused on the differences among four different systems used for delivering video over IP networks. These terms are often used in very similar contexts by experts, and care should be taken to clarify which version is being discussed. In the balance of this book, we will talk about IPTV as a video service that offers multiple channels of programming distributed on a real-time basis over a

[3]MobiTV press release, February 17, 2009.
[4]http://www.mobitv.com/about/press/releases/?page=press/release_042009b

private network to viewers who typically use an STB to watch the content on a television or other display device. We'll talk about Internet video, which consists of thousands or millions of discrete content elements (files) viewed over a public network on a monitor for a PC.

These differences are important because they affect the viewer's ability to control when and where specific content is viewed. Also, as we shall soon see, the business models and the technologies for these services can vary as well. As innovation continues, we are sure to see a variety of new and interesting IP video delivery technologies.

3 Business Models

*Information technology and business are becoming inextricably interwoven.
I don't think anybody can talk meaningfully about one without talking about
the other.*

Bill Gates

Regardless of the technology, the key to success in delivering video services to consumers is a profitable business model. A wide variety of models are being used in the market today for delivering video content over IP networks. Many different plans for user fees are being tried, ranging from completely free service to services that charge for each viewing of each piece of content.

Whether revenues come from subscriptions, "pay as you go," or pre-roll and interactive overlay ads, expect to see "new monetization forms that go for the new [online video] entertainment form," according to Google CEO Eric Schmidt.[1] "That's what we're seeking," says Schmidt. "That is the Holy Grail." With the advances of behavioral analytics and direct consumer relationships, it is forecast that ad-supported online video streaming will increase from $1.4 billion in 2007 to nearly $6.4 billion in 2012.[2]

In the long run, it is likely that a few selected approaches will dominate, but for now, it is smart to get an understanding of the many different models being used. This chapter is divided into two main sections. The first section looks at business models that are being used primarily for IPTV networks. The second section looks at models that are often used for Internet video businesses.

The lines can be blurry between these two groups, but here is the key point to remember: IPTV providers generally need to pay for installing and operating the network that delivers the services in addition to any costs for content, whereas most of the provider costs of Internet video services relate to content acquisition and preparation. Of course, there are a number of other costs that we will discuss, but network installation and operation expenses can be major portions of the overall system price tag.

---

[1]July 16, 2008, Google quarterly financial briefing.
[2]New Advertising Technologies and Platforms, Parks Associates, 11/08.

Corner Office View 1:

A Successful IPTV Model in Hong Kong

When it comes to IPTV, for one of the ultimate examples of an incumbent telecom firm moving into TV, you have to visit Hong Kong. When PCCW, the local phone company, launched a TV-over-broadband service in September 2003, everyone laughed; it had tried similar ventures twice before, in 1996 and 2000, and had failed on both occasions. But at the time, 85% of PCCW phone subscribers had access to broadband fast enough for video, and its new service, Now TV, proved a success, serving nearly 40% of all homes.

Hong Kong's population of nearly seven million people gives it the world's highest population density, making it easier to implement Internet and telephone services.[3] Several years ago, due to some of these factors, PCCW became one of the first incumbent operators anywhere in the world to stop the decline in fixed-line subscribers.

This is the kind of success that other telecom firms dream of: a new service that not only stops line loss, but beats the cable companies at their own game and brings in new revenue .... No wonder that "just about every phone company in the world" has come to visit PCCW, says Alexander Arena, the firm's finance chief. PCCW is now advising telecoms firms in several countries about how to emulate its successful roll-out of IPTV.[4]

—From "Tuning into the Future?", The Economist

Corner Office View 2:

A Google Internet Video Business Model

When it comes to Internet video, broadcast and Internet executives are seeking an efficient, scalable revenue model. Part of that quest is to "introduce new ad innovations so ad agencies really value what we're doing," says Disney-ABC EVP Digital Media, Albert Cheng. But wide commercialization has remained elusive. Here's one corner office point of view on monetizing Internet video from Keval Desai, GoogleTV's Director of Product Management.[5]

---

[3]Asia's Media Innovators, Stephen Quinn, 2008. "PCCW and the Now Business Channel in Hong Kong.
[4]"Tuning into the Future?," *The Economist*, October 12, 2006.
[5]Interview with Howard Greenfield, 3/30/09.

What's true for Internet video monetization (and video monetization in general) is that if there's not a lot of user interactivity associated with something, you can't monetize it. For short clips, advertising models such as overlay, interactive ads, text ads, or banners around the video are all fine. But I don't think that is where the majority of the dollars are going to come in.

I think an interesting trend to look at is what users are doing with video on the Internet. Most significant in my opinion is that they are looking at the same TV content they've been looking at for the last 20 years. Premium long-form content is going to migrate, or co-exist on your TV. Web monetization will come from in-stream video advertising of long-form content (which is basically the same model as we have on television).

When users start playing with their video, interacting with it, then you'll see interactive ads. If users are passively watching linear video, you'll see passive in-stream ads. A great example is the UK where people interact with their TV (there's a "buy" button on the Sky remote). So, user behavior is already established and interactive ads, telescoping, or video-on-demand make a lot of sense.

As an advertising strategy, all we're trying to do is follow the user. Follow the user and the rest will come. Trying to predict ad formats ahead of user behavior is the peril that most other video advertising efforts have fallen into.

I think monetization is a lagging activity and user behavior is a leading activity. So, when you're looking to monetize it, now or 6–24 months from now, you need to look at "what are users doing?" because if there's not a lot of activity, or traffic associated with the something, you can't monetize it.

Our AdSense for media online can be used by any publisher to monetize their long-form video. So, for example, we are monetizing a lot of old Bonanza shows on YouTube (who have the rights from the publisher to monetize that inventory).

IPTV

As discussed in Chapter 2, IPTV networks primarily deliver multiple streams of continuous content over private networks to viewers who watch the content on normal television sets. While this sounds simple, a significant amount of technology needs to be installed and managed to provide these services. Table 3.1 summarizes the key cost elements of an IPTV system.

Table 3.2 gives monthly programming costs for several popular television networks in the United States. Note that these costs are paid by the IPTV system provider to the content owners; part of the business plan for the IPTV network is devising a way to recoup these costs from viewers.

In addition to the costs given in Tables 3.1 and 3.2, other recurring costs must be covered. These include marketing, customer support, and network maintenance.

Table 3.1 IPTV System Cost Elements

Cost Element	Cost Basis	Description
Video Content	Recurring fee per month per viewer	Paid to content suppliers, such as broadcast networks
Delivery Network	Fixed, up front	Cost of IP network, part common equipment, part per-subscriber
STB	Fixed per subscriber	Often rented, sometimes purchased by consumers
Digital Head End	Fixed, up front	Receives video signals, converts into proper IP format
Content Servers	Fixed, scale with capacity	Used for on-demand and advertising
EPG	Recurring, scales with number of channels and subscribers	May be produced locally by IPTV provider or acquired from service bureau

Table 3.2 Programming Cost Examples

Network	Fee per Subscriber per Month (2008)
ESPN	$3.66
Fox Sports Net	$2.15
TNT	$0.93
Disney Channel	$0.86
NFL Network	$0.85
ESPN HD	$0.70
HD Net	$0.68
NHL Network	$0.53
USA	$0.52
MGM HD	$0.52

Source: SNL Kagan © 2009 with portions based on The Nielsen Company data © 2009, a division of SNL Financial LLC. All rights reserved; used with permission.

These costs can be hard to quantify before an IPTV system is deployed, but can have a significant impact on the overall profitability of a system.

The following sections describe some of the business models that can be used for IPTV systems.

Subscription

Subscription services are probably the most common methods used for funding IPTV systems. In this system, viewers sign up for a package of video services (channels) and pay a flat monthly fee. Subscribers are then allowed to watch as much or as little as they desire of any of the channels included in their subscription package.

Often, these services come in different tiers, with basic services (such as signals obtained from local over-the-air [OTA] providers) being the least expensive and premium sports or movie channels being the most expensive. Service providers try to group the channels into these tiers to maximize the number of subscribers at each level while minimizing the costs of the programming. This arrangement is similar to the pricing schemes used by many cable TV and satellite providers; hence it is normally well accepted in the marketplace.

For example, a basic tier of services may have several local OTA network feeds (which may have little or no programming costs to the IPTV provider), some news and weather channels, shopping channels, and other local content. A more expensive tier of services may include a variety of national entertainment, sports, and music channels, including channels such as those listed in Table 3.2. This tier could easily be priced at 100 to 200% premium over the basic tier. Even more expensive tiers could be provided, which include more variety, such as advertising-free channels or specialized sports channels.

À la Carte Channels

À la carte channel selection is similar in concept to subscription, except that each viewer is allowed to select exactly the channels they want to view so he or she does not pay for the undesired channels. As described earlier, the subscriber receives a monthly bill from the service provider, but only for the specific channels that have been chosen. The service provider in turn uses the revenue to pay content providers.

Within traditional cable TV and satellite providers, à la carte channels have not seen widespread deployment. For IPTV providers, there are two advantages to this approach. First, because each channel that a subscriber is viewing must be sent individually from the IPTV network to the viewer's STB, it is technically less difficult to deliver only a specific group of channels to each subscriber. Second, IPTV providers may capitalize on subscribers' desires to pay only for those channels they wish to view; an à la carte channel selection option could be used as a service differentiator and market entry strategy.

Local Advertising

Local advertising involves inserting advertisements from merchants that are targeted to local residents into network feeds before they are distributed to local viewers. The technology for doing this is well established—many national content providers include special indicators in their programming feeds that tell the local providers when to insert their local ads. These indications, called *avails*, are provided by the content owners under the terms of contracts with the local service providers. In some cases, a local service provider may earn enough revenue from the local ads to partially or completely pay for the cost of the programming.

Many cable TV providers have already designed their networks to take advantage of this important source of revenue. For IPTV providers, much of the technology is readily available. Specialized servers collect advertisements from a number of sources, and these servers can monitor multiple video channels simultaneously to locate avails. When one appears, the content from the server simply replaces the content of the programming feed.

The appeal of local advertisements is not limited to local businesses. Companies with global brands may wish to tie their advertisements to items of local interest, such as soft drink companies targeting fans of local sports teams. The challenge for a local service provider is to effectively market their selection of avails to the advertisers that will value them the highest.

Video on Demand

The idea of allowing viewers to watch any programming they desire whenever they want to watch it is not new. However, as technology advances and costs come down, *video on demand* (VOD) has become more and more attractive to service providers.

The basic concept of VOD is based on video programming that is stored and then delivered to a viewer when it is requested. This storage can either take the form of a centralized server equipped to send programming simultaneously to hundreds of viewers or take the form of more distributed storage throughout the network. At the limit, individual storage devices for each viewer can be located inside STBs.

Various forms of VOD have been tried over the years, and most of them still exist in one form or another. Table 3.3 lists the most popular types of VOD services.

One of the big controversies surrounding DVR service (described in Table 3.3) is the role of advertising in recorded content. Advertisers have two main concerns.

- Ad skipping, where viewers fast-forward through ads. This capability is often listed as the motivation for many consumer DVR purchases.
- Ad timeliness, where viewers watch programs at times far removed from their original broadcast date. This is a big concern for some advertisers who have their ad campaigns targeted for specific time windows, such as promotional ads for a movie that is being released to theaters the following day.

Service providers have a limited amount of control over content that has been recorded by a viewer on their own device for later playback. They have only slightly more control over DVRs that are embedded in a STB supplied by the service provider—at least they can ensure that the DRM function is working to protect any copyrighted content while it is on disk. Providers actually have the potential to influence viewers who use a networked DVR, where the video recordings are actually stored on the service providers' own video servers.

Network DVRs have exciting potential to make advertisers much happier than with other DVR technologies. Why? Well, consider what happens in a normal DVR scenario with an advertisement. The machine faithfully records the commercials along with the program content and gives the user the ability to fast-forward through any parts of the program or advertisements at their whim. For example, say the viewer recorded a program on December 20 and decides to watch the

Table 3.3 Types of Video-on-Demand Service

Type	Description
True Video on Demand	This is the purest form of VOD, where each viewer receives an individual video stream that they have complete control over. Viewers are able to start, stop, pause, rewind, and fast-forward the content. Viewers typically pay a fee for each title viewed; the charges are either debited from a prepaid account or included on a monthly bill.
Digital Video Recorders (DVRs)	These devices take incoming video programming, compress it, and record it to a hard disk that is typically located either in an STB or a standalone device. Viewers then control the DVR to play back content, including pause, fast-forward, and rewind capabilities. Also called *timeshifting*, viewers normally program their DVRs to record specific programs at specific times. TiVo is one of the pioneers of this technology, but most satellite companies now build DVR functions into their STBs.
Subscription Video on Demand (SVOD)	Same delivery technology and viewer control as VOD with a different payment system. In SVOD, subscribers pay a fixed monthly fee for unlimited access to a library of titles. In many systems, the library is updated monthly.
Free Video on Demand (FVOD)	A variation on VOD where payment is eliminated. In most systems, this content is restricted to long-form advertisements, how-to guides, and other low-cost content.
Everything on Demand (EOD)	For some technology visionaries, this is the ultimate form of video delivery system, where all programming is available to all viewers at all times.
Near Video on Demand (NVOD)	Similar to true VOD without the individual video stream control capabilities. One common form of NVOD is sometimes called *staggercasting*, in which multiple copies of a program are played starting at five-minute intervals, thereby limiting any individual viewer to no more than a five-minute wait before his or her program begins to play.
Networked Digital Video Recorders (NDVRs)	Offers similar functionality to DVRs, but recording is performed inside the service provider's network rather than in the viewer's location. Some content owners contend that this technology is so similar in capability to true VOD that it needs to be licensed as such.
Pay-per-View (PPV)	This precursor technology to VOD is used primarily to deliver live paid programming, such as concerts or sporting events. It is technically not VOD since the viewer has no control over the playback.

program on December 29. As you could imagine, the program contained a number of ads that pertained to special last-minute shopping opportunities for Christmas. Unfortunately, when the viewer watches the program, the sales are over and the ads are completely worthless to both the viewer and the advertiser. Now, consider the same scenario with a networked DVR and some advanced technology in the server. With this technology, the service provider is able to replace the commercials that were in the original program with ones that are timely and relevant whenever the viewer watches the content. In this example, the ads seen on December 29 might be for something great to do on New Year's Eve, which the viewer might actually be willing to watch, and an advertiser might be willing to pay for.

All that's needed to make this a reality is some pretty serious software inside the VOD server and some kind of legal framework to govern the "bumping" of one commercial by another. The industry may not quite be there yet, but the technology is certain to be available in the not too distant future.

Interactive TV

When viewers are given the opportunity to interact with broadcast content, the result is called *interactive TV* (iTV). This can take many forms, ranging from the simple press of a button to more elaborate menu schemes. Here are a few common applications for iTV.

- Ad response, where viewers can request more information about a product or service being advertised
- Camera angle selection, where the viewer can chose one or more different camera angles of live sporting events
- Voting/opinion polling, where the outcome of a television event is determined by a vote of the audience

The key requirement for iTV is a *return path*, where user actions are sent to the service provider. Particularly in satellite applications, this can be difficult to construct, requiring an Internet connection or, in older-generation technology, from the internal modem to an STB to the subscriber's telephone line. In contrast, in IPTV networks, the return path is already present, allowing for simple integration of iTV.

Triple/Quadruple Play

Triple play refers to multiple services being delivered by a single service provider, typically voice (telephony), data (Internet access), and television services. *Quadruple play* adds mobile telephony to the mix. Service providers normally offer discounts to customers who buy more than one service, which has proven to be a successful marketing ploy. The value proposition is that consumers benefit not only from lower prices but also the convenience of a single bill to pay (although the value of the latter is debatable).

From a service provider perspective, triple play services offer the combined cash flow from three separate services that can be used to pay for a common network that is capable of delivering all of them (such as networks based on IP technology). Of course, there are costs associated with installing the extra equipment and software needed to provide all three services, but these items can be paid for with moderate market penetration.

Certainly, triple play has been the beautiful face that launched a thousand networking ventures. Carriers that traditionally had separate spheres of influence (for example, video versus telephony) are now rushing to deploy networks that can support all three aspects of the triple play. And these forays have been met with some success—a number of telephone companies have acknowledged for many years that pricing and revenue for basic subscriber telephony services are declining, partially due to the combined effects of VoIP technology and mobile telephones.

"We have a triple-play offering that includes broadband access, voice-over-IP (VoIP), and IPTV," says Paula Souloumiac, director of France Telecom's International TV Content Division. "Our customer is getting IPTV, access to our VOD catalog, subscription offers, and a wide bouquet of channels—and all this coming from his broadband supplier."

"As you can imagine, the fixed-line business has been declining and the broadband business has been increasing," says Souloumiac. "So, we need to have a very strong position in the broadband market. And, in fact, by having a triple-play offer we've been able to attract customers. We also feel that having a TV proposition in the triple-play bundle makes it much stronger and our customers are being quite loyal. Today, for access providers, the TV element is becoming a 'must have.'"[6]

Internet Video via IPTV—The Walled Garden

IPTV providers have a dilemma. On the one hand, they want to be the sole (or at least very dominant) supplier of video content to their subscribers, which is one of the best ways of securing continuous subscription revenue flows. On the other hand, there is a huge amount of content available on the Internet, and there will certainly be pressure from subscribers to have easy access to this content. To resolve this dilemma, some IPTV providers have resorted to a concept called a *walled garden*.

A walled garden can almost be thought of as a protected copy of some portions of the Internet or possibly as a set of content offerings that have nothing to do with the Internet. It can also be thought of as a heavily censored and filtered view of the Internet. Either way, only a small fraction of all the content available on the Web is included in the garden.

Service providers see several advantages for using walled gardens. First of all, the wall can prevent viewers from accessing content that may not be technically compatible with the network equipment or content that possibly contains harmful viruses, worms, or Trojan horses. Second, the wall can help increase the amount of revenue that service providers derive from their content in the form of advertising revenue or payments for on-demand content. Third, the wall prevents viewer access

[6]http://www.iptv-news.com/—video interview, home page, April 27, 2009.

to content that may compete with what the service provider offers or content that may not be suitable for some groups of viewers, such as children.

The concept of a walled garden is not new. AOL tried to provide a walled garden of Web sites for all their subscribers in the early 1990s. For a while, this model worked, with a variety of custom content available only to AOL subscribers. After time, this model broke down as users started to demand access to sections of the Web that were not inside the wall. In addition, the cost of creating and preparing content to reside within the walled garden became very expensive, even for a large company like AOL with millions of subscribers. As the decade wore on, AOL eventually switched to allow subscribers to have more open access to the Internet.

Internet Video

Internet video delivery systems use the Internet as a means to deliver programming to viewers. As a result, the business models for this technology are significantly different from the business models used with IPTV systems. At the risk of completely abusing an analogy, there is no wall around this garden. Table 3.4 summarizes the major cost elements for an Internet video service provider.

Subscription-based pricing is much less common in Internet video than in IPTV, although Netflix, Amazon, and others are blazing a trail in this area, as examined later in this chapter. This is most likely due to the common perception that entertainment video is better suited to viewing on a television set than on a computer display (and sofas are typically more comfortable places to sit than desks). In addition, most Internet video delivery services are unable to offer anywhere near the video quality of a purpose-built television delivery service when both screen resolution and freedom from service interruptions are considered.

Some common elements are shared by both technologies. Both can rely heavily on advertising, although in the case of IPTV the advertising revenues tend to go more to the content providers, whereas in Internet video most of the ad revenues

Table 3.4 Internet Video System Cost Elements

Cost Element	Cost Basis	Description
Video Servers	Fixed, scale with number of streams provided	An adequate number of servers must be available to deliver streams to all of the simultaneous viewers of the content
Video Content	Often paid as a percentage of the revenue earned, if not free	Paid to content owners, such as performing artists and producers
Internet Access Bandwidth	Fixed, scales with number of streams provided	Fees paid to ISPs to supply high-bandwidth connections

are collected by the portal provider. Both architectures support a variety of VOD services, and both technologies have a wide variety of business models that have been used successfully.

The following sections describe some of the business models that can be used to operate Internet video services.

Pay-per-View

Pay-per-view is often used for high-value content such as Hollywood movies. In this model, the viewer purchases the right to view a specific piece of content over a specific time period (often 24 hours). The viewer is entitled to pause, fast-forward, and rewind the content, but loses all rights after the viewing window expires. Typically, the license only covers a single viewing device.

Part of the reason for these tight viewing window restrictions is simple profit maximization, but another part is security. If a viewer somehow devised a method to enable multiple devices to view content, the resulting "cracked" file would only be useful for a short period because of the display time limit. Such technologies help limit the incentive to devise these illegal techniques.

Rights Purchase/Podcasting

Much of the content delivered over Internet video systems is sold in the form of a permanent license, where the rights to store and view the content are delivered to the viewer for an unlimited time. Users are allowed to download the content onto their PCs or other viewing devices and play back as desired. Typically, there is a limit to the number of devices that can be used to play the content to prevent viewers from reselling the content to other parties.

One somewhat contentious issue for providers is the concept of backup copies. The current policy of Apple iTunes, like many online content services, is that backup copies for personal use are legal, but may not legally be distributed or sold to anyone by the original buyer.[7] Consumers want the right to make backups so they don't lose the rights to a valuable collection of content items as a result of a hard disk or other device failure. However, content owners fear that a liberal backup policy could result in widespread misuse of their valuable content.

Subscription

Some Internet video content is sold by subscription. Two business models are often used.

- Live video access, where viewers pay a monthly fee in exchange for the rights to view live streaming video (such as sporting events).
- Video library access, where viewers pay a monthly fee to have access to a collection of content that can be played.

---

[7]http://www.apple.com/legal/itunes/us/terms.html#SALE (intellectual property, 14a).

Subscription models work best when there is a collection of unique content and a group of viewers who are willing to pay. Examples include Major League Baseball in the United States, news programming from a variety of countries in different languages, and a variety of adult content. Another example is the tens of thousands of movies and TV shows available through Netflix and Amazon for streaming onto your television over the Roku device for a monthly fee. Financial success depends on controlling the costs of production (perhaps by sharing production costs with other television outlets, such as local television broadcast stations) and on establishing a subscriber base large enough to cover the system costs.

Advertising Supported

As with e-mail and Internet search portals, many Internet video providers started out by offering free services to viewers. As the user base grows, it becomes economically feasible for the portal owners to sell advertising space in the form of static ads displayed on the portal's Web page, as graphics overlaid on content display windows, or as video advertisements played immediately before the viewer's selected content.

Revenues derived from advertising can be used in three interesting ways, aside from filling the pockets of entrepreneurs and venture capitalists. One way is to use the revenues to purchase more content from suppliers, either as an outright purchase or in the form of revenue sharing. Another way is to hire people and purchase equipment to create a larger-capacity and more user-friendly portals that will attract more viewers and increase ad revenues. The third way to spend the revenues is on marketing, thereby attempting to increase the number of viewers using the portal. These choices are not mutually exclusive—many providers will choose to do all three as a way of increasing the success of their Internet video services.

Free and User-Generated Content

Human creativity knows no limits. The fortuitous combination of low-cost, high-quality camcorders, animation software, audio recording/mixing software, synthesizers, and professional-grade video editing software that can run on PCs has created an immense pool of people who have the means to produce their own digital video clips and programs. Certainly much of the content that is produced is only beautiful in the eye of its creator, but enough inspiring, intriguing, or amusing content is being produced to populate any number of Web sites with high-quality content.

One way for service providers to create revenue from this type of Web site is to charge users a fee to host their video content to simplify sharing between friends and family members. As demonstrated by a number of photography sites that have done this, it can be tricky to create a profitable business.

Another way to fund a "free" video Web portal is to sell advertising space on the portal itself or to push advertisements to viewers before the content is played. This can provide enough revenue for the service provider to cover their costs, particularly for bandwidth and storage.

A third common way to fund a "free" video Web portal is to offer previews of video content that needs to be purchased. For example, many professionally produced music videos are available for sale. A number of Web sites have been created that provide free previews of these clips, along with links to sites where they can be purchased and downloaded. Other types of preview content are available for movies currently in theatrical release or on DVD. Web sites that feature these previews can be funded by commissions or other "click-through" accounting methods.

Reality Check

Clearly, the scale of investment required to install and operate an IPTV system requires some form of payment from viewers. The following Reality Check takes a look at one local telecom supplier that has been able to successfully build and operate a fairly compelling IPTV delivery system.

Canby Telcom

Canby Telcom is an incumbent local exchange carrier located in Canby, Oregon, about 20 miles south of Portland.[8] The company has provided telephone service to local residents for more than 100 years. Currently, the company provides around 11,000 telephone access lines to 8600 customers.

The geography covered by Canby Telcom consists of a good deal of agricultural land. The company provides service over an area covering 84 square miles. A large number of Hispanic people have moved into the area to work on the flower and tree nurseries that are a common feature of the area.

In October 2004, Canby Telcom received approval for their business plan to deploy a full set of triple-play services to their customers. In addition to the voice services they traditionally supplied, the company decided to offer broadband data IPTV service using DSL technology. The company began offering service to their first customers using this new system in October 2005. They are currently in a secondary phase of upgrading their copper network to fiber to the home.[9]

Canby's basic offering includes voice, data, and video service using ADSL+ technology. Customers can receive broadband data service at up to 10.0 Mbps in the downstream direction, which they hope to raise to 20.0 Mbps in 2009. For subscribers within 5000 feet of a DSLAM, Canby is able to offer up to three simultaneous video streams. Customers between 5000 and 8000 feet from the DSLAM can be supplied with two simultaneous video streams.

---

[8]Information on Canby Telcom provided by interviews with company management (Keith Galitz, president, and others) in November 2006 and through other published sources.
[9]http://telecomengine.com/article.asp?HH_ID=AR_4687

System Construction

The Canby Telcom IPTV system was constructed using equipment and software from a number of different suppliers. This is the case with essentially all current IPTV deployments because of the wide variety of different technologies involved. The following list indicates some of the original building blocks and their respective suppliers.

- Content processors—Tut Systems Astria CP. These units are responsible for taking incoming programming from a variety of sources and converting it into the common compressed digital format that will be delivered to viewers.
- Remote terminals (DSLAMs)—Calix C7 Multiservice Access Platform. These units sit inside Canby Telcom's facilities and generate the DSL signals that are sent to subscribers. They also receive upstream data back from the subscribers.
- DSL modems—Best Data 542 Four Port Ethernet switch/router. These units receive the incoming DSL signals and separate the packets into up to four streams. Three streams can each be connected to one of the STBs, and one can be used to provide high-speed access for a PC.
- Middleware—Myrio. This software provides a number of functions, including supporting the channel change process and presenting information to viewers such as the EPG and the VOD selection menu.
- Encryption/DRM—Verimatrix. This software works in conjunction with the Myrio software to protect the digital content from being misappropriated by viewers or by third parties.
- STBs—Amino AmiNET 110. Small, powerful STB with Ethernet input. This supports standard definition MPEG-2 programming only.
- Today they are MPEG-4 based for the 36 HD channels they offer using the Entone STB.

Services Offered

Canby offers quite an impressive array of triple-play service options. Basic telephone service is available throughout the company's serving area. DSL service is available to 99.6% of the homes and businesses in the serving area. By November 2006, IPTV service was available to 3000 homes in the serving area.

The IPTV service offers 200 standard definition and 36 channels of broadcast DTV with a variety of basic and enhanced packages at $21.95 ("economy") and $55.95 ("essentials"). These packages combine local programming, video on demand, and caller ID on TV.

Investment

Canby Telcom was somewhat of an early mover in the IPTV market, due to the company's desire to roll out services beginning in 2005. This may have caused the cost of their system to be higher than what might be typical today for two reasons.

- The cost of MPEG-2 compression technology continues to decline, similar to other trends in the high-technology field.
- Some of the technologies that Canby had to use were quite new and had not been fully integrated with the other technologies. As a result, the integration costs may have been higher than what would be experienced for a similar system today.

Even with these higher costs, Canby was able to install their entire IPTV digital head end for less than $2 million of invested capital. The primary cost elements included the following.

- Digital head end, which includes content processors and other signal receiving and processing functions, accounted for 70 to 75% of this total.
- VOD system, including the disk drives that actually store the content and the servers that create the IP packet streams that deliver the content to viewers, accounted for 20 to 25% of this total.
- Other equipment, including the satellite receiver dishes and associated electronics, middleware servers, and initial licenses, accounted for the balance of the investment.

Results

Due to a combination of good engineering, affordable pricing, and relatively weak competition from the local cable TV company, Canby Telcom has been able to achieve good take rates. In November 2006, the company had 900 IPTV subscribers, out of a total of approximately 3000 homes passed, for a take rate of 30%. What's more, 77% of the IPTV customers took the full triple play of video, voice, and data from Canby, helping prevent erosion in the basic telephony population, which had been a concern of Canby's management. As of February 2009, the company's IPTV subscribers had grown to 1600.

Summary

This chapter discussed a variety of topics that relate to the business models being tried for both IPTV and Internet video. Because these technologies and their applications are so new, it is difficult to determine which business models will be successful and which ones will not pan out. Only with time (and some large sums of money) will these answers start to emerge.

We began by looking at both equipment costs and programming costs for an IPTV system. Then, we examined some of the methods that can be used to get viewers to pay for these services, including subscriptions, local advertising, and VOD. We then looked at several business models that have been used with Internet video, including pay-per-view, podcasting, subscriptions, and advertising supported. We also glanced at free video portals that have been supported primarily by investors with deep pockets who hope to devise a way to earn a return in the future. We concluded with an in-depth look at a real IPTV system that is meeting its financial goals ahead of plan.

4 Network Overviews

The American fascination with television and other video content is not easing up, as consumers keep turning to TV, Internet and Mobile at record levels. Viewers appear to be choosing the best screen available for their video consumption, weighing a variety of factors, including convenience, quality and access. It is clear that TV remains the main vehicle for viewing video, although online and mobile platforms are an increasingly important complement to live home-based television.

Susan Whiting, vice-chair of the Nielsen Company (February 2009)

IPTV and Internet video systems can be very complex puzzles to piece together. As any jigsaw enthusiast will say, it is hard to understand how each individual piece fits without an overall picture of the integrated whole. In this chapter, we hope to provide this big picture view of the technology components and how they work together.

A wide variety of network architectures have been used successfully to deliver IPTV and Internet video services. Describing all those variations is impractical in a single book, but it does make sense to look at typical network architectures for each delivery method. By understanding these reference models, readers will get a better understanding of all the elements that make up both types of video delivery systems.

Interestingly, in the IPTV section, we will spend most of our time describing hardware components, whereas when it comes to Internet video, we will spend a lot of time discussing software. Why the difference? The reason is because most IPTV networks have to be constructed from a number of hardware components to reach into viewers' homes, whereas Internet video delivery takes place over links to the Internet that are purchased independently by each subscriber. In other words, IPTV service providers usually need to build a network to reach their viewers, whereas Internet video service providers typically use existing infrastructure.

The Corner Office View:

AT&T IPTV 2005

When the first edition of this book was published, AT&T was on the verge of launching their IPTV product. Jeff Weber, SBC's vice-president of product and planning, said at NAB 2005, "At the highest level, the economics look dramatically different today [2005] than they did 10 years ago. . . The improvements in compression technology, the ability to do switched video instead of broadcast video, the technology development on a scale around the world makes [IPTV] real. As these standards evolve—and I think SBC can help provide that—the scale and the economics come down, driving the deployment costs [down]."

AT&T IPTV 2009

Five years later, AT&T U-verse^{SM} provides IPTV service to over 1 million subscribers, representing an increase of 264,000 in the final quarter of 2008 alone. The service is available to more than 17 million living units. Randall Stephenson, AT&T chairman and chief executive officer, reports "Our AT&T U-verse TV service continues to ramp. We completed the world's largest deployment of the fastest Internet backbone technology across our U.S. network. We further expanded our industry-leading network capabilities and product sets for the business market."

This chapter is divided into two sections, one focusing on IPTV networks and the other focusing on Internet video networks. Each section includes detailed descriptions of the major components, both hardware and software, that go into these networks. Reality Checks for both types of networks are included at the end of this chapter.

Constructing an IPTV Network

IPTV networks can be built to serve millions of subscribers or just a few thousand. Large systems can be national in scope and can be optimized to deliver hundreds of channels of programming across thousands of miles of networks. Small systems may service a local community with just a few dozen channels or a single company in one building. In either case, cost-effective deployment of both the central equipment and the delivery network is crucial to successful business operations.

One thing to keep in mind is that IPTV networks are typically designed for a phased deployment. Not all services are offered to all potential subscribers when a system is first launched, for the following two reasons.

- *Time is needed to test and kick-start revenues.* The complexity of deploying an IPTV network can require many hours of engineer and technician time from both system operators and their vendors for installation and system integration. Since staffing budgets are typically limited, services must be deployed only after they have been properly tested and integrated with the other network elements. Also, the equipment that is required to deploy advanced services may be too expensive to install until after enough customers have been acquired to provide an adequate revenue stream.

- *Building a subscriber base will occur gradually after launch.* Consumers will take varying amounts of time before deciding to subscribe to new IPTV service offerings, particularly if their television viewing needs are being met by other technologies. A prudent business plan recognizes that effort will be needed to convince customers of the benefits of a new television delivery method. It is simply not realistic to assume that 20% of the available customer base will sign up as soon as a new service is launched.

Because of these two factors, it is important to develop a construction and customer activation plan that grows over time. A first launch may see only a very small percentage of the available customer base signing up for service. Therefore, the network must be designed to keep the cost of the central equipment low during the early phases of deployment. Outside plant construction may initially target areas with high densities of customers, where the costs can be kept low relative to the number of residences that will be wired for service.

Two important metrics are used in financial plans for IPTV systems. The first is a calculation of the total number of *homes passed* by the network, which is essentially the number of residences where the network is physically present and available for connection to any customer who wants to become a subscriber. The second is a calculation of the total number of subscribers that have actually signed up with the IPTV service provider to receive video service. One sign of a deployment's success is the ratio of the number of subscribers to the number of homes passed the *take rate*. Initially, this ratio will be very low (in the single digit percentages) and increase slowly over time. Note that this ratio will never reach 100%, due to the availability of other technologies in most service areas (such as cable TV or satellite) and due to the fact that not all consumers will want to pay for television services at any price. We'll explore these concepts more in Chapter 9.

Typical System Architecture

For very large IPTV delivery systems, there is often a hierarchy of facilities constructed to deliver video signals across a large expanse of territory. One (or two, for disaster recovery) *super head end* (SHE) can serve millions of customers by processing the video channels that are common to all subscribers across the serving area. A *video serving office* (VSO) will be located in each region as required to handle local programming and channels specific to a single city or geographic area. A *central office* (CO) or *remote terminal* (RT) can serve as a *local end office* (LEO) that contains the equipment needed to actually deliver the programming to customers in a local area. This is typically a portion of an existing facility already owned and operated by a telephone company or other local utility. The roles of each of these facilities are explained in more detail in the following sections. Note that different companies may have different names for these various facilities; what's important is that each of the functions described is performed somewhere in the network. Figure 4.1 shows an overview of a typical IPTV system architecture.

Note that for smaller-scale IPTV systems, these three functions may be combined in a single location. The functions all need to be performed; they just might not be performed in separate facilities as described here.

Super Head End

A super head end is the primary source of programming for the IPTV system. It is responsible for gathering content from programming suppliers, converting it into the appropriate form for delivery over the IPTV network, and transmitting the content to

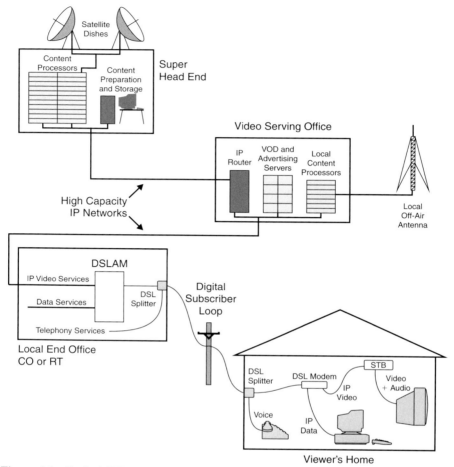

Figure 4.1 *Typical IPTV system architecture.*

the VSOs. The SHE may also be the location where content is prepared for storage on video servers that will be used to deliver VOD services. Let's look at each of these functions in the SHE content work flow:

1. *Content Aggregation.* Content must be gathered from a number of different programming suppliers. The programming can be anything that will be delivered over the IPTV system, such as standard television network feeds; specialty channels that may feature sports, news, music, drama, children's, or nature programming; premium movie channels; or other nonbroadcast feeds. In many cases, these video signals may be gathered from a group of satellite receivers or from a terrestrial video transport network. Most often, these incoming signals will be in an encrypted digital format so the appropriate receivers must be able to receive the necessary commands and decryption keys from the programming suppliers.

2. **Conversion.** Incoming content must be converted into the form that will be transmitted over the IPTV system. To simplify operations, each channel will likely need to be formatted in a very standard manner—standard bit rates, standard packet format, standard compression method, and everything else that will make it possible for the viewer's equipment to understand the video signal and how to process it.

Since programming suppliers are free to choose any type of compression, it is very common for *transcoding* to be required. Transcoding is the conversion of signals from one compression format to another. The input to the transcoder can be any type of video—uncompressed video, MPEG-2, MPEG-4, or VC-1—at whatever bit rate the content supplier has chosen. The output needs to be compressed with the proper codec and operating at the specified bit rate for the IPTV network.

3. **Transport.** The compressed video signals must then be transported over a network to each of the VSOs. In some cases, this network will be owned and operated by the IPTV provider; in other cases, network capacity will be leased from a long-distance network provider. In either case, these networks will tend to be terrestrial (with some exceptions for geography) because the large bandwidths needed to supply hundreds of channels to many locations may be too expensive for satellite.

In many cases, the networks connecting the SHE to each VSO will be redundant. This allows operations at a VSO to continue even if a major network failure has occurred. In very large systems—those serving hundreds of thousands of viewers or more—a second SHE will be constructed to prevent a single catastrophic failure from cutting off television service to a large number of viewers. In this case, the two SHE locations can be hundreds of miles apart to enhance survivability.

4. **Formatting.** Content intended for delivery to viewers on a VOD system can arrive in a wide variety of formats. Some content may arrive in one of the many different professional videotape formats or on DVDs. Content may also be delivered as data files sent over an IP network. Still other content may be transmitted over real-time broadcast links (such as fiber or satellite), requiring a mechanism to receive video signals and store them for further processing.

Regardless of the source of the content, several key functions must be performed on each VOD content element. The content must be transcoded and converted into a common format that can be interpreted by every STB, standardizing parameters such as bit rate and compression technology. The content will also need to be cataloged and labeled for reference, and software tags (known as metadata) will need to be added that indicate the duration of the video, describe the content for viewers, list any restrictions on the storage or delivery of the content, and so on. Formatting content into IP packets is not required at this step—that will be the function of the VOD servers that actually deliver the video signals to the users.

Advertising content may also need to be processed by the SHE. Most of the processing steps are the same for ad content as program content, with the exception that the result will be delivered to advertising servers instead of VOD servers. Ad servers may be located in the SHE for inserting ads into programs that will be delivered throughout the IPTV system, and they may also be located in individual VSOs for ads that will run only in specific regions. As with VOD content, proper labeling and delivery of advertising content files are crucial to success.

Distribution of the VOD and advertisement content to servers located in a VSO will typically be in the form of files sent over a standard data network. Since this content is not being viewed in real time, redundancy is typically not required. In the event of a failure of the network between the SHE and a VSO, the content can simply be transmitted again once the network is repaired. One thing that will be crucial on this network is security. Content owners will want strong assurances that their valuable titles won't fall into the hands of video pirates. Accordingly, the VOD file distribution system will use encryption and/or physically secure networks (such as private fiber optic links).

All of these different functions in a SHE will require hardware and software systems. Staffing will be required to monitor system operations, repair any failures in a timely manner, and perform tasks that require human intervention, such as VOD file processing.

Video Serving Office

A VSO provides video processing and delivery services for a geographic region, such as a city. Each VSO can receive content from a SHE, as well as local programming sources. It is responsible for distributing all of this content in real time to every central office/remote terminal (CO/RT) in the region. A VSO will also typically serve as the location of the VOD and other servers that deliver specialized content to viewers. Customer service, billing, and other related operations may also be housed in the VSO. VSO functions also include:

1. **Localization.** One of the most important functions of the VSO is to process content specific to the local region. This might be from local over-the-air broadcast stations or it might be locally originated programming from other sources, such as educational institutions, government sources, or public access channels. Similar to a SHE, local content can arrive in forms that need to be converted into the common IPTV delivery format.
2. **Compression.** Video content processors take many different types of video inputs and create video outputs in the format necessary for distribution. Content processors can take video signals that have been compressed at one bit rate and convert them into a different bit rate. They can also take video signals that have been compressed using one standard (such as MPEG-2) and convert them into a different standard (such as H.264). Some content processors can also take uncompressed video and compress it using any one of several compression standards.
3. **Stream Creation.** The VSO will also be the location where actual IPTV streams are created. These streams consist of packets that are sent out to COs/RTs. The level of sophistication of the remote equipment will determine the number of streams that need to be generated by the VSO. With simple remote equipment, the VSO will need to generate one stream for every active viewer. With sophisticated remote equipment capable of duplicating outbound video packets, only one stream for each broadcast channel will need to be generated. In this latter case, when multiple viewers are watching the same channel, the remote equipment will make as many copies as necessary (*multicast*) to feed one to each active viewer.
4. **Storage** VOD servers are also typically housed at the VSO. These systems are responsible for creating the individual (*unicast*) streams sent to each subscriber when viewing VOD content. With true VOD, each viewer has the ability to pause, fast-forward, and rewind the video stream. Because commands from each viewer need to be processed rapidly and uniquely, the control functions of the VOD server are as important as content playout.
5. **Local ads** can be an important source of revenue for the IPTV operator. These ads can be inserted (with proper approval) into both nationally and locally originated programming.

Ad servers are used to store advertisements after they are received from the SHE or other source. Ad inserters scan the active channels looking for avail signals, then retrieve the correct ad from the server, and insert the ad into the outbound video signal.

6. **Interactivity** is one of the main competitive weapons for IPTV as compared with satellite television. At the VSO, commands from individual STBs are gathered and processed. One of the main interactive functions is the selection, purchase, and viewer control of VOD content. Another is actual interaction with video content, such as voting for a game show contestant or making purchases on a shopping network. To support these functions, the VSO needs to be equipped with applications servers that run the software needed to process commands from viewers.

7. **STB authorization** is important to the financial well-being of the IPTV provider. Systems in the VSO will validate each STB is authorized before it can receive video content to eliminate unauthorized viewing. Two goals can be achieved through the use of scrambling and encryption: the IPTV operator can ensure that only paying customers are viewing content and that the content can be protected from unauthorized duplication and retransmission.

8. **Fiber delivery.** Typically, a fiber optic network consisting of multiple gigabit Ethernet links is used to connect the VSO to CO/RT locations. These can be packed onto relatively few fibers by using a different wavelength (color) of light for each GigE stream.

Central Office/Remote Terminal

Many IPTV networks use existing telephone company physical infrastructure, including buildings. Central offices contain telephone call switching equipment. Remote terminals, which are often located underground, contain systems that connect subscriber lines and digital or fiber optic links to the nearest CO. In both types of buildings, equipment can be installed to deliver IPTV services over DSL circuits. The equipment located in these facilities must perform several different functions.

1. **DSLAM function.** Inside each CO/RT are one or more digital subscriber line access multiplexer (DSLAM) units (which can also be called *video remote access devices* [VRADs]). The basic function of a DSLAM is to act as an Ethernet switch and connect video traffic arriving from the VSO to the DSL lines going out to each subscriber premises. To accomplish this, the DSLAM examines the IP address of each incoming packet and forwards it over to whichever DSL circuit connects to the subscriber device with that IP address.

2. **Multicasting technology** (usually based on *Internet group management protocol* [IGMP]) is useful for IPTV video broadcasting and is supported by some of the newer brands of DSLAM. With this technology, the DSLAM is capable of taking a single stream from the VSO and replicating it to feed multiple simultaneous viewers of a single channel. Without this technology, the VSO must create an individual video stream for every viewer.

3. **Connectivity.** The DSLAM must also connect the existing telephony system in the CO/RT. A DSL splitter or hybrid bridge is used to allow both the DSL equipment and the existing phone equipment to share a single pair of copper wires that leads to each subscriber's home.

4. **Combining services.** Several different services can all share the high-speed bandwidth offered by a DSL line to a consumer's premises. IPTV video services are, of course, one component. Another is high-speed data service for Internet access; this traffic can be separated by the DSLAM and connected to an IP data router for processing within the CO. Services such as VoIP could also be delivered to separate outputs of the DSLAM if configured appropriately.

Customer Premises

One of the most difficult environments for an IPTV operator is inside the viewer's home. IPTV devices require power, a physical location, and a network wiring system to connect to one or more STBs located around the house. Many different technologies have been employed here, including HomePNA, coax, and twisted pair, and some investigations are ongoing into wireless connections.

1. *A DSL modem* is installed in each home to receive the high-speed digital signals from the DSL circuit and convert data into forms that other devices can use. This device can be stand-alone or integrated into a home gateway.
2. *A DSL filter* is used in each home to prevent standard telephones from receiving the high-speed signals processed by the DSL modem.
3. *The home gateway* is an optional piece of equipment installed by some service providers to provide control of and communication to multiple STBs. This device can also serve to manage the home network to ensure that Web surfing from a PC in the home does not compromise high-priority video traffic. It can also serve to convert between the different types of cabling used inside the house and the high-speed DSL lines.
4. *The STB* supports much of the functionality within an IPTV system. It decodes the incoming digital video signals, produces on-screen graphics, supports user channel changing and other interactive functions, and many other tasks. Without a suitable STB for each television set, an IPTV system would be unusable.

Typical Software Capabilities

Software performs many key functions inside an IPTV network. As is the case for a PC, an IPTV system simply wouldn't function without software. The following sections describe a number of software functions typically found in IPTV systems.

Electronic Program Guide

The *electronic program guide* (EPG) is an on-screen display that tells viewers which content is available on which channels. This can include both broadcast channels available to all viewers simultaneously and VOD content available for viewers to watch individually. Program guide information can either be produced by the IPTV network provider or, as is most often the case, purchased from an external supplier.

Two main types of EPGs are available. The first is a scrolling program guide, where the content on each available channel is displayed in channel number order on a grid that slowly scrolls up the television screen. This scheme does not require interactivity from the viewer and can become annoying to users as the number of channels exceeds fifty.

The second type of EPG is called an interactive program guide. In this scheme, a grid of channels and content choices is displayed on the television screen, as described previously. However, in this case, viewers have the ability to navigate around in the grid using their remote controls. The viewers can scroll and jump up or down in the grid to view different channels and can also scroll to the right to see future programs.

System operators have two choices for handling EPG functions.

- Intelligent STBs with embedded EPG functionality can be used. In this case, data for an interactive programming guide are broadcast to all the STBs on a periodic basis. Each STB is responsible for storing the latest information and for creating the displays. This is done to enable rapid response to the viewer's commands and to eliminate the burden on central equipment of having to process scroll commands from every viewer. This is also why newly connected STBs can require time before being able to display an accurate program guide, as it may take a while for all the information to be received and stored.

- In other cases, the interactive program guide processing is centralized in the VSO. In this architecture, the STB simply sends viewer commands upstream and receives new display information downstream. This system has the advantage of reducing the amount of processing that takes place in the STB, but has the disadvantage of requiring more communication between the STB and the VSO.

Conditional Access System

A *conditional access system* (or CA system) controls which users are able to view which programming. For example, only viewers who have subscribed to a premium movie channel are allowed to have access to that content. This can be relatively simple to implement in an IPTV system because the system simply needs to ensure that streams are never delivered to users who are not authorized to receive them. In contrast, a different approach is needed in a satellite or traditional cable TV system, where all channels are present at the input to each STB. In these systems, the content must be scrambled, encrypted, or otherwise made unavailable to unauthorized viewers.

Video-on-Demand System

A VOD system provides users with content that can be viewed at their discretion. This typically consists of a set of content files stored on a server and played out under the control of users.

Software for a VOD system needs to perform several functions, some in conjunction with other software modules. The available titles need to be listed and described by way of the EPG. Any required payment must be collected. A network connection (possibly via several hops) needs to be set up between the VOD server and the viewer's STB to deliver the content. The proper keys for decoding any content encryption need to be sent to the STB by the digital rights management (DRM) system (covered in the next section). Viewer commands (such as pause, fast-forward, and rewind) from the middleware system need to be retrieved and processed rapidly to control how the content is played out. All of this needs to happen fairly quickly in response to user actions so that the system operates as "video on demand" and not "video when the system is good and ready."

Digital Rights Management System

A *digital rights management* system is designed to protect the property rights of a content owner. The focus of DRM is to control what the viewer can do with content after it is delivered, whereas a CA system controls whether the content will be delivered to a viewer. DRM typically involves some form of encryption or scrambling that renders the content unwatchable without the appropriate key. The key is usually some type of numeric value that controls the operation of a descrambler or decryption device. This topic will be covered in more depth in Chapter 7.

In addition to content scrambling, the DRM system needs to ensure that unauthorized copies or recordings of the content are not made. This usually takes the form of some type of scrambling or signal locking at the output of the STB.

Subscriber Management and Billing System

The revenue stream of an IPTV provider depends on an efficient, functional system for managing subscribers and gathering data needed to prepare accurate bills. Here is a brief list of functions that are normally required.

- *Device association,* where a specific subscriber is linked with a specific set of hardware, such as an STB. Accuracy in this process is essential to ensure that the STBs have been deployed correctly and that any charges incurred by an STB actually belong to the associated subscriber.
- *Subscriber services profile,* which indicates the services that the subscriber has ordered, such as a specific set of premium content channels. This system also needs to accurately track when customers call to add or remove services so that STB control settings can be adjusted appropriately.
- *Subscriber purchase history,* which records the specifics of any purchases such as premium VOD content.
- *Service call logging and repair dispatch,* which has a big impact on subscriber satisfaction levels when they call for repairs. Accuracy is essential, so subscribers can be told when to expect repair technicians to arrive and when their service will be restored. It can also help technicians understand the problems that were reported by the subscriber and any steps that have already been taken to isolate the fault.

It is not uncommon for specific types of content to require direct payments to the content owner. This might be a monthly payment per subscriber for a premium sports channel or a per-viewing charge for a new-release movie offered on VOD. IPTV providers who don't have good billing systems in place can find themselves in violation of contracts requiring payment to the content owners. In extreme cases, a poor payment or faulty security system could result in the IPTV provider losing access to premium content in the future.

It's interesting to note that many companies are coming to recognize the growing importance of customer service for IPTV and other systems. Amdocs, a leading supplier of customer management solutions to service providers, commissioned a survey of service providers in 2008. The results were quite interesting: "75% confirm that faster time to market will reduce customer churn—more than 90% recognize that decreasing time to market requires investment in OSS (Operations Support Systems)."

Emergency Alert System

In the United States, the federal government requires that television and radio broadcasters and cable television system operators implement an Emergency Alert System (EAS). This system can be used by the President to make an announcement to the public in a time of national emergency. Use of the system is also permitted for state and local agencies to warn of certain hazards such as tornadoes or other dangerous weather. The system must be capable of interrupting programming on all channels provided by the television system and of inserting an appropriate warning or other instructions. On-screen graphics may also be used. The EAS must be installed in each active system and must be tested weekly and monthly. Failure to have an operational EAS can result in significant fines for the system operator.

Constructing an Internet Video System

Building an Internet video system is easier in some respects than building an IPTV system but more difficult in others. Construction is easier because an IP network, with all of the accompanying packet delivery hardware, does not need to be built, as the Internet will be used. However, building a delivery system that has adequate capacity to handle the peak number of simultaneous users while also being affordable can be a difficult balancing act. Accordingly, many systems are designed to be scalable so that capacity can be added quickly and easily as demand grows. Some hosting companies offer this as a service, where system capacity can be rented incrementally as demand grows.

The basic elements of a content delivery system include a content preparation system, a Web site to serve as a landing point, a video delivery server, and a viewer device to watch the programming, usually a PC. A content delivery network (CDN) may also be used to assist deliveries to viewers. Each of these elements requires software for operation, much of which can be purchased off the shelf. The following sections discuss the principal hardware elements and then the software applications hosted on them.

Typical Hardware Architecture

The vast majority of the hardware needed for an Internet video delivery system can be housed in a single facility, although it does not need to be. The quality of connectivity between the different systems' elements and between the systems and the Internet is a primary determinant of system performance. In very large applications capable of delivering thousands of simultaneous streams to viewers, hardware distributed at several different geographic locations can actually help performance by eliminating bandwidth bottlenecks that might occur. For an overview of a typical Internet video system, see Figure 4.2.

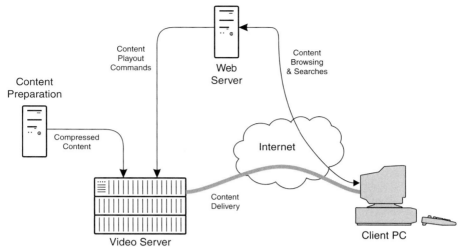

Figure 4.2 *Typical Internet video system architecture.*

Content Preparation System

Raw video content, such as a live image generated by a camera or video that has been recorded to a tape, is generally not well suited for streaming applications; the content needs to be processed to make it ready for streaming. Processing can include format conversion, video compression, labeling and indexing, and publishing for streaming.

Capturing and preparing content for viewing can be a simple or a highly complex process, depending on the goals of the users and their budgets for time and money. For some users, taking a home video camera and placing a compressed video image on their personal Web site is adequate. For others, professional production, with carefully edited images and graphics designed for Web viewing, is required.

Sometimes, multiple versions of a video file are required. This is the case if users are given the choice of two or more different media players or if the video is to be encoded at different bit rates. Low bit rate videos are delivered to users who have lower speed Internet connections. High bit rate videos deliver better images if viewers have access to high-speed Internet connections. Using software tools embedded in a video server, each user's connection speed can be measured automatically and dynamically so that the video bit rate can be increased or decreased as network conditions change, and the user is not aware of the changes. A different video file must be prepared for each bit rate and codec combination so that if two viewer types are supported and three different bit rates are offered, then six different files must be prepared; this can be done automatically by some authoring tools.

Web Server

Web servers are used in Internet video systems to assist viewers in selecting content to view. A typical page will contain descriptions of the videos, as well as selected stills from one or more videos. Some of these Web pages are configured to have embedded links to video content that begin video playback as soon as a user views the Web page. These Web pages can be viewed with a standard browser and searched by normal text-based search engines. Videos can be tagged with text labels by viewers to assist others in searching. Many pages also contain links to other pages of video with related subject matter.

Web servers often support a number of other functions. The following are some common Web server capabilities:

- *User and e-commerce administation.* Some sites require payments or user log-ins prior to viewing. Web servers often handle the whole process of managing user profiles, collecting payments, and encouraging nonmembers to enroll before entering the site.
- *User ratings.* Many sites allow users to rate or vote on particular videos. Web servers can gather this information from users, store and process it, and create pages that show the summarized details to other users.
- *User comments* form a huge part of many sites' appeal. Web servers are used to collect, manage, and display these comments. Care must be taken to ensure that the comments are associated with the proper videos and that any rules about the use of profanity or copyrighted material are followed.
- *Ad placement.* A number of video Web sites use advertising as a source of revenue. Web servers must be configured to deliver the correct, current advertisements. More sophisticated servers can deliver context-sensitive advertising, where the choice of ads to be displayed is based in part on the type of video featured on the page. For example, if a Web user is looking at a video that features a famous comedian, then the Web server could display an advertisement for a DVD of that comedian's most recent movie.

Video Server

The video server is the workhorse of an Internet video system. It is responsible for securely storing the video files that can be viewed. In addition, the video server must create the packet streams that are delivered to each viewer. The video server must also handle encrypting or scrambling the outbound video streams to ensure that they are protected from unauthorized use.

- *Storage:* The video server only needs to have enough capacity to store the video files it is providing. Accordingly, servers can have either large or small capacities. If multiple versions of the video files have been created, then the server needs to have enough capacity to store all of the different versions.
- *Stream creation:* The video server must be capable of delivering a stream to each requesting user. This is essentially always done on request so that each time a user wants to view a video, the server needs to create a stream of packets to send to that specific viewer. Every packet in the stream needs to be created by the server, because each one must contain the specific destination IP address corresponding to the viewer's device. While this is not an incredible burden for a few video streams, the workload on the video server increases as more users are added and more streams are requested.
- *Security:* Files stored on the video server are typically encrypted or scrambled for two reasons. First, by pre-encoding the files, it reduces the amount of work that needs to

be done by the DRM system when files are streamed to viewers. Second, in the event that an unauthorized third party gets access to the content on the server, the encoded files will be unwatchable. Content owners often specify contractually how their content is to be handled, and this may include the form in which the content is stored on the server.

Live Streaming Server

A live streaming server is a specialized device that enables scalable delivery of live video programming to multiple users simultaneously. It operates by taking in a single stream of content and producing multiple copies for delivery to multiple viewers in real time.

Typically, viewers who want to watch the live content will navigate to a central Web site that acts as a portal (covered in "Typical Software Architecture") for the content. Users who navigate to the portal are then redirected to the live streaming server as soon as they request to watch the video. Once they are connected to the streaming server, a copy of the source video is created inside the server. This new copy is then formatted into IP packets addressed to the viewer's device and sent out for delivery over the Internet.

Client PC

Most Internet video is delivered to PCs for viewing, although other devices are becoming available. Each PC must be equipped with software capable of receiving the incoming video packets and converting them into a video image on the user's display. In order for this software to work properly, adequate hardware must be present. Most recently produced PCs have enough processing power to decode and display standard-definition video images that have been compressed using standards such as MPEG-2 and MPEG-4. High-definition streams (which are becoming more common in Internet video) may require hardware accelerators found on advanced graphics cards in order to produce HD image output.

Typical Software Architecture

Software is a key element of any Internet video system. It plays a major role in enabling viewers to find and select content, delivering the content, and playing the content on the viewing device. Let's take a look at some of the major components.

Portal Web Site

A portal Web site typically provides a common launching point for viewers and content providers. From a viewer's standpoint, a successful portal has a wide range of content that can be easily searched and navigated through to locate content that will be interesting to view. From a content provider's standpoint, a good portal will attract a large number of potential viewers. Examples abound on the Internet, including YouTube and Hulu.com.

A well-constructed Web site will typically have a number of different ways to search for content. One method uses a standard text-based search on the title of the video. Another method uses tags (similar to keywords) that have been added to video files by viewers that describe particular attributes of the video, such as "turtles" or "funny." Still other methods may rank videos by popularity in a number of categories or display videos that are watched frequently by viewers who have watched the currently displayed video. Many Web sites also allow viewers to post comments or rate videos, thereby increasing the level of viewer participation.

Web sites typically consist of a number of Web pages that serve as the user interface to video content. Different approaches are taken in the design of the user interface. Some Web sites will have a single featured video per page, which will begin playing as soon as the user navigates to that page. Other Web sites will have a collection of links to still images excerpted from videos; when the user chooses one of the thumbnails (small pictures) to view, the video will begin playing in a new window or Web page. Choosing between the two methods is really a matter of preference, and both are widely used.

Examining the HTML code for a video Web site page reveals that the actual video content is not contained in the page itself, but is instead stored elsewhere. The Web site handles interaction with the user and provides links to the locations where the content is actually stored. One benefit of using this technique is that it avoids having the user's browser attempt to load a complete video file each time the user navigates to a new page of the Web site. Instead, what happens is that the Web site page loads to give the user a complete page image with everything but the video, and then an automatic process takes place to stream the video file to the viewer. What the user sees is a Web page with an active video window, but in reality these two items are delivered separately and united inside the user's Web browser software. If the user navigates away from the page (or presses one of the controls to pause, rewind, or fast-forward the content), then the Web page remains static, but the streaming engine reconfigures itself to deliver the user's new selection.

Streaming Engine

The *streaming engine* is a software module on the video server specifically designed to create a series of IP video packets for each outbound stream. Each IP packet must have source and destination IP addresses. In order for the video packets to reach the correct destination, the server must create headers for these packets with the correct IP destination address.

Since streaming is done on a real-time basis, the engine must also create well-behaved streams, meaning that the pace of the packets should be regular and consistent. The rate of the packets also has to be controlled such that the player receives only as many packets as needed to render the video and audio correctly. Too fast and the player would be required to store the extra packets before playback, creating havoc with the playback if the buffer overflowed. Conversely, if the pace slows too much, the player would be starved for data and would have to freeze or interrupt the user display to compensate while waiting for new data to arrive. Although software players normally include small buffers to smooth out the inevitable variations in packet arrivals caused by IP networks, the goal of a streaming engine is to deliver a 5-minute, 10-second stream in 5 minutes and 10 seconds.

Content Delivery Network

For popular Web sites, it is expensive to purchase enough video server capacity to handle peak loads when many viewers are trying to watch videos simultaneously. Service providers offer content delivery network services to Web site owners who are willing to pay to have their Web sites load quicker, both because of the greater quantity of CDN servers that can be brought online as demand peaks and because the servers are distributed geographically around the Internet to be close to viewers. A wide variety of CDN services are available; they can be purchased by both large and small Web site providers.

Web Browser

Web browser software resides on a viewer's PC, mobile phone, or other device and enables a viewer to view and navigate through Web pages that contain text, graphics, and other data. Examples include Microsoft Internet Explorer, Apple Safari, and Mozilla Firefox. Viewers use these programs to navigate through Web sites to find content to view. Web browsers work with static content such as text and graphics that can be described with HTML commands. One of the best features of HTML is the ability to embed hot links into documents—these have the effect of directing the browser software to a new Web site that is then downloaded and displayed on the viewer's device.

Browsers use multimedia plug-ins to support other functions such as video and audio playback. These plug-ins consist of pieces of software stored and run on the viewer's PC or other device that can interpret video, audio, and other special types of files, such as Flash. When a Web site contains content beyond the scope of normal HTML, special commands are used to put the correct plug-in into operation when the content is selected. We'll spend more time on browsers and plug-ins in Chapter 11.

It is common for a single PC to have a number of plug-ins to support a variety of multimedia types. Different plug-ins are used for different types of media; one type of plug-in is used for viewing Flash animation while another is used to play a compressed audio stream. Because the plug-ins are also closely tied to the internal workings of specific operating systems, a Quick-Time plug-in for a Macintosh won't be useful for playing Adobe files on a Windows PC.

Media Player

A media player is another piece of software resident on the viewer's device. Examples include Microsoft's Windows Media Player, Apple's QuickTime, and

Real Player from Real Networks. A media player performs a very similar function to a browser multimedia plug-in in that it takes a content stream and turns it into images and sounds that can be seen and heard by the viewer. However, there are differences between media players and plug-ins, which are covered in the following discussion, as well as in more depth in Chapter 11.

A media player is typically a stand-alone piece of software. It can be run by itself, without having a Web browser activated. Most players contain a library function that enables them to list a variety of content that can be played by a viewer. This list can include content resident on the local device (e.g., hard drive of the PC) and content available from the Internet. Most media players can access the Internet to locate and play files from a variety of sources. In contrast, a browser plug-in is only active when a Web page is delivering multimedia content, and there is no easy way to use the plug-in to play content that is not part of a Web page.

Most media players offer a significant amount of viewer control over content display. The video window can often be expanded or contracted. When an audio-only file is being played, some players offer visualization graphics that change shape in response to the sounds being played. A variety of skins can be chosen to change the appearance of the controls and the frame that surround the viewing window. This contrasts with the very limited control given to viewers by most Web pages—typically just pause, rewind, and fast-forward (if enough of the clip has been buffered).

Digital rights management is a key part of most media players that is used to ensure that the rules and limitations defined by content owners are obeyed. Another important function is copy protection, which prevents unauthorized copies of media files from being made. Both of these technologies are typically built into a media player, as otherwise it would be difficult to get content owners to agree to allow their content to be played by that brand of player. Browser plug-ins are typically not as sophisticated; they rely on the functions of browsers to manage Web pages and media streams reliably.

It is also interesting to note that many commercial media players have different versions of their software, some of which can be downloaded at no charge and other versions that require purchase. The purchased versions typically offer greater functionality, such as support for full-screen video display or more advanced video compression techniques. Some media players offer subscriptions to special libraries of content as well as user customizable programs.

Reality Check

The first Reality Check of this chapter takes a look at two modifications to the architectures that have been used successfully for providing IPTV services. The second Reality Check discusses aspects of the IPTV business that all prospective providers should consider before launching a project. The third Reality Check discusses a very simple Internet video delivery system that offers a minimum level of functionality.

Alternative Architectures

Systems with architectures similar to the IPTV network described in this chapter have been implemented at numerous large telephone companies around the globe. However, one of the great benefits of IPTV is that it does not need to be tied to a specific architecture. Here are some alternatives that have been used successfully by IPTV providers.

Shared Super Head End

There are an amazing number of small and geographically dispersed telephone service providers who could offer IPTV services if they were able to get access to programming. The costs would be very substantial if each one of these companies needed to create a SHE with multiple satellite receivers, content processors, encryption units, and subscriber management systems and if they had to negotiate contracts with a large bouquet of content providers. Instead, some services have sprung up to fill this need by offering a prepackaged set of programming distributed from a central location.

Avail Media is one example of an IPTV programming source that has stepped in to fill this need as a wholesale provider of managed content aggregation services through an integrated head-end infrastructure. Today, the company provides an end-to-end video solution to 118 service providers across the United States, the Caribbean, and the island of Guam, handling everything from transport rights to subscriber usage tracking to marketing support. Avail Media's business model is to provide a turnkey approach to simplify video deployment, allowing service providers to focus on subscriber-facing activities and the commercial launch of services.

The company has acquired a content library with transport rights from programmers such as ABC-Disney, Turner, NBC Universal, MTV Networks, and Fox Cable Networks. They also have Hollywood movie studio VOD rights, as well as niche, ethnic, and international content providers. The lineups of 300+ live SD and HD linear television channels are all encoded in MPEG-4, IP-encapsulated, encrypted, and transported via three satellites for reception directly at central offices via an IPTV gateway.

The IPTV gateway consists of satellite dishes and receivers; IP switching; a Management and Control System (MCS), which supports services such as alternate feed control for live regional sporting events (i.e., blackout management); and a fully redundant RF switch that feeds satellite receivers. After demodulation in the satellite receivers, content is transmitted to the Feed Control Manager (FCM), which provides monitoring of content streams, does transport stream multiplexing and scrambling, and provides an interface to conditional access systems. Encryption middleware and an MPEG-4 STB are required for the receipt of Avail Media-encoded content.

Once this equipment is in place, the local telco needs to negotiate a contract and install hardware to get content from any local television stations and add those signals to their IPTV channel lineup. The shared SHE vastly simplifies and reduces the cost process of installing an IPTV system for a smaller telephone company.

Alternative Circuit Technology

Not all IPTV services need to be delivered over DSL circuits, although they are certainly the predominant technology. For green-field installations, namely those where a large group of housing is being built in a single development, even DSL-oriented companies such as AT&T use *Fiber to the Home* (FTTH) technology to deliver voice, video, and data services over an IP infrastructure. Similarly, it is becoming more common to deliver IPTV services over a cable TV broadband system or a wireless IP system, provided that a suitable return path is installed.

Business Challenges

Several key challenges need to be overcome to create an IPTV system that will be accepted by viewers and profitable for the operator.

Return on Investment

One of the biggest challenges is to design an IPTV system that can be installed economically in enough viewers' homes to generate a decent return on investment. A huge amount of hardware and software must be purchased to build the content collection and processing offices. These costs don't vary much whether the system needs to serve 100 or 100,000 viewers, and the costs need to be spread over a large number of subscribers to make the business models work. In addition, there is a significant cost per user in terms of the devices that must be installed in each home and the costs of the transmission equipment required to distribute the signals. While these latter costs vary with the number of subscribers, the total costs for the system can still be fairly high.

Reaching Existing Homes

Another significant challenge is installing an IPTV system in an existing neighborhood. Economical ways must be found to reuse existing infrastructure (such as subscriber loops). Also, construction costs need to be watched carefully, as not all homes that have access to IPTV networks will actually purchase the services. Contrast this with the situation in newly built developments, where fiber optic connections can be made directly to each house for not much more of an investment than needed to install standard metallic subscriber loops.

Local Permissions

One challenge that cannot be overlooked is the need to get permission (often in the form of a renewable franchise) from the local government authorities to install and operate a system. Many communities have powerful vested interests in the form of existing video delivery services, such as cable TV or OTA broadcasters. While many governments favor having competitive network suppliers, the practicalities of encouraging new providers to install or upgrade their networks while at the same time maintaining fairness to incumbent providers can be difficult to balance.

The Low End of Internet Video

It's important to remember that Internet video systems come in many different sizes. In fact, it is instructive to look at a minimal system just to see how simply it can be done. Of course, with this system, performance will also be minimal, with perhaps a limit of a handful of viewers active at any one time. However, for some applications, that is all that is really needed.

Here is what a basic system could consist of:

- A stand-alone PC or server with a reasonable amount of processing power and a high-performance network interface card.
- A basic Web server package to provide the user Web pages.
- Content preparation software, which could be as simple as the video-editing functions built into PC operating systems.
- A video streaming server package, which is available for low cost from several different sources.
- A broadband network connection.

Of all the aforementioned expenses, probably the most expensive one—on a long-term basis—is the network connection. All of the other equipment and software can be purchased for less than $1000.

Summary

This chapter discussed the basic architecture of both IPTV and Internet video systems. The first section of the chapter focused on IPTV and went through the primary system hardware elements, including the SHE, VSO, and CO/RT. It also discussed some of the software functions that make up an IPTV system.

The second section of this chapter described the key elements of an Internet video system. It covered the basic hardware, including content preparation, Web server, video server, streaming server, and client PC. It also discussed software elements, including the Web site, streaming engine, Web browser, and media player.

In many real deployments, some of the aforementioned systems will be combined with others, but the functions must still be performed. Although the tasks may be accomplished in different locations or packages, each of them is essential to the end-to-end flow of video to viewers.

5 IP—The Internet Protocol

The Internet is not just one thing, it's a collection of things—of numerous communications networks that all speak the same digital language.

Jim Clark

IP is the most successful computer networking technology ever invented. A recent count shows more than 570 million host computers connect directly to the Internet.[1] Every new desktop or laptop computer produced today comes equipped with a networking connection that supports IP.

After reading the basic descriptions of IP networking in this chapter, our discussions about IP video will be much easier to understand. This chapter discusses the basics of IP transport, explains the concept of a packet, and shows how IP fits into the overall scheme of data communications. It then covers unicasting and multicasting, two key concepts in video networking.

The Corner Office View

The remarkable social impact and the economic success of the Internet are in many ways directly attributable to the architectural characteristics that were part of its design. The Internet was designed with no gatekeepers over new content or services. The Internet is based on a layered, end-to-end model that allows people at each level of the network to innovate free of any central control. By placing intelligence at the edges rather than control in the middle of the network, the Internet has created a platform for innovation. This has led to an explosion of offerings—from VoIP to 802.11x Wi-Fi to blogging—that might never have evolved had central control of the network been required by design.

—Vinton Cerf, Chief Internet Evangelist, Google Inc., and coinventor of TCP/IP[2]

A Simple Analogy

To understand the principle of the Internet Protocol, a simple analogy may be appropriate. In some respects, an IP address is like a telephone number. If you know someone's telephone number, there is a pretty good chance you can pick up your

---

[1]From Internet Systems Consortium, Inc., www.isc.org. This number doesn't include the millions of computers that are connected within private networks and share an Internet connection.

[2]Vinton Cerf, letter to U.S. House of Representatives Committee on Energy and Commerce, November 8, 2005, googleblog.blogspot.com/2005/11/vint-cerf-speaks-out-on-net-neutrality.html

phone and call him or her. It doesn't matter what country the person is in, as long as you dial correctly (adding country code when required), and it doesn't matter what kind of technology that person is using—mobile phone, cordless phone, fixed rotary, or tone-dialed phone. Several different network voice technologies may be used to complete the circuit, including copper cable, fiber optics, microwave links, satellite links, and other wireless technologies. No matter how convoluted the route, the call goes through.

For data networks, an IP address provides the same function as a telephone number: it is a mechanism used to uniquely identify different computers and to enable them to contact each other and exchange data over a huge variety of different network technologies.

Stretching the analogy a bit further, simply knowing someone's telephone number doesn't mean you're going to be able to communicate with him or her. A call might be placed when nobody is there to answer the phone. The phone might be engaged in another call and not available. The call might go through just fine, but if both speakers don't use a common language, communication won't occur. The same is true with IP networking—simply knowing another computer's IP address doesn't mean that two applications running on two different machines can communicate with each other.

Of course, it is important to remember that IP networking and telephony are two very different technologies. Telephony is "connection oriented," meaning that a circuit must be established between the sender and the receiver of information before communication takes place (such as a voice conversation or a fax transmission). In a call, all the information flows over the same path. IP, however, is "connectionless," meaning that the information (such as data, voice, or video) is broken up into specific IP subunits, called packets, prior to transmission. Each packet is free to take any available path from the sender to the receiver.

What Is a Packet?

An IP *packet* is a unique container for data. It consists of a string of data bytes that has a defined format, including a header and a block of information bytes. Each packet can be a different length (within limits).

The header of each packet contains information about the packet. Most important is the destination address, which is the IP address of the destination for the packet. The header also includes the IP address of the source of data so that two-way communication can be easily established between two devices. This also enables packets from different sources going to different destinations to share a single communications link. Devices at either end of the link (called *routers*) can sort the packets out and deliver them to different destinations based on the IP addresses in each packet's header.

The biggest strength of an IP network is that many different packets, all containing data from different applications, can share a single packet transport link. This permits the tremendous flexibility of an IP network—once a device does the hard work of converting a particular data stream into packets, the rest is easy because the IP network will take care of delivering the packets to their destination. Once they are delivered, it is again the responsibility of an application to take data out of the packets and put data to work. This isn't a trivial process—the receiving application must deal with any IP network delivery errors.

How IP Fits In

IP provides a very useful mechanism to enable communications between computers. IP provides a uniform addressing scheme so that computers on one network can communicate with computers on a distant network. IP also provides a set of functions that make it easy for different types of applications (such as e-mail, Web browsing, or video streaming) to work in parallel on a single computer. Plus, IP enables different types of computers (mainframes, PCs, Macs, Linux machines, etc.) to communicate with each other.

IP is very flexible because it is not tied to a specific physical communication method. IP links have been successfully established over a variety of different physical links. The most popular technology for IP transport is Ethernet, which is often used for local area networking. Many other technologies can support IP, including dial-up modems, wireless links (such as Wi-Fi), DSL, SONET, and ATM telecom links. IP will even work across connections where several network technologies are combined, such as a wireless home access link that connects to a cable TV system offering cable modem services or a DSL line, which in turn sends customer data to the Internet by means of a fiber optic backbone. This adaptability is one of the things that makes IP so widespread.

IP doesn't do everything. It depends on other software and hardware, and other software in turn depends on it. IP fits between the function of data transport performed by physical networks and the software applications that use IP to communicate with applications running on other devices. Figure 5.1 shows how IP fits between applications on the top of the networking hierarchy and physical communications on the bottom.

IP is not a user application or an application protocol. However, many user applications employ IP to accomplish their tasks, such as sending e-mail, browsing the Web, or playing a video. These applications use protocols such as the *HyperText Transfer Protocol* or *Simple Mail Transfer Protocol* for necessary services within the IP framework. For example, one of the services provided by HTTP is a uniform method for giving the location of resources on the Internet, which goes by the abbreviation URL.

Internet Protocol by itself is not even a reliable means of communications; it does not provide a mechanism to resend data that might be lost or corrupted in transmission. Other protocols that employ IP are responsible for that. Using the telephone analogy again, IP can connect the telephone call, but it doesn't control what happens if, for example, the person being called isn't home or if the call gets interrupted before the parties are finished talking. Those occurrences are the responsibility of the protocols that use IP for communication.

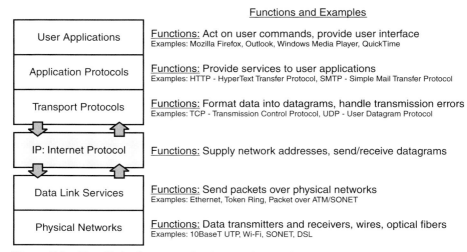

	Functions and Examples
User Applications	**Functions:** Act on user commands, provide user interface Examples: Mozilla Firefox, Outlook, Windows Media Player, QuickTime
Application Protocols	**Functions:** Provide services to user applications Examples: HTTP - HyperText Transfer Protocol, SMTP - Simple Mail Transfer Protocol
Transport Protocols	**Functions:** Format data into datagrams, handle transmission errors Examples: TCP - Transmission Control Protocol, UDP - User Datagram Protocol
IP: Internet Protocol	**Functions:** Supply network addresses, send/receive datagrams
Data Link Services	**Functions:** Send packets over physical networks Examples: Ethernet, Token Ring, Packet over ATM/SONET
Physical Networks	**Functions:** Data transmitters and receivers, wires, optical fibers Examples: 10BaseT UTP, Wi-Fi, SONET, DSL

Figure 5.1   *How IP fits between other layers of networking protocols.*

Types of IP Networks

Many different types of physical networks can be used to transport IP video. This section reviews some of the most popular ones and describes where they are commonly used.

Ethernet

Ethernet is the most widespread data communications network in the world. Ethernet is used in local area networks to connect computers, printers, servers, IP routers, and many other types of devices. There are three commonly used speeds for Ethernet connections: 10 Mbps, 100 Mbps, and 1 Gbps. The first two technologies are often called 10baseT and 100baseT, respectively, and the fastest of the three is often called GigE. 10GigE links that operate at 10 Gbps are used inside providers' networks and in backbones for the Internet and corporate networks; they are not commonly used for connections to end-user workstations.

Ethernet is a *Local Area Network* (LAN) technology. This means that it is not suitable for use in *Wide Area Networks* (WANs) or *Metropolitan Area Networks* (MANs). The reasons for this are that Ethernet has some fairly short distance limitations (2000 meters in many instances) for timing reasons.

Basic Ethernet cabling usually consists of special twisted pairs of conductors called CAT5 or CAT6, depending on the speed rating (the higher number rating is capable of faster speed). An Ethernet network can also be implemented over optical fibers; this is reasonably common for GigE links and very common for 10GigE links.

Ethernet networks are abundant in modern office settings and are often used in home networks. Many networks that were originally set up to share a printer with a small group of PCs have expanded to cover hundreds of devices throughout a building. These networks will often contain a variety of servers and network interfaces, including Internet connections. Many home Ethernet networks were originally installed for the sole purpose of enabling multiple PCs to share a single high-speed network connection.

Wireless Ethernet

Wireless Ethernet is becoming very popular for many applications, including connections to laptops and other portable devices. A couple of popular names for this technology are 802.11 (the number of the IEEE standard) and Wi-Fi.

Most Wi-Fi networks are configured with a fixed central *access point* (AP) that provides a common node for all the portable devices. Typically, the AP provides a connection to a high-speed network that supports Internet access or access to a corporate network.

Wireless transmissions can be affected by a number of different factors in the local environment, and data transmission speeds can change rapidly. As a result, systems will use automatic packet retransmission to ensure that data get delivered. Unfortunately, this can cause the data transmission speed to fluctuate rapidly and without warning. This can make it extremely difficult to reliably send live video streams. Applications using file transfer or download and play technologies over wireless connections will fare better, although their performance may be inconsistent.

Wi-Fi is used inside many homes for connecting PCs to each other, printers, and the Internet. The main advantages are portability and elimination of the need to string cables to every location in the home where a PC is going to be used. Wi-Fi hot spots (locations where one or more APs are located) are very common in public areas such as coffee shops, hotels, and airports. Wi-Fi is not used often for professional video networks because of the limited bandwidth and the highly variable delay.

Another wireless technology, Wi-Max or IEEE 802.16, has been standardized, but not yet widely deployed in the United States. Similar to Wi-Fi, this service uses licensed radio spectrum to deliver data from an access point to nodes located within a range of several miles. This service is particularly attractive for mobile applications (it is sometimes referred to as fourth-generation [4G] mobile technology); however, the cost-effectiveness of using Wi-Max for IPTV delivery is questionable.

Cable Modems

Many cable TV companies provide a variety of services to customers with the goal of capturing a larger portion of their customers' monthly telecommunications expenses. As a result, many customers have been extremely pleased with these reliable high-speed services offerings.

Cable modems work by taking digital data signals and converting them into high-frequency signals that flow over cable TV cabling in place of some of the television content. The relevant standards for these signals are called DOCSIS, for Data Over Cable Service Interface Specification, developed by a consortium led by CableLabs. Because data services are bidirectional, transmission must take place in both directions on the cable TV system.

Cable modem termination system (CMTS) shelves are located at the cable TV head end. These provide high-speed data connectivity to hundreds or thousands of cable TV subscribers. The output of the CMTS system is one or more *RF* signals that are combined with normal video signals distributed to all of the viewers in an area. At each broadband user's home, a cable modem is installed that tunes to the required frequency and selects data addressed to that user's home. Data packets are converted into standard Ethernet format and delivered to the user's PC or other device (such as a home router or Wi-Fi access point). On the return trip, the cable modem accepts data from the end-user device and transmits it back to the CMTS by way of an RF channel on the cable TV return path.

Cable modems are quite popular in the United States, with over 35 million residential subscribers.[3] IPTV services can be delivered over cable modems. However, because cable TV systems already have a video delivery system, they are not often used for IPTV, except for VOD services. Internet video services are frequently delivered over cable modems. Outside the United States, cable modems are less popular but are still used for a significant number of broadband households.

Digital Subscriber Lines

Digital Subscriber Lines (DSL) provide broadband data services over long twisted pair cables. They were developed to enable companies with telephone lines installed to customer homes to offer high-speed Internet connections without having to install a whole new network.

Sophisticated techniques are required to get high-speed digital data to move reliably over cables that were designed just to handle low-frequency voice signals. There are trade-offs between speed and distance—longer distances allow more subscribers to be served from a single office, but at lower speeds.

Special technologies have been developed to modulate data onto the twisted pairs and to cancel any echoes that may occur during transmission. This technology requires advanced digital signal processing, with very high-performance chipsets that are undergoing constant improvement. DSL lines are popular in the United States with over 27 million residential customers.[3]

DSL is used primarily in networks that already have twisted-pair networks installed. It makes little sense to use DSL technology in new construction areas, as there is not a tremendous cost premium for installing fiber optic systems in a completely new network build. Even major proponents of DSL, such as AT&T, typically install fiber in new housing developments.[4]

---

[3]FCC press release, January 16, 2009.
[4]From a presentation at IBC on September 9, 2006, entitled "AT&T U-verse TV" by Paul Whitehead of AT&T.

Fiber Optic IP Networks

Optical fibers have a number of advantages for high-speed data transport, and these benefits certainly apply to IP networks. These advantages include an extremely high data-carrying capacity,[5] isolation from outside interference, long transmission distances (including undersea cables), and low cost per kilometer.

IP packets can be sent over optical fibers in a number of different ways. One popular method involves sending GigE and 10GigE signals directly over fiber. Another method involves mapping packets into SONET/SDH-compliant signals and transmitting those over an optical network. A third method involves sending IP packets over fibers in a format designed for fiber to the home transmission.

Both IPTV and Internet video signals can be transmitted over optical fiber, and at some point, essentially all streams do pass over fiber between video sources and viewers. Fiber is often used for distributing broadcast television content on a national and international level, and it is virtually always used for long-distance Internet transport. Fiber is normally used to distribute content from VSOs to DSLAMs. Fiber-to-home systems often use IPTV technology to deliver VOD and other video services to individual subscribers.

Internet Protocol Addresses

IP addresses are easy to recognize due to their special "dotted decimal" format. IP addresses consist of a series of four numbers separated by periods (or dots). A dotted decimal number represents a 32-bit number, which is broken up into four 8-bit numbers. For example, 129.35.76.177 is the IP address for http://www.elsevier.com. Most folks who have configured their own home network or laptop connection have probably seen information in this form.

Of course, being human, we have a hard time remembering and typing all of those digits correctly (even when writing a book). So, the *Domain Name System* (DNS) was invented to make life easier. DNS provides a translation service for Web browsers and other software applications that takes easy-to-remember domain names (such as "elsevier.com") and translates them into IP addresses (such as 129.35.76.177).

IP addresses are key to the operation of an IP network. They form the unique identification that each device must have to be able to send and receive packets. On any network, each device must have a unique address; otherwise the network wouldn't be able to deliver packets properly. Private networks that contain several devices and one Internet connection can use private IP addresses inside the network while sharing a single public IP address for access to the Internet.

---

[5]Nippon Telegraph and Telephone Corporation reported a speed of 14 terabits per second on a single fiber in a September 29, 2006 press release (http://www.ntt.co.jp/index_e.html. This is equivalent to 14,000 gigabit Ethernet links on a single fiber.

Key Parts of an IP Network

Many different types of equipment can be used to construct an IP network. Because purchasing, installing, and operating these devices can represent a large portion of the cost of an IPTV or Internet video system, it makes sense to describe some of the key system elements.

- *Ethernet hubs and switches* are used to physically move data packets from one device to another inside a physical location. Hubs have essentially no packet processing intelligence—they simply take any packets that come in on one port and transmit them out all the other ports of the hub. Switches are more intelligent—they can determine where each packet is going and send each packet out on the proper port. Switches are invaluable for connecting the hundreds of IP devices found in even a medium-sized corporation. Switches have a limited scope, however—they only pay attention to directly connected devices. Switches do not have the ability to look at a packet and figure out that in order to get to destination Z the packet needs to be sent first to devices X and Y. That is the function of an IP router.
- *IP routers* are the workhorses of an IP network. They are essential for delivering packets across a large network because they are able to figure out a route for each packet. These routes can travel great distances through multiple devices over many different kinds of physical networks, such as wireless, fiber optic, twisted pair, and DSL links. It is not uncommon for a router to manage several thousand different packet routes, even though it may only be connected to a few dozen other devices. As a result of their flexibility and intelligence, IP routers can be quite expensive, particularly ones that can handle large bandwidth loads found in video networks.
- *Web and data servers* provide a wide variety of data sources for a broad spectrum of purposes. These servers need to support the IP protocol to operate on the Internet and the World Wide Web. Typically, these units are set up to respond to transactions that have been initiated by client devices, such as user PCs.
- *Client devices* cover a wide range of different technologies, form factors, and uses. They can range from desktop PCs of many different vintages and capacities to an array of portable or handheld units and even set top boxes. These units are typically set up to run applications that users can invoke to accomplish specific tasks.

In a typical transaction over an IP network, a user at a PC types in a command to do something, such as read an e-mail or news article. This is accomplished by means of an application running on that user's device, such as an e-mail application or a Web browser application. These applications provide the user interface that appears on the user device, including images on the device display and a mechanism for the user to point and click or type an instruction.

When the user's command is completed, the application software will typically create a command output by sending data through a protocol such as HTTP. Referring to Figure 5.2, this process can be visualized as a downward movement through the different protocol layers. The command created by HTTP is then passed on to a transport protocol such as TCP, where it is given addressing information and formatted into packets for handling by IP. The IP layer takes the packets and makes them suitable for transport over the actual data network such as Ethernet.

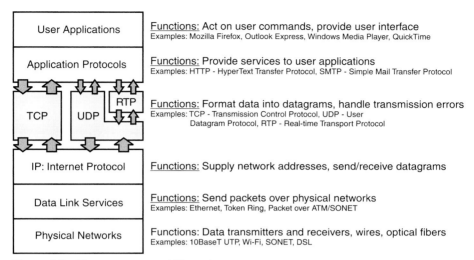

Figure 5.2 *Transport protocol hierarchy.*

Ethernet is then responsible for actually transmitting the packet data over a physical cable to another machine, where the process is reversed, that is, data are passed back up through the protocol stack on the receiving device. Eventually, data from the user are delivered to an application on the receiving machine. At this point, the user's request can be responded to either automatically (as in the case of a Web server) or manually (as in the case of an e-mail).

When the response is ready, the process is reversed. In the responding machine, data are passed down through the various protocol layers and onto the physical connection back to the user's machine. The response is then passed back to the user's application, and the transaction is completed.

The real beauty of this way of handling messages is that each protocol layer has well-defined, specific responsibilities. This also makes it possible for one layer to change without having to rework all of the other software. Consider the introduction of wireless networking over the past 10 years. While it is true that various operating systems (such as Windows or Mac OS) had to be rewritten to accommodate these changes, most user applications (such as Microsoft Outlook or Adobe Acrobat) did not. Similarly, new versions of applications can be released without having to change the basic underlying protocols.

Transport Protocols

Transport protocols are used to control the transmission of data packets in conjunction with IP. We discuss three major protocols commonly used in transporting real-time video.

- *User Datagram Protocol* (UDP) is one of the simplest and earliest of the IP protocols. UDP is often used for video and other very time-sensitive data. In UDP, the originating device can control how rapidly data from a stream will flow across the network. In other protocols (such as TCP, covered next), the network can drastically affect how data transfer works. For video and other real-time streams, UDP is a logical choice for the transport protocol, as it does not add unneeded overhead to streams that already have built-in error correction functions. Because UDP does not require two-way communication, it can operate on one-way networks (such as satellite broadcasts). In addition, UDP can be used in multicasting applications where one source feeds multiple destinations such as IPTV networks.

- *Transmission Control Protocol* (TCP) is a well-established Internet protocol widely used for data transport. The vast majority of the devices that connect to the Internet are capable of supporting TCP over IP (or simply TCP/IP). TCP requires that a connection be set up between the data sender and the data receiver before any data transmission can take place. One of the essential features of TCP is its ability to handle transmission errors, particularly lost packets. TCP counts and keeps track of each byte of data that flows across a connection. The automatic flow control mechanism will slow down data transmission speeds when transmission errors occur. If this rate falls below the minimum rate needed by a video signal, then the video signal receiver will cease to operate properly. One advantage of TCP for video delivery is that most firewalls allow TCP traffic to pass, whereas many firewalls block UDP traffic.

- *Real-time Transport Protocol* (RTP or Real time Protocol, if you prefer) is intended for real-time multimedia applications, such as voice and video over the Internet. RTP was specifically designed to carry signals where time is of the essence. For example, in many real-time signals such as video, if the packet delivery rate falls below a critical threshold, it becomes impossible to form a useful output signal at the receiver. For these signals, packet loss is better tolerated than late delivery. RTP was created for these kinds of signals—to provide a set of functions useful for real-time video and audio transport over the Internet. Overall, RTP adds a lot of functionality on top of UDP without adding a lot of the unwanted functions of TCP. RTP also supports multicasting, which can be a much more efficient way to transport video over a network, as discussed in the next section.

In the networking hierarchy, all three protocols are considered to operate above the IP protocol because they rely on IP's datagram transport services to actually move data to another computer. Figure 5.2 shows how UDP, TCP, and RTP fit into the networking hierarchy. Note that RTP actually uses some of the functions of UDP; it operates on top of UDP.

Multicasting

Multicasting is a key concept for IP networking. However, there are two very different meanings of the word that can apply to the field of IPTV:

- In over-the-air digital television broadcasting, multicasting means delivering multiple video programs simultaneously over a single DTV broadcast channel.
- In IP networking, multicasting means delivering a single stream to multiple viewers simultaneously.

Broadcast multicasting became feasible with the advent of terrestrial digital television. Within a standard digital channel (19.38 Mbps in the United States) it is possible to have multiple video channels, each occupying a portion of the total bandwidth. For example, ION Media Networks has more than 50 digital broadcast stations across the United States—each one capable of delivering at least four different SD programs simultaneously using DTV multicast technology.

In IP multicasting, a single video stream is sent simultaneously to multiple users. Through the use of special protocols, copies of the video stream are made inside the network for every recipient. All viewers of the multicast get the same signal at the same time.

Most of the IP networking equipment delivered over the past 5 to 10 years is capable of supporting IP multicasting, but it has been disabled out of fear of an excessive burden on networks. For example, IP multicasting is not currently enabled on the Internet, restricting the use of multicasting for IP video streaming to private networks. However, within IPTV systems, multicasting is a key enabling technology and is widely deployed.

Internet Protocol Unicasting

To get a better understanding of IP multicasting, it is helpful to compare it to the process of IP *unicasting*. In unicasting, each video stream is sent to exactly one recipient. If multiple recipients want the same video, the source must create a separate unicast stream for each recipient. These streams then flow all the way from the source to each destination over the IP network.

Each user who wants to view a video must make a request to the video source. The source needs to know the destination IP address of each user and must create a stream of packets addressed to each user. As the number of simultaneous viewers increases, the load on the source increases, as it must continuously create individual packets for each viewer. This can require a significant amount of processing power and also a network connection big enough to carry all the outbound packets. For example, if a video source were equipped to send 20 different users a video stream of 2.5 Mbps, it would need to have a network connection of at least 50 Mbps.

An important benefit of unicasting is that each viewer can get a custom-tailored video stream. This enables the video source to offer specialized features such as pause, rewind, and fast-forward video. This is normally practical only with pre-recorded content but can be a popular feature with users.

Unicasting is the norm for Internet video for two reasons. First, because the Internet is not multicast enabled, it is not feasible to use multicasting.[6] Second, most Internet video viewers expect to be able to control video streams (i.e., pause, rewind, fast-forward), which is hard to do with multicast streams.

---

[6]Alternatively, a streaming server or a Content Delivery Network (CDN) could be used to handle the load of creating multiple packet streams.

Internet Protocol Multicasting

In multicasting, a single video stream is sent simultaneously to multiple users. Through the use of special protocols, the network is directed to make copies of the video stream for every recipient. This process of copying occurs inside the network rather than at the video source. Copies are made at each point in the network only where they are needed. Figure 5.3 shows the difference in the way data flow under unicasting and multicasting.

In multicasting, the burden of creating streams for each user shifts from the video source to the network. Inside the network, specialized protocols enable the network to recognize multicast packets and send them to multiple destinations. This is accomplished by giving the multicast packets special addresses reserved for multicasting. There is also a special protocol for users that enables them to inform the network that they wish to join the multicast.

Keep in mind that multicasts operate in one direction only, just like an over-the-air broadcast. There is no built-in data return-path mechanism to collect data from each of the end points and send it back to the source (other than some network performance statistics such as counts of lost packets). This means that any interactivity between the end points and the video source must be handled by some other mechanism.

Multicasting in IPTV

Multicasting is a key technology for IPTV because it enables a single source signal to be sent to multiple destinations. This can enable hundreds, or even thousands, of viewers to simultaneously watch a single television broadcast.

In an IPTV network (as described in Chapter 4), there are several points inside the distribution network from the SHE to the viewer where multicasting can be used to great effect.

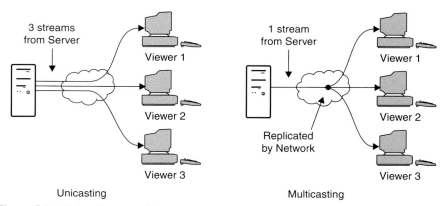

Figure 5.3 *Unicasting vs multicasting.*

From the SHE output, multicasting can be used to take a single live stream and distribute it to multiple VSOs. This saves the expense of constructing a high bandwidth streaming server inside the SHE. This also greatly reduces the size of the network connection required at the output of the SHE.

When it comes to distributing broadcast television streams to viewers, multicasting is almost always used. This technology enables a viewer's STB to connect to a program feed simply by joining a multicast. However, where this happens is greatly dependent on the capabilities of the DSLAMs. Most current DSLAMs are multicast enabled.

- When the DSLAMs are not multicast enabled, a unique video stream must be sent for each viewer all the way from the VSO to that viewer's STB. This requires a high bandwidth connection from the VSO to each DSLAM, with enough capacity to handle all of the active viewers simultaneously. This approach has the advantage of reducing the complexity (and therefore the cost) of the DSLAMs.
- When the DSLAMs are multicast enabled, the connection between the VSO and the DSLAM can be simplified, with only one copy of each broadcast channel needing to be sent. Requests to join and leave the multicast are received from STBs and processed inside the DSLAM; copies are made as necessary for each STB. Even though this approach increases the complexity of the DSLAM, it does significantly reduce the amount of bandwidth needed to feed signals from the VSO to each DSLAM.

Issues with Multicasting

Multicasting is not enabled on all IP networks because there are some noticeable drawbacks to the technology. These include network resource burdens, management complexity, and unverified file transfer. Let's explore each of these in more detail.

As mentioned in previous sections, one drawback of multicasting is the additional burden that it places on the network, primarily routers. Routers are impacted in two main ways—processing the overhead packets containing multicast join and leave instructions and processing the live streams. In most IPTV systems, broadcast channels (such as prime-time network TV) are broadcast using multicast technology. Each time a channel change takes place from one multicast stream to another, several messages must be processed, including instructions to stop delivering one stream and to start delivering a new stream to a user's STB. In addition to this overhead processing, the IP router needs to be able to make a copy of every single multicast packet for every destination served by that router. In some cases, the copies will go to another router downstream toward the destination. In other cases, the copies will go directly to a STB. If a router has to serve hundreds or thousands of STBs, each with a multicast stream, this can require a lot of processing power.

Multicast networks can be complicated to manage. In the most popular multicasting protocol, there is a built-in mechanism to gather feedback from all of the distant end points. This protocol is designed carefully to minimize the amount of traffic coming back from the end points, with the trade-off being that each end point reports less often as their number goes up. This can make it difficult to determine when only a few end points are having difficulty with a particular stream.

Bit-for-bit file copying using acknowledgments is not compatible with multicasting. Normally, when perfection is demanded (say in a million-dollar financial transaction), the end points are designed to handshake with each other after each block of data is delivered successfully. Any mistakes require resending the damaged or missing packets. This is impractical for a multicast, as it is unlikely that all end points would always experience the same errors at the same time. Accordingly, other protocols (such as TCP) should be used to transmit data when errors must be totally excluded.

Reality Check

This chapter's Reality Check takes a look at the immense growth of broadband services that has taken place over the past decade. While the growth rates have slowed in some countries as penetrations increase, millions of broadband lines are still being installed each month around the world. All of these lines service potential customers for IPTV and Internet video.

Broadband Network Growth

For IPTV and Internet video to operate with any level of user satisfaction, a broadband network connection is essential. While it is technically possible for a dial-up user to view a video signal, the long delays needed to download even a short clip at very low resolution make dial-up impractical. So in order to get a feel for the market for IPTV and Internet video, we must restrict our focus to broadband users.

A good working definition of a broadband connection is one that offers more than 256 kbps of throughput. This is adequate for low-resolution, low-frame rate video in real time. It may also be enough for a user to download a short video clip from a Web site in a reasonable amount of time. This kind of speed simply cannot be achieved with a dial-up modem operating over an analog voice line.

There are many different ways to look at broadband network statistics. One way that makes sense is to look at the worldwide deployment of broadband links, as this comprises the total available market for IPTV and Internet video services. Figure 5.4, based on data from Point Topic, shows the worldwide-installed base of broadband circuits in from June 2005 to December 2007 for three different technologies: DSL, cable modem, and *fiber to the node/fiber to the home* ("other" on the diagram).

Expansion of this market has been quite rapid, growing from a total of 79.7 million lines at the end of Q2, 2003, to 359.8 at the end of Q2, 2008. This amounts to a cumulative growth rate of just over 35% per year. Interestingly, there is still a great deal of room for future growth: compare this to the 1.263 billion fixed line

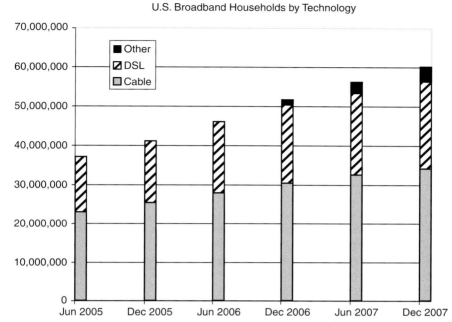

Figure 5.4 *Worldwide broadband technology from 2005 to 2007.*[7]

telephones in use and to the 2.168 billion mobile/cellular phones in use around the world in 2005[8] and it is easy to see the continued growth potential for broadband services.

Summary

Internet Protocol has changed the world of data communications and impacts the physical world around us more all the time. As telecommuting, videoconferencing, and an increasing array of social networking and online video applications reduce the need for travel for communication's sake, alternative work schedules and life-styles have opened up. As the Internet continues to grow, most people will be able to learn about whatever they want from the comfort of their own homes. More and more devices are becoming IP enabled, from cell phones to refrigerators, and they will all end up connected somehow, over networks that are becoming IP-centric. The opportunities created will be enormous due to what IP helps make happen.

This chapter began with a basic discussion of the properties of IP and looked at some of the roles that IP plays in the hierarchy of data communications. It then described some popular types of devices that support IP communication and

[7]http://www.msnbc.msn.com/id/25513994
[8]CIA Factbook http://www.cia.gov/cia/publications/factbook/geos/xx.html

examined some of the higher level protocols, such as TCP and RTP, that use IP to transmit Web pages and video. This was followed by a look at multicasting, which is one of the key enabling technologies for IPTV. The Reality Check showed how large the market has become for broadband services and how much room exists for future growth. It's amazing to consider that essentially every broadband subscriber is a potential customer for IPTV or Internet video.

6 Video Compression

Once you get past a few hundred kilobits-per-second, it's possible to deliver pretty good quality video and sound.

Vinton Cerf

Video signals used to deliver IPTV and Internet video are always compressed. Compression means reducing the number of bits required to represent the video image. This is an important topic because choosing a suitable compression method can sometimes mean the difference between the success and failure of a video networking project.

This chapter begins by explaining the reasons for compression and looks at some of the factors that determine what form of compression is suitable for an application. Then, it examines MPEG video compression, as it is the most widely used technology for video and audio compression. After that, the chapter looks at some of the other compression systems available for use with video and audio signals. The chapter concludes with a brief discussion regarding some of the licenses needed to use various forms of compression technology.

The Corner Office View

[itvt]: What directions do you see [compression] heading in the near future?

Cooney: It's not difficult to see where it's going. Yesterday's compression technology was MPEG-2; tomorrow's compression technology is one of two options: MPEG-4 or Microsoft's VC-1. Both of those technologies, by about a factor of two, outperform MPEG-2. So, half the bit rate, double the channels—however you like to look at it.

[itvt]: Is the cable industry eager to switch to the more advanced codecs?

Cooney: If you're a telco that's getting into the IPTV space and that has no installed base of set-top boxes, and you're asking yourself, "How do we implement the next generation of compression," the answer is easy: if you're making technology decisions today, you might as well pay for the best technology available, which in the case of compression is MPEG-4 and VC-1. Actually, as it happens, if you're a telco, you're going to need to use those codecs anyway, as MPEG-2 isn't good enough to get video through your relatively small pipes. So for telcos, there's really no decision to make: they have to use next-generation compression. But for the other operators, both cable and satellite, there are definitely decisions to make, and commercial implications are the drivers of those decisions.

—*Eric Cooney, president and CEO, Tandberg Television,*
as interviewed by Tracy Swedlow of itvt[1]

Why Compress?

Video compression as a subject matter may seem really dull, but the real-world benefits of using the latest technology can radically increase the versatility of your IP network. Put simply, better compression means greater flexibility—the more efficiently data are handled, the more choices you have with your existing resources. An existing network can support more cameras, better audio–video quality, or both.[2]

Many communication systems that have become commonplace over the past decade depend on compression technology. For example, MP3 players use compression to take files from audio CDs and make them small enough to fit into the memory of a portable player. Compression fits a two-hour movie onto a four-inch DVD or Blu-Ray disc. Cable TV, local television broadcasters, and satellite television systems can now use compression to place multiple digital video channels into the space formerly occupied by a single analog video channel, allowing hundreds of video channels to be distributed economically to viewers.

Here are some of the main reasons why compression is used for IPTV and Internet video systems.

- Compressed streams can be transmitted over lower bit rate networks than uncompressed streams. For Internet video applications in particular, this can mean the difference between getting the stream to a user or not. For example, any home user who has an Internet connection based on older technology may not be able to receive data above the range of 1.5 Mbps. Unless a digital video stream is substantially compressed, it will not fit into this bandwidth.
- More compressed streams can fit into a given bandwidth. This is particularly important for IPTV systems that have a fixed upper limit on bandwidth for a given distance. For example, ADLS2+ has a limit of just over 10 Mbps at a distance of 9000 ft (2750 m). With normal compression techniques, 10 Mbps has enough bandwidth for two to four SD video signals, or one HD and some SD videos. As compression technology advances, more signals can be squeezed into the same amount of bandwidth.
- Raw, uncompressed HD video signals occupy 1.5 Gbps of bandwidth, which is roughly 1000 times the capacity of a standard ADSL link. Without compression, there would be no way to deliver HD video to a viewer over any of the normal IPTV, satellite, or cable TV networks.

[1]Interactive TV Today blog, August 31, 2005, blog.itvt.com/my_weblog/2005/08/eric_cooney_pre.html
[2]http://www.sourcesecurity.com/news/articles/co-3289-ga.2806.html

- A compressed video or audio file will occupy less space on a disk drive or other storage medium than an original uncompressed file. This enables users either to put more content in a given amount of storage or to use less storage for each file.
- In many real-world video signals, there is a large amount of redundancy and under-used bandwidth. Often a good portion of each video frame is identical to the frame immediately before or after it. A good compression technique can use this redundancy to greatly reduce the amount of bandwidth.

Of course, there are compromises that must be made in order to achieve these benefits, such as the following.

- Compression introduces delay into a video or audio signal, at both compression and decompression stages. This occurs because most video compression systems need to store several frames of video in order to extract the differences between adjacent frames of the input signal. Similarly, audio signals are compressed through the use of calculations based on successive short sound clips.
- Compression can be difficult on signals that have a lot of noise in them, such as static or other interference. When there is a lot of noise in a video signal, the compression system has difficulty in identifying redundant information between adjacent video frames.

Overall, the benefits certainly outweigh the drawbacks, particularly when you consider that IPTV and Internet video providers really don't have a choice about using compression.

Groups of Pictures and Why They Matter

Users of any MPEG system will quickly encounter a variety of frame types, including *I frames*, *P frames*, and *B frames*, as well as the term *group of pictures* (GOP). These terms all describe the way picture data are structured in an MPEG stream or file.

A frame is a single image from a video sequence. In NTSC, one frame occurs every 33 milliseconds; in PAL, one frame occurs every 40 milliseconds.

- An I frame is a frame that is compressed solely based on the information contained in the frame; no reference is made to any of the other video frames before or after it.
- A P frame is a frame that has been compressed using data contained in the frame itself and data from the closest preceding I or P frame.
- A B frame is a frame that has been compressed using data from the closest preceding I or P frame and the closest following I or P frame.
- A GOP is a series of frames consisting of a single I frame and zero or more P and B frames. A GOP always begins with an I frame and ends with the last frame before the next I frame. The GOP is usually a fixed, repetitive pattern that is configured on the compression device. Different content suppliers may use different GOPs for different channels, but they are normally fixed within each channel.

To understand why MPEG uses these different frames, let's look at the amount of data required to represent each frame type. With a video image of normal complexity, a P frame will take two to three times less data than an I frame of the same image. A B frame will take even less data than a P frame—a further reduction by a factor of two to five. Figure 6.1 shows the relative amounts of data for each frame type in a typical MPEG GOP.

Impacts of GOP Length

One parameter that system providers have a lot of control over is GOP length. Choosing the right length can be quite controversial.

Remember that a GOP always begins with an I frame. To determine the length of a GOP, simply count the number of B and P frames between each consecutive I frame and add one for the I frame. For example, in the frame sequence shown in Figure 6.1, the GOP length is 12: one I frame, three P frames, and eight B frames.

A GOP is considered short when the GOP length is low, say three or five. Some systems use GOPs that are quite long; values of 15, 30, or even 60 have been used in some applications.

Selecting a suitable GOP length can have a big impact on a video network. Many system performance factors are affected by GOP size, including the bit rate of encoded streams, the channel change time, and the ability of the stream to tolerate errors. Let's examine each of these factors in more depth.

Bit Rate

As Figure 6.1 clearly shows, I frames contain more data than P frames or B frames. With a short GOP length, the total number of I frames in the stream is increased, thereby increasing the average amount of data that needs to be transmitted for each frame. This translates into greater bandwidth, which can affect the performance of both IPTV and Internet video services. With longer GOPs, there are fewer I frames per second, so the aggregate data rate drops.

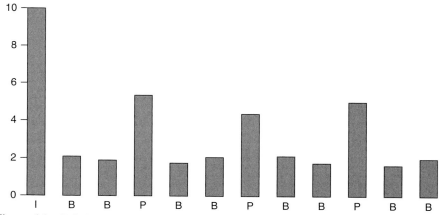

Figure 6.1 *Relative amounts of data in each MPEG frame type.*

Channel Change Timing

Whenever channel changing occurs in a video stream, the decoder has to have enough data to accurately produce a new image sequence. The ability of the decoder to do so depends on which type of frame it receives first after each channel change. If the decoder receives an I frame first, then everything works smoothly because each I frame contains all data to completely reproduce one frame of video. If the decoder receives a P frame or a B frame first, then it has a problem because these frames only contain enough data to tell the decoder about any changes that have happened since an earlier frame. So, what typically happens after each channel change is that the decoder waits for the first I frame of the new video channel to arrive before it begins to produce an image.

With a short GOP of, say, five frames, channel changing isn't much of a problem. In a 30-frame-per-second system (such as those used in the United States), this means that the decoder needs to wait, at most, 166 milliseconds for the first I frame, and that amount of delay is insignificant to viewers. If, however, the GOP is 30 or 60 frames long, it could mean that the decoder may need to wait one or two seconds before the first I frame arrives. This can be quite annoying to viewers.

Two different approaches have been demonstrated to address this issue. One method uses a server that stores copies that are compressed using only I-frames of all the videos present on an IPTV network. When a user changes channels, the STB connects momentarily to the server to get a sequence of I frames for the new channel and then rejoins the regular long GOP stream once a new I frame is delivered. This approach can deliver very fast change times, but this technique can be difficult to scale to thousands of users all changing channels simultaneously, as could occur during a major live sporting event.

Another system actually makes available two versions of each stream for use by STBs—one with low resolution and a short GOP and another with normal resolution and a long GOP. Normal viewing is with the long GOP, normal resolution stream. When a channel change occurs, the STB connects to the low-resolution stream and *up converts* it to a normal size picture. Once the normal stream is ready (i.e., when an I frame arrives), the STB switches back to the normal stream.

This latter method has the advantage of not requiring any special servers or targeted streams to be delivered to each STB, but it does require two versions of each stream to be available. The low-resolution streams can also be used for picture-in-picture applications when they aren't being used for channel changing.

Error Tolerance

One major benefit of an I frame is that it permits the STB to wipe out any memory that it has about previous frames. This contrasts with P and B frames, which require the STB to store a copy of the preceding frames so it can create the new frame properly. Consider what happens if one of the incoming frames in the middle of a GOP has an error. This error can persist in the STB for a while, until the next I frame arrives. Once this happens, the error can be cleaned out.

Moving Pictures Experts Group

The *Moving Pictures Experts Group* has developed some of the most common compression systems for video around the world and, given these standards, the common name of MPEG. Not only did this group develop video compression standards, including MPEG-1, MPEG-2, and MPEG-4, but it also developed audio compression standards, which are discussed later in this chapter.

MPEG standards have enabled a number of advanced video services. For example, MPEG-based DVDs and Blu-Ray discs replaced videotape as the preferred medium for viewing Hollywood movies in the home. Digital television, including over-the-air broadcast digital TV, digital satellite television, and digital cable TV, is based on the MPEG video compression standards. Also, much of the content for streaming media on the Internet is compressed using MPEG or closely related technologies.

What Happened to MPEG-3?

Some readers may be curious about the lack of an MPEG-3 standard. In fact, there was originally a working group called MPEG-3 set up to develop a standard to focus on multiresolution encoding. Because this group's work was completed before the work on MPEG-2 was completed, the work was simply incorporated into the MPEG-2 standard.

Readers should be careful not to confuse the MPEG audio coding standard called Layer III, often abbreviated as MP3, with the nonexistent MPEG-3 video compression standard. MP3 audio files are popular in many music file-swapping and portable player systems.

MPEG-1

MPEG-1 was the first standard developed for video compression by the Moving Pictures Experts Group. It was intended for use in creating video CDs, which had some popularity in computer multimedia, but never completely caught on as consumer movie rental or purchase format, and it is rarely used today. It is interesting to note that MPEG-1 is allowed as a video compression method for DVDs, and many DVD players will play video CDs. MPEG-1 does not support interlacing, so standard full-resolution PAL and NTSC signals are not usable with MPEG-1.

MPEG-2

MPEG-2 is one of the primary standards for MPEG video. It is used in a wide variety of applications, including production for satellite television and cable TV, as well as for over-the-air DTV broadcasting. Each day, thousands of hours of MPEG-2 video are recorded, processed, and played back by television broadcasters around the world. Plus, millions of hours of MPEG-2 recordings are sold to the general public each day in the form of DVDs.

MPEG-2 supports standard NTSC and PAL signals at full resolution, as well as 720p and 1080i HD signals. MPEG-2 also enables multiplexing of a number of video and audio streams, so applications such as multichannel satellite television become possible. MPEG-2 also supports five-channel audio (surround sound) and the Advanced Audio Coding (AAC) standard.

Many MPEG-2 devices, including highly sophisticated MPEG-2 encoder and decoder devices, are in their third or fourth generations. There are literally hundreds of millions of televisions, STBs, digital satellite receivers, and DVD players installed in consumers' homes that can decode MPEG-2 signals. A wide variety of MPEG-2 equipment is available for functions such as statistical multiplexing, bit rate converters, telecom and IP network adapters, and more.

With sufficient processing power and memory, a PC can be used to create an MPEG-2 stream in real time. However, for many applications, such as program editing and production, real-time performance is not necessary, and even moderate-performance PCs can create MPEG-2-compressed video files for later playback.

Overall, MPEG-2 is a well-defined, stable compression system with a large installed base of equipment. Hundreds of millions of devices installed around the world are capable of receiving and decoding MPEG-2 video in a wide variety of flavors. MPEG-2 is the dominant standard throughout the United States for DTV broadcasting, and new televisions are required to be equipped with MPEG-2 decoders. However, the video and audio quality of MPEG-2 is not competitive at stream rates below 2.5 Mbps, and most recent vintage IPTV and Internet video equipment and systems are deployed with more efficient compression systems such as H.264, as we shall soon see.

MPEG-4 and H.264

MPEG-4 is a more recent product of the standards process; the first version became formally approved in 2000. As would be expected, MPEG-4 incorporates a whole range of new technologies for video compression. The most advanced version of MPEG-4, called *Advanced Video Coding* (AVC) or H.264, makes it possible for high-definition signals to be encoded at bit rates well below 10 Mbps, opening up a much bigger range of technologies for transporting HD video signals.

Prior to the introduction of H.264, the MPEG-4 AVC standard, MPEG-4 did not offer truly dramatic performance improvements over MPEG-2 for compressing live natural video sequences, including most types of news, entertainment, and sports broadcasts. Basic MPEG-4 provided a number of advantages for synthetic (computer-generated) video and deeply penetrated IP video streaming applications (e.g., Apple's QuickTime has fully migrated to MPEG-4). Most desktop PCs can decode MPEG-4 video using media player software freely available on the Internet.

H.264 is a more recent offering (circa 2004) and has superseded MPEG-2 in most new applications. This is because H.264 can achieve quality levels that compare favorably to MPEG-2 at half the bit rate. Of course, there is a cost to this in terms of the greater processing power needed to encode and decode the signals.

One potential drawback of H.264 is that decoders are more complex than those for MPEG-2. According to the MPEG-4 Industry Forum (www.m4if.org), an H.264 decoder will be 2.5 to 4 times as complex as an MPEG-2 decoder for similar applications. This means more powerful hardware devices and greater demand on processor resources for software decoders. Although most recent–vintage devices can easily handle H.264 in a video delivery system, it is still a good idea to test any user devices (STBs, desktop PCs, laptops, etc.) that will be used to decode the video signal prior to widespread deployment.

H.264 offers a wide range of different performance points, called profiles, for various applications. Each of the fifteen defined profiles specifies the complexity and number of features required in the decoder. Similarly, there are sixteen different performance levels that govern the image sizes (in lines and pixels) and the maximum allowed bit rates. Not all combinations of profiles and levels are allowed, but there are still a large number of combinations allowed within the H.264 standards. As a result, there is a wide variety of different hardware and software technologies that can correctly be deemed to meet the H.264 standard, but only some of them will work for any particular application. Service providers may need to avoid using some of the advanced features of H.264 and stick to simpler profiles and lower levels, depending on the capabilities of the equipment selected.

Overall, MPEG-4 is a powerful collection of technologies that has greatly increased the amount of video information that can be squeezed into a given amount of network bandwidth. Through H.264, much more efficient video coding is possible, and the variety of object types available makes integration with computer-generated graphics simple and extremely bandwidth efficient. Because of these advances, and because of the greater processing power available in set-top boxes and personal computers, H.264 is now the most common choice for IPTV and Internet video deployments.

Audio Compression

Just like video compression, MPEG has a variety of audio compression options. There are three layers of MPEG audio, which are conveniently called Layers I, II, and III. A more advanced audio compression standard called *Advanced Audio Coding* has been introduced, along with two more recent high-efficiency variations: HE-AAC and HE-AAC+. This section takes a short look at each one of these. Note that any of these audio compression methods will work with any type of MPEG video compression, except that MPEG-1 streams do not handle the AAC series of audio methods.

MPEG audio Layer I is the simplest compression system. It uses 384 input samples for each compression run, which corresponds to 8 milliseconds of audio material using 48-kHz sampling. Each band is processed separately, and then the results are combined to form a single, constant bit rate output. Layer I can achieve a compression ratio of 4:1, which means that a 1.4 Mbps CD-quality stereo audio signal can be compressed to fit into a 384-kbps stream with no noticeable loss of quality. Compression beyond this—to 192 or 128 kbps—results in lower quality.

MPEG audio Layer II uses more samples for each compression run, 1152 to be exact. This corresponds to 24 milliseconds of audio at 48 kHz sampling. This enables frequencies to be resolved more accurately. Layer II also eliminates some of the redundancy in Layer I coding, thereby achieving better compression, up to 8:1. This means that CD-quality audio can be achieved with a stream rate of 192 kbps.

MPEG audio Layer III uses the same number of samples as Layer II, but uses them more efficiently. Layer III has an audio mode *called joint stereo*, which capitalizes on the strong similarities between the signals that make up the left and right channels of a stereo program. It also uses variable-length coding to pack the compressed audio coefficients into the output stream more efficiently. As a result, Layer III encoders can pack CD-quality audio into streams as small as 128 kbps, achieving compression ratios as high as 12:1. This format is widely known as MP3 and is used extensively in portable music players and online stores that sell music.

MPEG AAC is available only with MPEG-2 or MPEG-4 video streams. It supports up to 48 audio channels, including 5.1 audio. Very good-quality results for surround-sound applications can be achieved with AAC at 192 kbps, and CD-quality stereo can be achieved at a bit rate of 96 kbps. HE-AAC+ can do even better, with near-CD quality at a bit rate of 48 kbps, although at a cost of greater end-to-end delay (more than half a second) and greater complexity for the encoder and decoder. A number of portable music players are capable of playing this format, as well as PCs with the appropriate software.

Dolby AC-3 Audio

Dolby AC-3 audio coding is also commonly known as Dolby Digital. It offers a high-quality audio experience with good compression characteristics and has been approved for use both in DVDs and in digital television broadcasts in the United States. Dolby AC-3 audio is included in some versions of MPEG-4 and H.264 and is used on a number of satellite television systems.

Overall, MPEG audio is flexible and does not require near the magnitude of processor involvement of MPEG video. As the layer number goes up, the complexity of both the encoder and the decoder go up, but so does the compression ratio. Software-only Layer III decoders can run smoothly in a wide variety of personal computers. AAC decoders are easily within the range of current processor performance, and support for AAC has become widespread in portable devices and mobile phones. When choosing an audio-encoding method, remember that the overall transport bandwidth must be high enough to carry the video signal, the audio signal, and some overhead to make the streams operate correctly.

Microsoft Windows Media and VC-1

Windows Media Player is a general-purpose software package designed for PCs that uses the Microsoft Windows operating system. It can support a wide variety of video compression formats and is capable of processing a wide variety of Internet video streams.

Microsoft also designed a video compression system that was originally called Windows Media 9 and was subsequently formalized in the 421M standard by SMPTE. Some IPTV providers who have implemented systems based on Microsoft technology have adopted this standard, which is known informally as VC-1.

Some readers may wonder about the differences between VC-1 and H.264. Both codecs offer significant advances in coding efficiency (i.e., fewer bits for a given picture quality) as compared to MPEG-2. To date, there hasn't been any compelling evidence to say that one is clearly better than the other for any large group of applications. Interestingly, many vendors of encoders and decoders are designing their hardware to support both technologies through the use of general-purpose digital signal processing (DSP) hardware and downloadable firmware.

Other Compression Technologies

MPEG and Microsoft are not the only games in town. Here are a few other compression technologies that bear consideration for service providers, primarily those in the Internet video market.

JPEG

Standards developed for compressing photographic (still) images by the *Joint Photographic Experts Group* are called JPEG files. These standards have been adapted for video use by treating each frame of video as a separate picture and compressing it. The approach brings some benefits, most importantly is the ease in which motion sequences can be edited. Because each frame of video is compressed individually, there are no structures like the GOPs of MPEG and therefore no restrictions on when one frame sequence can be stopped and another started. JPEG files are used in some video editing systems precisely for this reason.

JPEG2000

JPEG2000 is an advanced form of still image compression that was finalized in 2000 (hence the name). It uses a completely different technology for image compression than JPEG (called wavelets), but performs the same tasks. Because JPEG2000 also compresses each frame of video individually, the technology is not able to take advantage of the similarities between adjacent frames. As a result, streams tend to be higher bandwidth than those used commonly in IPTV and Internet video applications.

Proprietary Codecs

A number of proprietary video and audio *codec* systems are on the market, and many of them are suitable for use in Internet video networks. Because they are proprietary, the exact details of their operation are normally not provided for general publication. In addition, because the different codec manufacturers engage in competition, product cycles are short and performance and other specifications can change rapidly. Let's look at two codec suppliers for the video streaming market: Real Networks and Adobe.

Real Networks is a supplier of proprietary codec technology. Most of Real's products are targeted at the video streaming market. As with Microsoft's products, a number of third-party tools (from suppliers such as Adobe) can be used to create compressed video streams in both real-time and off-line production environments. Content is available for streaming on the Web in Real's Sure Stream format, which is designed to automatically adapt to suit the wide range of different network connection speeds used around the globe.

Adobe's video compression system, called Flash, is widely used in Web site design and Internet video, including popular video portals such as YouTube. Video compression is even offered as a Web service, where video files can be uploaded to a server and then connected to a Web site for viewing.

One distinguishing feature of both of these codec suppliers is their willingness to provide a free software client (player) for receiving their compressed video streams. Literally hundreds of millions of personal computer users have downloaded and installed these players onto their desktop and laptop computers. In addition, most of these companies also supply a free encoder with limited functionality. More sophisticated encoders are generally available for a fee; these versions often contain advanced features that can make the job of creating content files easier, as well as using more efficient compression algorithms.

There are no easy answers when deciding whether to use proprietary codecs. The main software-based codec suppliers have a long and distinguished track record of innovation and customer service. The same can be said for many hardware-based codec suppliers. Nevertheless, any users of a proprietary codec run the risk that their supplier will, for one reason or another, stop providing products. Prudent users will assess this risk and have a contingency plan in place. Here are some advantages and disadvantages of proprietary codecs.

Advantages of Proprietary Codecs

- *Innovation:* As compression technology advances, innovations can be incorporated into proprietary codecs very rapidly. Industry standards tend to have a slower rate of change because of the need to achieve agreement between many different parties.
- *Pricing:* Many proprietary software codec suppliers offer basic versions of their players (decoders) for free and have free or low-cost encoder options.
- *Backward Compatibility:* Proprietary codec suppliers have a strong incentive to ensure that new versions of their codecs work with previous versions and have typically done a good job in this area. This may not be as true with designs based on standards, unless backward compatibility is defined explicitly in the specification.

Disadvantages of Proprietary Codecs

- **Portability:** Because a single vendor controls when and how proprietary codecs are implemented, versions for alternative platforms may be late to arrive or never produced. This can limit users' choices, particularly in the selection of operating systems.
- **Change Control:** Major codec suppliers determine when new features are released to the market and frequently encourage end users to upgrade their PC applications to the latest version. This can make it difficult for large organizations to ensure that all users have the same application version and to ensure that the codec software doesn't interfere with other applications.
- **Platform Requirements:** As codecs become more powerful, the minimum requirements for other system components (operating systems, processor speeds, etc.) can also increase. This can force users to deploy system upgrades in order to use the latest versions of some software codecs.
- **Archival Storage:** As with any rapidly evolving technology, long-term storage of encoded video files is useful only as long as suitable decoder software is available. In the case of proprietary codecs, the supplier controls software availability over the long term.

Digital Turnaround

Digital turnaround is the process of taking video and audio signals encoded in one format and converting them into another format. This normally occurs under the control of a service provider to help standardize the operation of a multichannel system and is a widespread practice in IPTV systems. Once each stream has the same compression technology, GOP length, and bit rate, the process of channel changing is simplified greatly: one compressed stream simply replaces another stream with compatible compression formats whenever a viewer decides to switch. Digital turnaround usually consists of two tasks: transcoding and transrating.

Transcoding is the process of converting a video signal that is encoded in one technology (say MPEG-2) into another technology (say H.264). The best-quality results can usually be obtained if the signal is never fully decompressed or recompressed, enabling the output signal to closely match the original video feed.

Transrating is the process of changing the bit rate of video streams. Most IPTV providers convert all of the incoming content into a common bit rate, using one range of bit rates for all SD content and a second range for HD content. Transrating needs to happen frequently because many content suppliers use a higher bit rate for distributing their content than the rates that most IPTV and Internet video service providers choose to use.

Reality Check

This chapter's Reality Check discusses the licenses necessary to use some of the compression technologies described here. Every DVD player and every DVD disc sold includes the cost of a mandatory license fee collected for each unit produced. Service providers need to consider license terms when analyzing the costs of installing a video delivery system.

Disclaimer

Neither the authors of this book nor the publisher claim any expertise in licensing law or in the terms of the MPEG LA license agreement. Readers should consult with MPEG LA and any other licensing bodies to confirm all details of the required licenses prior to installing a video network that relies on this technology.

Technology Licensing

As we have seen in this chapter, a huge number of clever technologies have been applied to the art and science of video compression. Even though much of this technology is governed by international standards, not all of this technology is in the public domain. In fact, many of the key technologies used in MPEG and other compression systems were developed by individuals and corporations who still retain ownership of their technology in the form of patents and other legally protected rights. For example, the patent portfolio for MPEG-2 technologies includes 630 patents from around the world.

Fortunately, the owners of these technologies banded together to set up an organization known as the *MPEG LA* (the LA originally stood for Licensing Administrator, but now LA is the official name). MPEG LA is responsible for establishing and collecting the license fees on the technology and for distributing the collected funds to the patent owners. This central clearinghouse provides big benefits to the users of this technology, as one simple payment to MPEG LA satisfies the patent obligations for the covered technology. Contrast this with the headaches and complexities that would be involved in negotiating separate license agreements with the 201 companies that have patents included in the MPEG-2 technology pool.

The license fees are assessed on a per-item basis and are officially described on www.mpegla.com. For example, the fee listed on the Web site for an MPEG-2 decoding device (such as a DVD player, STB, or computer with a DVD player, whether hardware or software) produced after 2002 is $2.50. Other fees are assessed for MPEG-2 encoders, MPEG multiplexers, and other devices. Fees are also assessed for recorded media, such as DVDs, but the fees are relatively low (e.g., $0.03 for a single-layer DVD disc, although there are a number of different ways of calculating the fee).

There are similar fee arrangements for H.264 devices. In addition, fees are based on the number of streams created and on the number of subscribers served in cable and satellite television systems. There are also fees for individual titles sold to viewers on a DVD or via pay-per-view, such as a VOD system. These fees have created some controversy in the industry because they include charges for the device itself (similar to the MPEG-2 charges) and also charges for viewing content using the device. Also note that the same type of fee structures apply for VC-1 and other common codecs.

Where does this leave the owner of a video networking system? First, it is important to understand that because fees for devices are normally collected from the device manufacturers, end users of equipment generally don't need to worry about technology fees. Second, publishers of media, such as DVDs, are also responsible for paying the fees required for those items. Third, most of the H.264 license fees that are payable on a per-stream or a per-subscriber basis are targeted at companies that are charging users to view the videos. Because the licensing terms are complex, it would be prudent to perform a thorough legal review of any licensing fees prior to beginning a major service deployment.

Summary

Video compression is a requirement for essentially all IPTV and Internet video systems. This chapter began with a discussion of why compression is so important. GOP length, a very important topic for service providers to consider, was discussed in depth. The chapter then took a look at the varieties of MPEG for both video and audio applications, as well as other compression systems, including Microsoft's VC-1, JPEG, and offerings from Real Networks and Adobe. It concluded with a brief look at digital turnaround and a discussion of licensing issues.

Any service provider needs to make a careful evaluation before choosing a compression technology. Each technology has benefits and drawbacks in terms of performance, cost, availability, and scalability that can have major impacts on business plans, deployment schedules, and viewer experiences. This choice cannot be taken lightly, as providers will need to live with their choices for years to come.

7 Maintaining Video Quality and Security

Television is like the invention of indoor plumbing. It didn't change people's habits. It just kept them inside the house.

Alfred Hitchcock

Quality and security are important for any video delivery system. Quality is a prerequisite to keeping viewers happy (and therefore paying their monthly subscription bills) and to providing advertisers and content owners with image quality complementary to their desired public images. Security is needed to keep viewers from watching content they aren't authorized to view and to prevent them from making unauthorized copies of content that only they are authorized to view.

This chapter begins with a discussion of the main factors that affect quality and how they can be controlled. It then examines the role of conditional access, which manages which viewers have the ability to watch which content. The chapter concludes with a discussion of digital rights management and how it relates to the types of video signals that are often used with IP-based delivery systems.

The Corner Office View

Service providers understand the importance of video quality to their bottom line yet feel they do not currently have the right solution for monitoring and managing video quality from the content ingest point at the head end to the customer premises equipment (CPE) in the home.

—Gary Schultz, president and principal analyst of MRG[1]

Factors That Affect Video Quality

A wide range of factors can affect the quality of a delivered video signal and have important impacts on the viewer experience. Managing the video delivery system to optimize these factors will result in more satisfied viewers.

---

[1]http://telephonyonline.com/iptv/news/iptv-video-quality-0219/

Audio/Video Synchronization

In real life, as people move their lips while talking, the sounds change accordingly. Similarly with sounds from physical objects—when a person's shoe hits a hard pavement, a sharp sound can be heard. Viewers find it objectionable when the sounds don't match the image being displayed in a video presentation. When a mismatch occurs, it is called a loss of "lip sync" or a loss of audio/video synchronization.

One potential source of lip sync problems is clock differences between the transmitting and the receiving ends of a video link. Careful management to ensure that both the encoder and the decoder in a link are referenced to a common clock signal— and that these clock signals are transmitted properly along with the compressed video stream—will help ensure that synchronization doesn't become an issue.

Assuring lip sync can be difficult on IP networks, which are inherently asynchronous. The solution lies in careful network provisioning (to ensure that adequate bandwidth is available for all the traffic) and in making sure that there are no processing bottlenecks (such as overloaded routers) that can delay or scramble the order of packets. Some IP receivers (including STBs and PCs) can be configured to use large incoming packet buffers to smooth out any delay variations or to realign packets that arrive in the wrong order. This has side effects of delaying the signals flowing through the device and increasing channel change time to allow the buffers to be filled with new content. Both of these effects should be limited as much as possible.

Source Image Quality

As with many complex processing systems, the adage "garbage in, garbage out" applies to IP video transport. For example, source signals that have a lot of noise (i.e., random changes in the video image that are not present in the source scene) can greatly affect the performance of MPEG encoders. When this happens, the encoders see the noise as changes in the image that need to be captured in the compressed data stream, thereby creating more work for both the encoder and the decoder. This can divert processing power away from other portions of the image that could otherwise benefit.

Several things can be done to improve source image quality. First, service providers can work with content providers who have high-quality source images and get the content directly from them rather than through intermediate sources. Second, high-quality video links using little or no compression can be used to bring the programming from the sources to the network. Third, noise reduction equipment can be used to clean up noisy video signals, making them easier to compress.

Macroblocking

When images are compressed using MPEG or other block-based compression technologies, the image is broken up into groups of pixels before the compression operation begins. For MPEG-2, the pixels are grouped into macroblocks that measure 16 pixels on a side. Borders between adjacent macroblocks on a video screen can be quite noticeable to the eye if there is an abrupt change in color or brightness between adjacent blocks. This can occur if the image has been compressed excessively; that is, there are not enough bits in the MPEG stream to accurately reproduce the source image in each block. When these borders appear, the perceived image quality for human viewers drops significantly, and steps are often taken to prevent this.

Macroblocking is more likely to be noticed in scenes with a lot of motion, with subtle gradations of color or in scenes where the overall light level in the scene is moving higher or lower (i.e., a fade to black) when essentially every pixel on the screen is simultaneously changing intensity. When macroblocking reaches an extreme state, each of the four 8 × 8 image blocks contained in a macroblock may be represented as a single color (also called pixelation), which can be very objectionable to viewers.

To prevent macroblocking, video providers need to make sure that the bit rate of the video stream is high enough to handle the motion and detail levels in the original pictures. In addition, many MPEG streams use error correction to prevent minor bit errors from causing macroblocking.

If longer duration errors occur in the path between the encoder and the decoder, then some data needed to reconstruct the picture are lost or corrupted. When this happens, the decoder is not able to recreate the source image correctly, and the output for that block of data may be corrupted. To the viewer, this loss of data often appears as one or more macroblocks with very poor resolution. This problem can be corrected by eliminating the errors in the data path or by at least reducing them to a low enough frequency that error correction can be effective.

Sound Quality

The quality of audio signal delivery has a significant impact on television viewers. Unsurprisingly, viewers prefer high-quality sound to low-quality sound. Much more interesting is the correlation between delivered sound quality and perceived image quality—studies have shown that viewers will rate the image quality of a video signal higher when the quality of the audio is improved without any change in the displayed image.

In some ways, audio delivery is more complicated than video. The ear is much more difficult to deceive than the eye—even short interruptions in an audio signal (less than 10 milliseconds) will be noticeable. In contrast, an isolated loss of a full 33-millisecond video frame can easily be concealed by duplicating the previous frame so that most viewers will never notice the interruption.

Fortunately, compressed audio signals typically require much less bandwidth than compressed video signals. This makes it possible to add more error correction to the audio signals without having a significant impact on the overall signal bandwidth.

Resolution

The resolution of a video image refers to the number of pixels present. Images with higher pixel counts have higher resolution (unless the image has been degraded in some other manner). In IPTV systems, image resolution is normally matched to the display resolution, so an SD signal for an NTSC system would have 720 pixels on each of 480 lines. In Internet video, many different video resolutions are used, ranging from QCIF at 176×144 to full HD at 1920×1080 pixels and everywhere in between.

Delivered resolution needs to be managed carefully. Viewers typically prefer higher resolution signals to lower ones, but high resolution can carry a high price in terms of system design. If the number of pixels in each dimension (vertical and horizontal) doubles, the total number of pixels in the image goes up by a factor of four. This not only adds to the amount of bandwidth required for a signal, it also adds to the amount of processing power needed to encode and decode the signal. Higher resolutions generally increase the burden on the entire system, from start to finish.

Many Internet video systems deliver signals at less than full SD resolution, both to save bandwidth and to make images easier for PCs to display. Virtually all IPTV systems offer SD resolution video (comparable to broadcast, cable TV, and satellite systems) and most offer HD video.

Internet Protocol Artifacts

Artifacts are image or sound impairments that are detectable to a viewer. They can be caused by noise, encoding errors, transmission errors, decoding errors, poor cabling, display errors, and other sources too numerous to name. Let's focus on three common causes of artifacts in an IP video delivery system (bit errors, packet loss, and packet jitter) and see how they can be avoided.

Bit Errors

Bit errors occur when the digital information delivered to the user device is different from data originally sent. Bit errors are caused by a wide range of physical phenomena on any network, including over-the-air broadcast, fiber optic, and satellite systems. When errors occur, they can affect any data used to create the picture. Some errors are harmless, affecting only a single pixel, whereas others can be quite serious and affect multiple frames of video. Unfortunately, because bit errors tend to be distributed randomly, there is no good way to predict whether a given bit error is going to be harmful or not.

There are a number of schemes for correcting bit errors. One method involves retransmitting errored packets; this is the method used by the TCP protocol. As discussed in Chapter 5, this isn't usually the best solution for streaming video due to the potential delays in retransmission.

Another method to handle bit errors is called *forward error correction* (FEC). With FEC, additional data are added to each packet of data that enables the receiver to correct a limited number of bit errors in each packet. One popular method for calculating FEC data that is part of the MPEG standard is called Reed–Solomon, based on a seminal 1960 paper by I.S. Reed and G. Solomon.[2] Even a modest

---

[2]"Polynomial Codes over Certain Finite Fields," *J. Soc. Indust. Appl. Math.* Volume 8, Issue 2, pp. 300–304 (June 1960).

amount of FEC can have a significant impact on the system bit error rate. However, this protection comes at a price—extra FEC data consume bandwidth on top of that needed for video and audio data. As a result, not all service providers use FEC, depending on their overall system error rate performance targets and network quality expectations, among other factors.

Packet Loss

Packet loss is one of the most common errors that can happen on an IP video delivery system. It can be caused by many sources, including bit errors that corrupt IP packet headers (forcing them to be discarded), overloaded links that force routers to discard packets, inadequate or malfunctioning networking equipment, and other sources. Packet loss is a routine occurrence on the Internet, and Internet video delivery systems must be designed to handle it. One way to handle Internet packet loss is to use large buffers at the receiver and enable retransmission of lost packets, which can be done with download and play delivery techniques. Another option is to use error concealment in the decoder. A final option is to use packet-level FEC.

One popular packet-level FEC technique is defined in SMPTE standard 2022 (also known as COP3). Using this method, packets are grouped into rows or columns and an FEC packet is added to each row (or column) of data. If any single packet in a row (or column) of data is lost, the FEC packet for that row (or column) can be used to recreate the lost packet. Of course, this method can add significant delay to the overall transmission system (due to the need to process whole rows of packets to add the FEC and recover from errors) and it can also add significant overhead (if, for example, the row length is set to 10 packets, then 1 FEC packet is added to each row, resulting in FEC overhead of 10%). COP3 has been widely adopted for transmitting professional-quality video over IP networks and can be used for any video delivery link.

In IPTV systems, packet loss can be minimized through the use of careful system design practices (such as building in surplus bandwidth) and by careful control of the amount of traffic allowed to enter the system to avoid overloading the links. However, occasional packet losses that cannot be completely avoided must be handled in a graceful manner by the decoder equipment.

Packet Jitter

Packet jitter is created when the packets that make up a data stream do not arrive in a smooth, continuous flow. For example, if an application was trying to send 100 packets per second in a smooth stream, it would try to send 1 packet precisely every 10 milliseconds. If these packets were sent across a jitter-free network, they would arrive with the same timing: 1 packet every 10 milliseconds. When this pattern is disturbed—packets start arriving too soon or too late—jitter occurs. This causes the gaps between the packets to be either too short or too long—say 9 milliseconds or 11 milliseconds.

For normal data, such as e-mail or a Web page, jitter is not an issue because this information is not time based. It really makes no difference if the Web page is displayed a few milliseconds early or late because such differences are imperceptible to people. However, for data streams containing audio or video information, such variations can be very harmful.

To understand how jitter affects a video stream, recall what makes up a video stream. It is, in effect, a series of pictures taken 30 times per second (25 times per second in most countries outside the United States and Japan) that, when played back one after the other, gives the illusion of motion to the human eye and brain. This technique works fine when the series of pictures is displayed in a smooth, continuous flow. However, when the picture display times vary excessively, the illusion of motion can be broken, and the video becomes uncomfortable to watch. Jitter also makes the synchronization of video and audio data more difficult because clock variations can affect the two data streams differently, causing timing errors in the decoding process.

In actual applications, jitter will affect both uncompressed and compressed video data. This is due to the clock information carried with a compressed signal. These clocks are fundamental to the operation of MPEG and other types of decoders. When these clocks get disturbed, there can be many different impacts on the video signal. For example, excessive jitter can cause the receiver buffers to overflow or run out of data. In either case, the video image can be disturbed by suddenly freezing when data run out or by losing picture information when the buffer overflows.

There are two main ways to fight jitter in an IP network—prevent it or use a buffer to fix the timing at the receiver. Many successful systems employ both techniques to keep jitter under control.

Preventing jitter is simply a matter of ensuring that any packets containing video data are not delayed at any point during their transit through the network. This means there needs to be an adequate available bandwidth on each link, minimizing the random chance that video packets will be blocked or delayed by other traffic. In addition, the data routers that form the core of many networks need to be able to send certain types of packets (such as those containing video files) as a priority over other packets, reducing the chance that they will be delayed.

Buffering incoming packet data is also commonly used to reduce jitter. The buffer is set up on a FIFO basis (first in, first out), with the size of the buffer limited by the amount of delay that can be tolerated. Incoming packets are put into the buffer as soon as they arrive, at a variable rate due to any accumulated jitter. Packets are removed from the buffer according to an evenly spaced clock signal so that any accumulated jitter is cleaned out. This clock rate needs to be tuned carefully to make sure that the buffer doesn't overflow with too many packets or underflow with too few packets. The clock may also have to adapt to changes in the underlying packet rate.

One disadvantage of buffering is that it adds delay to the overall delivery system, which increases the amount of time it takes the system to recover from a failure or to switch to a different packet stream due to a channel change or other event. As a result, there is a lot of pressure to minimize the amount of buffer used while still providing enough to handle the amount of jitter expected at the input.

Signal Availability

Availability is a measure of the amount of time that a signal is active and meeting minimum performance levels. Availability is calculated by measuring the duration of any interruptions in the signal and dividing by the total length of the program being delivered. For example, if a program lasts 100 minutes, and it was unwatchable for one-tenth of a minute (six seconds), then the availability of that signal would be 99.9%.

Generally, for IPTV networks, availability statistics need to be quite high to provide acceptable levels of consumer satisfaction. A system that offers 99.9% availability for a year can be expected to be unavailable to every viewer for an average of 8.7 hours. This probably won't be acceptable to most subscribers if all of the unavailability occurs in one day. As a result, many systems are built to offer 99.99% availability to each viewer and 99.999% availability in the common core (routers, feeder networks, etc.) of the network.

Conditional Access

Conditional access (CA) is a group of techniques used to ensure that only viewers who meet certain conditions are given access to specific content. The basic technology for doing this involves encrypting or scrambling the content so that an unauthorized viewer who receives the signal is unable to view it. Authorized users are supplied with numeric keys that permit the operation of special hardware or software within an STB or PC that is able to decrypt or descramble the signals. CA systems are available from a number of vendors; typically these are integrated middleware systems that provide both content scrambling/encryption devices and control the distribution of the keys required to view the content.

Encryption can take many forms, but most major systems have a few core traits in common. First, the encryption and decryption must be computationally easy to perform when the key is known. Second, decryption must be difficult when the key is not known. Third, the keys must be manageable so that they can be distributed to the appropriate viewers.

Many different encryption management systems have been designed that embody these core traits. Some of the more common ones are described next.

Smart Cards

One traditional form of key distribution for STBs is the smart card. These cards are called "smart" because they incorporate a processor and memory that can be used by a variety of applications. Billions of smart cards are sold around the world each year for a variety of uses, including identification cards, mass-transit fare tickets, prepaid telephone cards (outside the United States), debit/credit cards, and a host of other applications. Typically, a smart card contains a processor capable of performing basic calculations and executing simple programs, as well as memory that can hold both variable and permanent data.

Smart cards must be connected to a reading device in order to operate. In some cases, this connection is made physically, using gold-plated contacts. Some cards can also connect wirelessly to special readers using short-distance radio signals, eliminating the need to physically insert the card into the device.

A key feature of many smart cards is their ability to store data securely. The cards can be programmed to store secret information, such as the private part of a public/ private key pair. Any unauthorized attempts to read that data would result in the card becoming permanently damaged and data destroyed. The internal processor of the smart card can be used to decrypt data using this stored private key, and results can be sent back out of the card without ever exposing the key to any external device.

For video applications, smart cards are one way to deliver descrambling/decryption keys for video content to a user device. Each content stream (or television channel, if you prefer) has a unique descrambling key that is created when the content is scrambled for broadcast. This key must be delivered to the viewer's device for it to be able to descramble the content properly. One way of doing this would be to simply send the key to the viewer's device; however, any other device that was connected to this communication path (think of a satellite link) would also receive this key and be able to decrypt the content. Instead, the descrambling keys are encrypted before they are sent to a viewing device.

When smart cards are used for delivering descrambling keys, each viewer device must be equipped with a smart card reader, either built in (as in many STBs) or connected through an external port (such as a USB port on a PC). When an authorized viewer wants to watch scrambled content, the viewer's device sends a request to a central server. This server checks to see if the viewer is authorized to view the content. If so, the server locates the correct descrambling key for the desired content and encrypts it using the appropriate public key that corresponds to the user's smart card. The server then sends the encrypted descrambling key out over the communication path to the viewer's device. When it arrives, the encrypted key is fed into the smart card, and the smart card performs the decryption operation to produce the descrambling key. The viewer device can then use the decrypted descrambling key to process the incoming signal and play the content for the viewer.

Smart cards offer a lot of benefits for service providers. The cards are portable and can be associated with a single viewer. For example, a card could be used to control access to adult content in a viewer's home, with one card issued to the family and another to the adults. Smart cards can also be delivered separately from the STB, making it more difficult for thieves to get access to both components.

One of the big downsides to smart card management is that they need to be kept physically secure (under lock and key). If stolen, they can be deactivated, but this can be a difficult process. Also, smart cards can lock a service provider into a single encryption vendor for long periods of time, as it is difficult and expensive to swap out cards that are in the hands of thousands of viewers. This is particularly true in the unlikely event that the encryption system is cracked by malicious users. If this happens, it is very expensive for the system operator to reprogram all the STBs and to issue a whole new set of smart cards.

A range of modern encryption technology providers have designed a replacement system for smart cards that is based on software, not hardware. In these systems, secure software modules are loaded onto each user's device (such as an STB or a PC) that provide a similar function to the smart card. A big advantage of software-based systems is that they can be upgraded and/or replaced much more easily than hardware-based systems because any required software updates can be delivered over a data network. Also, according to the suppliers of this technology, the software-based systems provide a level of security that is equal to or better than the hardware-based systems.

Watermarking

Watermarking is the process of inserting data into video or audio streams to track usage or prove ownership of the streams. It is similar in concept to some of the techniques used to protect currency and checks against forgery or counterfeiting. The basic idea is to insert identification without impairing the user's enjoyment of the content. Digital photographs can be watermarked to show copyright ownership and terms; these watermarks can be read by most of the major image-editing software packages. Video and audio content can also be watermarked with copyright data that can be read by some video recording and playback equipment to prevent unauthorized copying or distribution.

With digital content files, inserting a pattern into some of the less important bits in the file can be quite effective for watermarking purposes. For example, in a file with 16-bit audio samples, the least significant bit of any sample represents 1/65536th of the total output signal. When these bits are subtly manipulated, a watermark pattern can be inserted in the file with essentially no impact on the sound of the resulting piece.

Watermarking is implemented in different ways depending on the objectives of the creator of the watermark. A watermark can be specifically designed to be fragile so that any change to the file destroys the watermark, thereby proving the file was tampered with. Alternatively, a watermark can be designed to be so robust that even if the file is significantly altered, the watermark can still be discerned. Some watermarks are robust enough to remain embedded within content even when it is recorded by using a camera pointed at a video display. The latter is useful for tracking content that has been duplicated without permission; there are even Web crawlers that spend their time looking at millions of Web pages to see whether they have unauthorized content that contains certain watermarks.

Watermarking helps in rights enforcement when a unique watermark is created for each individual user. Individual watermarks can serve as a deterrent to unauthorized use of the content, as any misappropriations can be traced back to the specific source of the leak. Some middleware providers have started to provide systems that can produce a unique watermark inside every STB to allow traceability to a single subscriber. If users know that any misappropriated files can be traced back to them, it can be a powerful incentive to *not* share files illegally.

Personal Computer Security

Providing security for valuable content in PCs is a very difficult task. A major factor is that because a determined user can read essentially all data contained on a hard disk drive, it is very hard to keep information secret. The solution is to have a robust encryption scheme for the content and to ensure that the keys used to unlock access to the content are very secure. Two main forms of key protection are used on PCs: hardware based and software based.

In hardware-based key protection systems, a physical device must be connected to the PC for it to be authorized to decrypt or descramble the content. This device can take the form of a smart card attached to a reader connected to the PC. Another approach is to encapsulate a small processor (like those found in smart cards) into a device that can be attached to a serial port or a USB port. With either device type, the hardware must be physically attached to the viewer's device for the content to be unlocked. Descrambling keys are obtained from the device through a process of handshaking that prevents secret data stored within the device from ever being revealed.

In a software-based key protection system, special modules of software loaded onto the user's device control access to the key. These modules of software are not stand-alone—they must be in communication with a central server that ensures that the modules on the user devices have not been corrupted or had their security compromised. Software-based key control offers a big advantage over hardware-based systems because it enables complete system updates on a regular basis without the difficulty and expense of changing out a large number of deployed hardware devices.

Digital Rights Management

Digital rights management (DRM) is a set of software and hardware technologies designed to protect ownership rights of a content provider. The goal of DRM is to directly control the ways in which a viewer can use specific pieces of content. DRM systems will typically control uses such as repeated viewings, time windows when content can be viewed, copying or recording the content to other devices, or recording the content to removable media such as a CD or a DVD.

The concept of DRM is very close to that of CA. In fact, the two systems often work in close harmony in many digital video delivery systems. The key difference is that a CA system controls whether a viewer is allowed to view content, whereas a DRM system controls what the viewer can do with the content during and after viewing. In other words, CA governs which viewers can get access to content, whereas DRM governs what viewers can do with the content they have. Thus content that is downloaded for subsequent playout (e.g., podcasts) is often protected by a DRM system.

Reality Check

This chapter's first Reality Check looks at one of the most widely deployed (and widely discussed) systems for protecting audio and video content from unauthorized use. Development of a reliable DRM system was essential to Apple's successful negotiation of contracts with the major record labels to supply content through iTunes. The second Reality Check takes a look at why it makes sense, in some circumstances, to provide DRM for free content.

Apple's Fair Play DRM System for iTunes

Apple Computer's iTunes music store has been very successful in selling billions of compressed digital music files to millions of iPod owners. FairPlay, which is Apple's name for its DRM system, is an integral part of the iTunes software client and the iPod operating software.

The Fair Play system is quite comprehensive and is able to control a variety of different content uses. Controls on purchased content include limits on the number of computers that can share the content, limits on the number of CDs that can be burned with a single playlist that contains the content, and other restrictions. Many of these limitations were imposed as the result of negotiations with the recording industry that surrounded the launch of iTunes because of the perceived revenue impact of file-sharing systems.

In February 2007, Apple Computer published a letter by Steve Jobs[3] that outlined his thinking on DRM for digital music. He made the following points:

- DRM has never and will never be perfect. Hackers will always find a method to break DRM.
- DRM restrictions only hurt people using music legally. Illegal users aren't affected by DRM.
- The restrictions of DRM encourage users to obtain unrestricted music that is usually only possible via illegal methods.
- The vast majority of music is sold without DRM via CDs, which has proven successful.

Beginning in January 2009, DRM for most of the music sold on iTunes was removed, after Apple had received approval from the music industry. However, FairPlay restrictions remain in place for video content and games and utilities for the iPhone and iPod Touch. Also, most gaming platforms (PlayStation, Xbox) have pervasive DRM protection for their titles.

In 2008, a number of major Hollywood studios, electronics retailers, and consumer electronics manufacturers formed the Digital Entertainment Content Ecosystem (DECE). The idea behind this group is to create a DRM system that works with multiple content providers and across multiple consumer platforms

---

[3]Steve Jobs, "Thoughts on Music," http://www.apple.com/hotnews/thoughtsonmusic, February 6, 2007.

so that consumers would have more flexibility in how they purchase and consume content.

So the question becomes: Will DRM for video content be more persistent than DRM for music? One major difference that separates the video business from the music business is the fact that video has never been sold directly to consumers without some form of copy protection. VHS videotapes had a built-in copy protections scheme, as have DVDs and Blu-Ray discs. Another difference is the existence of an active rental market for video content (e.g., Blockbuster and Netflix), which indicates that there is a significant number of consumers who have become accustomed to paying for the rights to watch content once. Both of these factors may mean that DRM can survive in the video marketplace, but only time will tell.

Of course, any IPTV or Internet video services provider needs to recognize one overriding fact: they will not be able to get access to content unless they have agreement with the content owners regarding DRM or lack thereof. Without a content supply arrangement, no service provider will be able to stay in business.

DRM for Free Content

At first it may seem paradoxical for content available for free on a Web site to be protected by DRM technology. After all, once the content owner has decided to deliver the content for free to any viewer who wants to see it, why should they care if someone makes an unauthorized copy? Well, there are a couple thoughts to keep in mind.

- If any portions of the content belong to a third party (such as some of the songs on a movie soundtrack), the content owner may not have the right to allow others to make copies of that content. Similarly, the content owner might wish to establish a certain time window for the content to be available, say for a cinematic movie preview. If downloads are controlled by an effective DRM system, a time window is relatively easy to enforce. Without DRM, a time window is essentially impossible to enforce once there are unsecured downloads of the content circulating within the viewer base.
- If the goal of the service provider is to get viewers to look at advertising on their Web portal, then clearly allowing viewers to simply pass the content from one viewer to another will work against that goal. By protecting the content on the Web site and by allowing users to freely share links to content pages, the service provider can drive more viewers to their portal. This in turn will create more page views and more exposure for the advertisements.

Summary

This chapter focused on describing some of the techniques used to protect video quality and security. It began by discussing a number of potential video impairments and how they can be avoided or corrected. It then discussed network impairments as well as those caused by the video signal processing itself. It took a look at the various types of errors that can occur in IP networks and what system designers have done to minimize or compensate for those errors. The second part of the chapter took at look at the several different techniques used to provide CA functions for service providers, including the benefits and drawbacks of each. It also looked at DRM and how it is closely linked to but slightly different from CA. The chapter concluded with a look at two interesting aspects of DRM.

8 Sizing up Servers

While you are destroying your mind watching the worthless, brain-rotting drivel on TV, we on the Internet are exchanging, freely and openly, the most uninhibited, intimate and, yes, shocking details about our "CONFIG.SYS" settings.

Dave Barry

Media storage and delivery technology may seem dry to some, but when it comes to video, it has a crucial role to play in bringing digital content to the masses. One of the most commonly used devices in digital video production and delivery is the video server. Almost all content ends up on a server during some part of its life cycle, whether for production, delivery, archiving, or playout. Each of these applications has its own set of requirements and group of manufacturers offering specialized products. Because servers can be some of the more expensive items to purchase in an IP video delivery service, it is important to understand the demands of each type of application.

This chapter begins with a brief description of the major types of servers used in video applications. Then it examines a few of the categories in detail as they pertain to IPTV and Internet video. The chapter concludes with a table that compares the key performance parameters for several types of servers.

The Corner Office View

A few years ago, a magnetic recording density milestone was announced with a press release that read:

SEAGATE BREAKS WORLD MAGNETIC RECORDING DENSITY RECORD—421 GBITS PER SQUARE INCH EQUIVALENT TO STORING 4000 HOURS OF DIGITAL VIDEO ON YOUR PC

The announcement discussed the results of a magnetic recording demonstration on the 50th anniversary of the hard drive that set this world record:

The demonstration is evidence of the continued momentum in disc drive innovation and reaffirms the disc drive as the undisputed king of storage when capacity and cost-effectiveness are both required. At the demonstrated density level, Seagate expects the capacity ranges to result in solutions ranging in 40 to 275 GB for 1- and 1.8-inch consumer electronics drives, 500 GB for 2.5-inch notebook drives, and nearly 2.5 TB for 3.5-inch desktop and enterprise class drives. At 2.5 TB capacity, a hard drive would be capable of storing 41,650 hours of music, 800,000 digital photographs, 4000 hours of digital video, or 1250 video games. Seagate anticipates that solutions at these density levels could begin to emerge in 2009.

"Today's demonstration, combined with recent technology announce-ments from fellow hard drive companies, clearly shows that the future of hard drives is stronger than ever," said Bill Watkins, CEO of Seagate. "Breakthroughs in areal density are enabling the digital revolution and clearly indicate that hard drives can sustain their advantage to meet the world's insatiable demand for storage across a wide range of market segments."[1]

The state of the art continues to advance reaching 803 Gbits per inch by TDK (nearly doubling Seagate's achievement) recently. There does not seem to be an end in sight according to Katsumichi Tagami, director of the SQ Research Center, TDK Technology Group, who says "we've got a feeling that we will be able to achieve up to one terabit per square inch."

Video Servers

Video servers perform two main functions: storage and delivery. Storage is the physical act of keeping files of digital video content (usually on hard disk) for pro-cessing or playout. Delivery is the act of transmitting video content over a network to viewers or other devices that need the content. Depending on the application, servers may be optimized for one task or the other or may need to strike a balance between them.

Video servers are often made up of a number of physically separate hard disk drives and processors. This is done both for greater reliability and for better performance. Reli-ability is increased through the use of Redundant Array of Inexpensive Disks (RAID) technologies, which store extra data for each file. Extra data can be used with a simple algorithm to replace any data lost due to a failure or replacement of one of the disk drives. Multiple disk drives are used to increase the storage capacity of the total system beyond what is available on a single disk and also to increase the speed at which files can be written or read from the disk array. Similarly, multiple processors are used to enable the system to continue operating even if one processor fails and to provide greater computing power than would be available from a single processor.

Here are quick descriptions of some of the different applications where video servers are commonly used.

- *Ingest servers* are used to collect content from a variety of sources and make it avail-able for use in a variety of applications. Video content can come directly from a stu-dio camera or satellite feed, from a videotape that has just been removed from a camera or from archival storage, from another storage device such as a hard disk inside a camera or a remote server, or from essentially any other source that can pro-duce a video signal. Once the video has been ingested, it can then be handed off to a variety of other devices for further processing and storage.

[1]http://www.techspot.com/news/31867-tdk-claims-hdd-areal-density-record.html

- *Metadata tagging.* One of the most important roles of the ingest server is the proper tagging and description of each of the ingested video files. This information, called *metadata*, which can be produced automatically but usually requires human intervention, is crucial to the later processing and manipulation of the video content. If, for example, a mistake is made in the date of a video file, then an editor looking for the latest version of a shot may not be able to find it. High-quality data capture can be aided by the software that operates inside the ingest server to support rules for entering these data and processes that require proofreading of data by a second person once it has been entered.
- *File servers* are used in the video production process to handle content that is being manipulated into its final form. For example, a file server may be used to temporarily store a video clip from a color correction workstation before it is moved to another workstation that will be used to overlay graphics. The file server may also be used to store content or other data that are used repeatedly in the production process, such as theme music for a recurring program or common graphic elements.
- *Production or playout servers* are used to take finished video content that is ready to air and play it out in a continuous, highly reliable stream. With these servers, reliability is key because any failures can cause a broadcaster to go off the air. Various technologies can be used to provide redundancy and fail-safe operation; these features are commonly found on this type of server.
- *Archive servers* are designed to store massive amounts of content. This can be from all types of sources, such as live feeds, news clips, purchased programming, and so on. Archive servers typically emphasize large amounts of storage at a low cost, with speed of access being a secondary consideration. Archive servers can also be used to keep video records of programming as it has actually been broadcast in order to show compliance with government regulations and to answer queries from advertisers.
- *Video-on-demand servers* are designed to store content that viewers can order for viewing. These servers are typically designed to generate as many simultaneous streams as possible, often multiple copies of the same content. High bandwidth network connections are almost always used, whether the connection is to a private IPTV network or to the Internet.
- *Advertising servers* take advertising spots and play them back live inside video feeds. Although they typically don't need a massive amount of storage, they do need to interface to multiple simultaneous video channels and to carefully synchronize content playout to fit into the allotted advertising window. These servers need to be able to accept video content in a variety of different formats from multiple sources. In addition, these servers need to provide flexible scheduling tools that can be reconfigured easily to comply with rapidly changing advertising campaigns and keep good records of the ads that have actually run to support advertiser billing.
- *Live streaming servers* take live video streams and create multiple copies for transmission on the network. Although they need practically no storage, they need to have a large amount of processing capacity to create IP packets that are individually addressed to each recipient of the stream. Live streaming servers also need high bandwidth network connections to transmit all of the streams that they generate out into the IP network.

Because the last three types of servers just listed are often used in IPTV and Internet video applications, we will go into a bit more detail regarding these devices in the following sections.

Video-on-Demand Servers

Video on demand (VOD) is a common form of delivery for both IPTV and Internet video networks. By enabling users to select content from a library at any time, this technology can be a powerful draw for attracting viewers to a service provider. It can also be a competitive weapon against services that rely on broadcast distribution, such as satellite and digital terrestrial networks. Most IPTV and Internet video services providers, as well as many cable TV systems, offer VOD.

VOD servers must perform the following four main functions.

1. Video content storage, which is essentially the same function as any other video server. However, the server must be capable of transmitting multiple, asynchronous copies of a single piece of content (more on this later).
2. Network interface, which again is similar to other video servers, with the exception that a very large number of simultaneous streams may need to be supported.
3. User interaction support, which enables a viewer to pause, rewind, and fast-forward video content. This can require some sophisticated software to manage all of the viewers and to interface to the middleware systems that process user commands.
4. Catalog and ordering support, which provides support for the systems used to display the list of available content, as well as the transactions necessary to capture payment from the viewers.

Content on a VOD server is essentially always stored in a compressed format that is ready for play-out to the viewer. This simplifies the delivery process by eliminating the need to process the video before it is delivered. Because many IPTV systems have a narrow range of allowed video signal rates and normally support only a few compression formats, all of the content stored on the VOD server must be stored in compatible formats.

Accordingly, all incoming content must pass through a video compression device before it is placed on the VOD server. In some cases, the content supplier does the compression, and compressed files are simply copied directly into the server. In other cases, content may arrive in an uncompressed format and must be compressed before it can be placed on the server. This compression can be done in real time as the content is streamed or it can be done off-line on a file basis.

In still other cases, content may arrive compressed using a different bit rate or type of compression. If an incompatible format is delivered, transcoding is used to convert it to a compatible format. If the bit rate of the content needs to be changed, transrating is used to convert the content. Note that transrating is normally only done to reduce the bit rate of video content.

When purchasing a VOD server, it is important to match the capabilities of the server to the task that needs to be performed. The amount of storage can be large or small, and the number of streams supported can be large or small. These are not correlated; it is perfectly sensible to have a server with lots of storage yet little streaming capacity if it is being used to hold video content that is rarely viewed. Conversely, it is also sensible to have a server with relatively little storage (say, 50 to 100 hours of video content) but very high stream capacity if it is being used to serve first-run Hollywood movies to many viewers simultaneously.

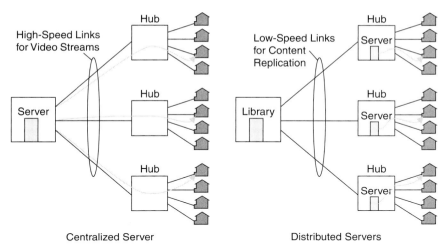

Figure 8.1 *Centralized versus distributed servers.*

IPTV service providers have two main philosophies of network server distribution, as shown in Figure 8.1. The first is centralized, where large, high-capacity servers are installed in central locations and the streams for each viewer are delivered over high-speed communication links to each local service provider facility. The second is decentralized, where smaller servers are located at each facility and provide streams only to local viewers. A central library server provides content to the distributed servers whenever necessary. On the one hand, the decentralized concept makes sense because it helps reduce the amount of bandwidth needed between locations. On the other hand, the centralized concept is appealing because it reduces the number of servers that must be installed. It also reduces the costs of transporting, storing, and managing redundant sets of content in multiple locations. In reality, both centralized and decentralized systems are deployed depending on system architecture, capabilities, and user viewing habits that affect VOD traffic patterns.

Service providers need video servers capable of delivering video streams to hundreds or thousands of simultaneous viewers. For this application class, specially designed servers are required. These units typically have a large number of disk drives and use multiple processors in parallel to format streams and deliver the content. The capacity of these systems is staggering; in order to supply 1000 simultaneous users each with a 2.5 Mbps stream, the server needs to be able to pump out 2.5 Gbps of data. Since no single disk drive or processor in a typical server is capable of this amount of data, servers use load sharing among the devices. This means that each piece of content is spread out across multiple disk drives and that a high-speed back plane interconnects the different drives to the different processors.

Calculating Server Storage Capacity

In order to properly calculate the amount of storage needed for a VOD server, two things must be known: (1) the number of hours of content to be stored and (2) the nominal bit rate of the video signal. With this information, calculating storage capacity is fairly straightforward.

Let's look at an example. Consider a one-hour video signal (with accompanying audio, of course) that runs at a bit rate of 2.5 Mbps. Recognizing that there are 8 bits in a byte and 3600 seconds in an hour, you easily calculate that the total file will be 1.125 billion bytes, or about 1.05 GB. Note that this value is approximate, as the exact format of the file on a hard disk will be different. In addition, a small amount of metadata will be added to the file to provide a description of the video and make it easier to transmit in multiple copies.

Here are a few more examples of required video server sizes for various amounts of content.

- 200 hours of SD content at 2.5 Mbps = 210 GB
- 500 hours of SD content at 4 Mbps = 840 GB
- 10,000 hours of SD content at 2 Mbps = 8.2 TB
- 300 hours of MPEG-2 HD content at 14 Mbps = almost 1.72 TB
- 500 hours of H.264 HD content at 6 Mbps = 1.22 TB

It is also interesting to note that some content owners place limits on how much compression can be applied to their video streams. Sometimes there are even contractual terms regarding the type of compression algorithm to be used. These limits are put in place to help ensure that the end viewer receives a high-quality image. This can be very important to large production companies who have a public image to maintain and who stand to lose credibility or viewers if their products are over-compressed. One example of such a company might be a broadcaster who holds the rights to a large number of sporting events. If local IPTV providers use excessive amounts of compression, then not only will that group of local viewers get an inferior video feed, but there could also be a negative impact on the broadcaster's brand image in other aspects of their business.

Advertising Servers

An advertising server can be a key revenue producer for IPTV systems and may also have a role to play in live streaming Internet video applications. The server's job is to insert advertisements into video streams at specially indicated times called *avails*. The result is a video stream delivered to a viewer with specialized advertising inserted.

Let's look at an example of how this technology works. A national broadcaster such as CNN designs their programming to accommodate advertisement inserts throughout the day. Many of these time slots will be sold to national advertisers and broadcast by CNN to every viewer in a country. Other time slots will be made available for local providers to sell to local advertisers. During these slots, CNN will include audio tones or special digital codes that indicate that these times are available for local ads to be inserted. The ad server will recognize the indicator and replace the feed from the network with a video file stored on the local server. Any viewers watching CNN through the local provider will see the local ad in place of the ad broadcast by CNN. Because the timing of each avail is under the control of CNN, the network can make sure that local ads are not inserted in place of high revenue national ads, but rather in place of ads that may not bring direct revenue to the network, such as advertisements for upcoming programs.

In the case of Internet video, ads are commonly delivered in two ways. One way is as a banner graphic or video clip on a Web portal, where viewers navigate to select the clip they want to view or download. The second way is as a video spot advertisement delivered to the viewer immediately before (called *pre-roll*) or sometime during (called *mid-roll*) the requested content.

From a business standpoint, local advertising can be a big source of revenue to any video delivery system operator. Over-the-air, cable TV, and satellite broadcasters all utilize this technology, and IPTV and Internet video operators can earn revenue as well. This revenue can be used to help offset the costs of programming and delivery systems, such as IPTV networks or Internet video servers. Both local and national advertisers will use local advertising for certain purposes. For example, it makes no sense for a local automobile dealer to advertise on a national basis. National advertisers may also want to deliver advertisements selectively to local audiences, such as a beverage company that may have an advertising tie-in with a local sports team.

Live Streaming Servers

Live streaming servers are used to support broadcasts over the Internet. They are necessary because each video stream delivered must be made up of packets specifically addressed to each individual viewer's device—there is no mechanism on the Internet to make copies of a video stream and deliver it to multiple users (i.e., multicasting). Another way to describe a live streaming server would be as a unicast replication server, because their principal job is to take in one unicast stream, make multiple copies, and then send them on toward multiple viewers.

Unicasting is the standard mode for sending packets over the Internet. In this mode, each packet has a single source address and a single destination address. If a source wants to send packets to multiple destinations, it must create a unique packet for each destination. This requires processing power because each packet needs to have a correctly formatted header, with a destination IP address, a correct set of flags, and a properly calculated header checksum. Once the packet is created, it flows essentially intact directly from the source to the destination over the Internet.

Live streaming servers need very little storage because the content is moving through in real time. Instead, these servers need a lot of processing power because they need to receive incoming streams, make copies for each viewer, and create properly formatted IP packets in a continuous stream for each viewer with little or no delay. In addition, the servers must be capable of processing transactions to add and drop viewers as people tune in to watch the video or tune out when they have seen enough or want to switch to other content. These servers may also need to capture data as required to produce invoices for paid content, although that task is normally the responsibility of the Web portal that authorized the user to view the video.

In contrast to most other types of servers, live streaming servers don't have to be purchased by each company that wants to use them. Instead, service bureaus will (for a fee) provide processing power and Internet bandwidth when a company wants to host a live event. These bureaus, often called *content delivery networks* (CDNs), will also host normal Web site content for delivery to Web surfers located around the Internet.

Encryption and Rights Management

Purchasing and installing a major server system can be challenging. However, getting the rights to enough content to fill the server can be a much more daunting task. Owners of the content will often refuse to permit their programming to be placed on a server until they are satisfied with the security arrangements. Securing these rights often involves direct negotiations with the content owners and may depend on certification of the DRM system.

A number of vendors of DRM systems have taken the necessary step of proving the security of their systems to the satisfaction of major content owners, such as Hollywood movie studios. At a minimum, a DRM system must ensure that the content is unusable (for viewing or copying) unless the viewer has been provided with the proper key. There are a number of mechanisms for controlling and distributing these keys, which were discussed in Chapter 7.

DRM is not only important in a VOD delivery network, but also for the content storage itself, directly within the VOD server. This is to prevent unauthorized uses of the content, which could occur from an outside intruder gaining access to the server or from an inside user misappropriating the content. Content owners will typically insist on protection of their property both in storage and during delivery.

VOD vendors have taken a number of steps to protect stored content within their systems. In addition to standard encryption techniques used in DRM, some vendors have developed a proprietary file system that is separated from the normal server-operating system. This can help prevent hackers and viruses from reaching the stored content. A second security technique involves breaking the content up into small files and distributing those files to physically separate hard drives. In the event that one of the drives is stolen or compromised, the content is useless because it is only a small portion of the overall file. This system also provides extra reliability because error correction data can be stored along with files so that all files can be properly reconstituted even after a drive fails.

Reality Check

This chapter's Reality Check discusses three different server implementations. The first two examples discuss ways to use servers to increase revenue, and the third discusses a way to change the physical location of the stored video content.

Selling Space on a VOD Server to Advertisers

On most VOD servers, there is a significant amount of space allocated for expansion. While this space may eventually be used up, the space is simply empty for a good part of many system life cycles. Some clever system operators have figured out a way to leverage this asset: selling space to advertisers.

In this situation, the advertisements are not the normal 30- or 60-second spot ads. Instead, they are long-form ads designed to appeal to the relatively small proportion of viewers who might want to get more information about a specific product or service. For example, a manufacturer of an innovative flooring product may want to sponsor an instructional video that shows consumers how easy it is to install and maintain their product, a luxury automobile manufacturer may want to host a program that shows a classic car rally featuring their products, a golf equipment manufacturer may want to sponsor a golf training video, or the visitors' bureau for a tropical island may want to host a tour of their natural features. There are many possibilities.

To make this successful for both system operators and advertisers, a few conditions must be met. First, there must be a way for viewers to find out about the content and navigate to it. This will certainly involve the use of listings in the interactive program guide, but may also involve splash screens or inserts in more popular pages to inform viewers that the content exists. Second, the system operator may want to exercise a minimal amount of editorial control to help ensure that the sponsored content doesn't end up being larded with hard-sell infomercials that have little value for viewers. The system operator may also want to gather some viewing statistics to see which types of content are popular and to provide feedback to the advertisers on the effectiveness of their offerings.

Advertisements Attached to VOD Content

As discussed earlier, not all VOD content needs to be paid for by viewers on a per-transaction basis. As discussed in Chapter 3, many different models can be used to pay for on-demand content. Deciding how to implement an advertising-supported VOD system can be quite interesting.

One of the most basic decisions that must be made is to decide when the advertisements will appear. Many viewers have become accustomed to pre-roll advertisements, where a few short spot ads are played before the desired content begins to play. This is, of course, common practice in movie theaters (previews of coming events, reminders to not smoke, and advertisements of the snack bar in the lobby are common themes). Pre-roll advertising is also common on Web sites and is part of many purchased content items such as DVDs and VHS tapes. The secret to not upsetting viewers is to ensure that the ads are brief and few in number.

A more controversial form of advertising consists of advertisements actually inserted into the content itself. This technique certainly does not appeal to some viewers. However, if the service provider makes it clear that advertising is required in order to pay for the content, then viewers are more likely to understand.

One very controversial aspect of advertising and VOD content is whether commercial *zapping* should be allowed. Commercial zapping occurs when a viewer decides to fast-forward past a commercial. Most live video recording devices (such as DVRs) allow users to fast-forward through advertisements.

Legal Blues for SonicBlue

Today, viewers regularly skip or *zap* commercials using DVR devices. This technology, which was included in Replay TV units sold by SonicBlue, ended up being the subject of a lawsuit against the company by a number of major media companies. SonicBlue ended up in bankruptcy in 2003 before the case was decided so there wasn't a clear ruling in the United States about the legality of this technology. However, TiVo, other DVR devices, and zapping continue to thrive, resulting in an ongoing content provider struggle to retain the attention of their audience through more inventive ads, interactive features, and product placement.

Servers and storage will continue to play a key role in the emerging broadband video delivery world as new content providers find that going online is the easiest way to penetrate a competitive U.S. or global programming market. "The broadcast era is over, content is not king anymore ... distribution is king," says MMAX Enterprises sports channel executive Chuck Vaughn. "Maybe that's a temporary situation," says Vaughn, "but the fragmentation has shifted everything on its head which is why everyone in Hollywood is nervous."

The two sides of the controversy regarding VOD service ad monetization can be summarized as follows.

- If zapping is not allowed, then users who are not willing to see advertisements will become less likely to watch the content. This in turn could translate into fewer overall viewers, meaning that revenues that depend on viewers (such as subscription fees) will drop.
- If zapping is allowed, then advertisers will be less likely to pay for advertising, as there is a lower probability of their ads being viewed. Service providers may then find it necessary to charge more for VOD content.

Of course, it is not necessary that this decision be made on an all-or-nothing basis—service providers are free to vary the amount of advertising for different types of content. They can also experiment both with advertisements that allow zapping and with ads that don't, at the risk of truly confusing viewers.

Push VOD as an Alternative to Centralized Servers

Push VOD uses hard disk storage located inside the viewer's STB to store content locally that can be viewed on demand. Push VOD is being used to provide VOD over networks that don't have interactive capabilities. This is certainly the case with satellite networks, which simply don't have the bandwidth to create a separate video signal stream for each user.

In an IPTV system, push VOD may be useful for a few reasons. First, by storing video files locally in each user's STB, the burden on the network could be reduced when a viewer is watching a VOD program, and the load on centralized VOD servers is lightened. Second, locally stored content could be used to provide entertainment or troubleshooting information to users in the event that their network connection failed. Third, local storage could be used to provide highly interactive programming or entertainment (such as games) that would be difficult or impossible to provide from a centralized server.

Of course, some factors must be considered before using push VOD. First, a very strong DRM technology will be required, as push VOD content is literally sitting in a hard drive in the viewer's home. Second, a fairly sophisticated control system will be needed to manage which content gets delivered to each STB and to collect the payments from viewers who chose to watch the content. Vendors are appearing that offer to manage both of these issues for service providers, and as hard drive capacities increase, more content can be stored.

One interesting concept that can benefit both viewers and service providers is installing a partitioned hard drive in an STB. In one partition, the service provider can push a dozen or two popular movie titles being featured for VOD. The other partition can be used to give the viewer a DVR capability for their favorite broadcast shows. This combination gives system operators two ways to pay for the extra expense of purchasing and maintaining hard drives in STBs—by selling push VOD content and by increasing the rental fees to viewers for STBs that include DVR capability. STB manufacturers have responded to this market by placing large hard disk drives into STBs and supporting partitioning in the STB operating software.

Summary

This chapter discussed a variety of different server types and examined in detail three types often used for IPTV and Internet video systems. VOD servers can be large or small, centralized or distributed, but they are always rated on the number of simultaneous streams they can support. Advertising servers are typically not

Table 8.1 Key Attributes of Different Types of Servers

Server Type	Capacity	Speed	Cost	Key Attribute
VOD	Varies	High stream capacity	Low to moderate	Bandwidth—number of simultaneous streams
Archive	As large as possible	Not important	Lowest cost per terabyte	Large capacity at low cost
Playout	Low	Low	High	Reliability/redundancy essential
Advertising	Low	Able to handle multiple channels simultaneously	Medium	Easy to operate software, excellent record keeping
Live Streaming	Very low	High stream capacity	Medium	Bandwidth—number of simultaneous streams
Ingest	Low	Low	Medium	Flexibility for video inputs, good software for metadata workflow

large or hugely powerful, but they need to be able to monitor multiple live network feeds, insert ads reliably, and keep good records. Live streaming servers need almost no storage but are rated like VOD servers on their total throughput in terms of number of simultaneous streams. Table 8.1 summarizes some of the similarities and differences among the various types of servers.

9 The Importance of Bandwidth

Here we go again! First music, then TV shows, and now movies.

Steve Jobs

Both IPTV and Internet video services are critically dependent on adequate bandwidth as more and more media content moves from on-air to online networks. Without it, Internet video files can be excessively slow to download and streaming video won't work. IPTV simply cannot operate without sufficient bandwidth to carry the signal. As a result, ensuring adequate network capacity is extremely important for operations and quality of service (QoS).

Only a few years ago, skeptics maintained that state of the art in broadband was not sufficient to deliver bandwidth-hungry television channels. One complaint has always been that operators would be "challenged to ensure that they have enough bandwidth over their DSL infrastructures to compete with cable." Well, times have changed. "IPTV is cooler than cable," AT&T now boasts about their popular U-verse service.

As mentioned in Chapter 4, U-verse has grown rapidly and surpassed a million subscribers in 2008, just four years after the telco giant announced that it was going into the television business. Having launched across the United States in 2006, they now even offer IPTV through the world's largest retailer, Wal-Mart.

According to AT&T, their goal is to provide a better experience than cable. They will match the quality of SD and HD content offered by cable companies, says spokeswoman Destiny Varghese, and then surpass them with interactive features for programming U-verse's DVR from PC or mobile phone and the ability to create custom TV weather, sports, and stock displays by setting preferences from your Internet portal. "We've only begun to scratch the surface of what IP is capable of "says Varghese" when integrated with wireless devices, PCs, and your cell phone."[1]

The Corner Office View

Greenfield: Forrester says there will be a huge bandwidth crunch for telco, cable, satellite providers. What do you think?

Mark Cuban: [That] is right. There isn't enough bandwidth for all the existing TV networks; some will die, some will stay standard definition, some will go HD.

Any IP video solution depends on adequate bandwidth from head end to home viewer. Just as building a fire requires a balance of fuel, heat, and oxygen, elements

---

[1]Interview with Howard Greenfield, October 2008.

needed for the IPTV consumer experience are equipment, network services, and content. Bandwidth is what sparks and sustains the combustion. Without understanding how to supply adequate throughput for data packets to produce smooth playout, the quality of service will degrade and subscribers will not pay. The standard has already been set by conventional TV service. An audience will accept an occasional dropped pixel or an audio blip, but realistically, the threshold for picture defects, blocky video, or frozen frames is low.

By provisioning enough bandwidth to deliver on the exciting promise of personalized, interactive IPTV content, a whole new market opens up. However, the QoS issues that accompany scalable, bandwidth-intensive HDTV and triple-play service offerings will increasingly go with the territory. To date, these challenges and costs for infrastructure investment have been significant, but most industry analysts see these as a minor speed bump along the way. Among the initial solutions for addressing improved bandwidth, which is discussed later in this chapter, are advanced DSL technologies with higher bit rates or greater range, media compression advances, and deployment strategies, such as constructing remote terminals closer to the home.

Bandwidth requirements vary greatly depending not only on the type of content being transmitted, but also on the quality of service expected. In the 1980s, a modem speed of 2400 bps allowed for basic text communications. Networks soon reached ISDN speeds at 128 Kbps but were still too limited to carry significant multimedia content. Today's global DSL speeds average 1.5 Mbps with many at much higher speeds, such as cable modems at 6 Mbps and higher. It is forecasted that over 32 million homes in the United States will have 10 Mbps or higher by 2012.[2] We are fast approaching a widespread, mass commercial IPTV capability.

Advances in compression are steadily making headway in delivering video services over broadband. MPEG-2 video broadcast, once standard for digital television and DVD, requires 4 to 6 Mbps for standard definition signals. However, new and more efficient codecs, such as MPEG-4 H.264 and VC-1, only need 1.5 to 2.5 Mbps and can render DVD-quality video within 2 Mbps. Decent-quality HD signals can be achieved with 5 to 8 Mbps. Additionally, more recent classes of DSL can carry far higher bandwidth than before, such as ADSL2+ and VDSL2 at roughly 24 and 50 Mbps, respectively.

Nonetheless, the bandwidth bar is continually being raised as more and more network services are bundled together for delivery to each subscriber. The next section examines various forms of DSL and their capabilities.

Digital Subscriber Line Technologies

Twisted pair–based DSL facilities are widespread, with more than a billion telephone lines globally; of the 350 million broadband subscribers worldwide in 2008, an estimated 66% are DSL based—a number forecasted to grow by a 13%

[2]"U.S. Broadband Update," Parks Associates, 2008.

compound annual growth rate (CAGR) through 2011.[3] As an incumbent technology, DSL is a popular, cost-effective way for telcos and other service providers to enter the new market for delivering broadband and video services without having to lay new cable and reconstruct a system. Also, because of the popularity and prevalence of high-speed data DSL telephone lines, many consumers are aware that they can purchase DSL service for Internet access. Many service providers now routinely offer video content using DSL service.

To understand the mechanics of DSL, it is useful to consider the main components in data and video traffic over DSL transport. All DSL systems make a trade-off between speed and distance: longer distances must operate at lower bit rates because losses in the cable increase as the length of the cable increases. As technology improves, these limitations are easing, but network designers still need to plan accordingly and usually make compromises due to these constraints.

The following are key DSL network components (Figure 9.1):

1. The main hub, or central office (CO), the source of the signal
2. Remote terminals (RTs) positioned between the provider's main offices and customers
3. The feeder plant where fiber-based voice, video, and data signals often travel over different transmission equipment
4. The DSLAM, located strategically relative to the homes being served, which generates the DSL signals and places them onto the pair of copper wires (or local loop) leading to each home

Among the more crucial factors in this equation is the DSLAM, which we'll learn more about later in this chapter. Every DSL customer must install a DSL modem to

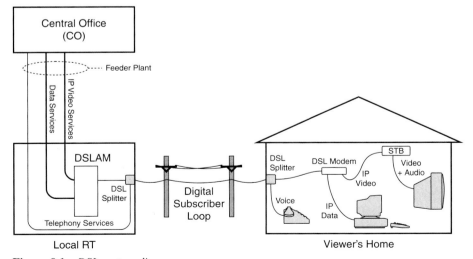

Figure 9.1 *DSL system diagram.*

[3]http://www.researchandmarkets.com/reports/598386/2008_global_broadband_market_demand_for_faster

receive DSL signals from the DSLAM and convert them into the proper form for the customer's other devices, such as a PC, a data router, or a television set. The modem also takes data signals from the customer and transmits them back to the service provider.

Of the more common types of DSL services available, each has its advantages and disadvantages. These can be summarized at a high level as shown in Table 9.1.

Actual bit rates that can be achieved on a DSL circuit can vary somewhat and depend on many factors, including the length of the subscriber's loop and the amount of noise or interference present on the line.

In addition to using existing wires already run to many homes and businesses for telephone service, another advantage of DSL circuits is that they are normally designed to fail gracefully. This means that if a customer loses power or the DSL equipment fails, normal telephone calls can still be made. A disadvantage of DSL services for video is that only a handful of broadcast-quality signals can be sent down a DSL line. Also, a separate stream must be dedicated to each television or other video-receiving device (VCR, digital recorder, etc.) and each must be equipped with an STB.

We've learned the basics of how DSL technology works. It's equally important to see how IPTV systems are implemented over advanced ADSL and VDSL circuits to understand the dynamics of home delivery and regional penetration.

Table 9.1 DSL Service Type Options for Broadband and IPTV

	Bandwidth	Advantages	Disadvantages
G.lite	Up to 1.5 Mbps downstream; up to 512 kbps upstream	Provides greater reach; does not need the splitter required on ADSL circuits to separate voice and data signals	Not fast enough for video
ADSL	Up to 8 Mbps downstream; up to 1 Mbps upstream	Mature technology	Will handle a few SD channels or at most one HD; splitter required to separate voice and data signals
VDSL	Up to 50 Mbps downstream; up to 12 Mbps upstream	Better bandwidth at short distances	Maximum distance is quite short ($\sim$1000 feet)
ADSL2+	Up to 24 Mbps downstream; 1 Mbps upstream	Smoother roll-off; as you go further from the source there is a gradual decrease in performance	May not work on all existing copper cable

More about VDSL and ADSL

It is said that there is broadband and then there is broadband, varying widely depending on geography, standards, and adoption rates. Most companies deploying IPTV currently use VDSL and ADSL2+, and roll-outs abound worldwide. In Germany, Deutsche Telekom, which has invested EUR 10 billion in its DSL technology[3] since 1999, has opened up its VDSL wholesale service in parallel with the German government's explicit goal of delivering 50 Mbps broadband to 75% of all households by 2014.[4] CenterTelecom in Russia is about to offer IPTV over its ADSL in the Moscow metropolitan area[5] while performance continues to advance as Ericsson has announced 500 Mbps VDSL2 over copper.

Compared to what's ahead, prior generation DSL technologies, such as *Asymmetric Digital Subscriber Line* (ADSL), provide relatively limited amounts of bandwidth from the service provider to the consumer and even more restricted links from the consumer back to the provider (hence the "asymmetrical" element of ADSL). With H.264 compression technology, this is barely enough for one SD video and audio stream, with a little left over for Internet access.

To keep overall speeds reasonable and to enable other services (such as Internet access) on the ADSL link, it is normal to find only one, or at most two, video signals on a single ADSL circuit. However, ADSL2+ has become more prevalent for IPTV because, for one thing, its downlink speed is twice that of ADSL. Also, ADSL2+ is capable of 24 Mbps performance (in theory) and supports port bonding, which doubles bandwidth again wherever the DSLAM supports it. Performance is dependent on the proximity of the home to the exchange. ADSL2+ provides a smoother performance roll-off than ADSL as this distance increases, but has the disadvantage of not being compatible across all existing copper cable and modem devices.

Very high-speed Digital Subscriber Line (VDSL) technology supports significantly more bandwidth on each subscriber line. Accordingly, more video channels can be transmitted to each VDSL subscriber, with three or four simultaneous videos possible. HD video signals could also be transmitted (possibly multiple ones), VDSL speed permitting. One drawback to VDSL is that the range of operational distances is less than that of ADSL so subscribers need to be closer to the service provider facilities (which is one reason why VDSL is more popular in Europe and Asia where housing densities tend to be greater). Also note that the speed of DSL services varies with distance, so good planning for varying data rates is essential (Figure 9.2).

Each television set that receives IPTV signals over DSL requires an STB to decode the incoming video. Some STBs can act as the residential gateway in the home and provide connections for other voice and data communications equipment.

Because of DSL speed limitations, each time a viewer changes channels on the DSL IPTV system, a command must be sent back to the service provider to indicate that a new video stream needs to be delivered. We'll look more closely at both home gateways and channel changing latency issues later in this chapter.

[4]http://www.fiercetelecom.com/story/dt-opens-vdsl-network/2009-03-02
[5]http://www.iptv-news.com/iptv_news/march_09/russias_centertelecom_to_launch_iptv_in_q2

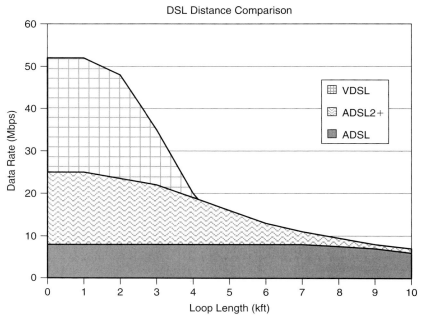

Figure 9.2   *ADSL, ADSL2+, and VDSL rate and distance performance.*

DSL Deployment: Homes Served, Homes Passed

Calculating ROI on IPTV and DSL business cases can become a complex calculation. There are many costs to take into account, including network infrastructure,
operations, and maintenance; content rights and royalties; and customer marketing.
One way to keep an eye on the bottom line is to use a deployment measure, *homes
passed* (HP), which refers to the number of potential subscribers who are ready to be
served, although they may not actually choose to subscribe to the service. Creating a
network with a significant quantity of homes passed is an up-front investment for
provisioning full service to communities.

In traditional OTA and satellite broadcast settings, the ratio of homes passed to
homes served (HS) is not a significant issue because the ability to broadcast to a
region is mostly about skillful broadcast tower and satellite transponder deployment:
essentially, a single transmission reaches all. In IPTV implementations, however,
covering a region requires more planning and deployment steps to connect a line
to pass in front of every home and arrive at an optimum, profitable ratio of homes
served to homes passed. The penetration ratio of HS to HP is what counts. One rule
of thumb for achieving adequate ROI is that penetration must reach 20% at an early
stage of deployment.

Because most business case data about IPTV systems is a closely guarded secret,
there is not enough public information to determine what's working and what

strategies should be adjusted. With no magic formula, creating a system of measurement is essential. Until you have subscribers, there's no additional cost. However, with IPTV, providers must continue to build out the network and be prepared to provide full-coverage service on a risk/reward basis.

Digital Subscriber Line Access Multiplexer

One of the main delivery service elements in IP video transport that makes it all happen is the Digital Subscriber Line Access Multiplexer (DSLAM), supporting connections between IP telephone or PC devices and the Internet. The DSLAM provides a high-speed data conduit between multiple DSLs and the network backbone's vast bandwidth.

DSLAM technology performs a mission-critical function in digital media data routing and transport. If we start with a look at the legacy of the communications world, plain old telephone service (POTS) provided telephony and served telecoms customers. POTS systems were never designed to operate as data lines and typically do not offer guaranteed data transfer rates.

The modern digital counterpart of POTS is IP switching, which provides reliable data flow and supports the switching of video and audio signals. In the IP switching model, each digital video or audio signal is converted into a stream of IP packets and is sent onto a local area network where actual switching is done by standard IP networking equipment. The great advantage of this digital approach is that many different types of signals can be carried over IP, such as video, audio, voice, and other signal types. Bringing all these functions together on a single network means that connections can be consolidated, network management can be simplified, and flexibility can be increased.

Location, location ... well, you've heard it before. To facilitate faster traffic flow and allow for the efficient transport of data—be it for phone, video, or Web content—DSLAMs must be physically located at the right points and proper distances along the network. However, regardless of the strategic deployment of DSLAMs and their seamless interoperation with server and network, another challenging demand placed on the new IPTV architecture is channel changing performance, which is examined later in this chapter.

Home Gateway

A DSL home gateway provides data connectivity to various devices in the home. It connects the networked devices in the house with any server storage and the Internet through a high-speed DSL modem and communications ports. Benefits to consumers include connectivity with IPTV content, PC downloads, and media, as well as virtual private network and security features.

The On-Demand, Network-Smashing Future

In what *Wired* magazine called television's "fast-forward, on-demand, network-smashing future," the promised land, you might say, is a single, seamless infinite world of content. This means aggregation of the previously separate communication domains of video, music, Web pages, movies, Internet search, telephony, and games. It also means that whether by Web, TV, or mobile phone, whether through prime-time TV channels or amateur user-generated channels, your home is the intersection where this is about to take place.

The home gateway supports DSL and accommodates the expanding functionality and a converging set of devices. In what some refer to as the "living room war," an increasing market share of broadband content, combined with broadcast over IP, offers a new commercial prize for service providers: delivery billing for a new array of entertainment programming and information services.

Cable: Coax and CAT6

The central plumbing system, as it were, for connecting this in-home media entertainment complex is the various internal wire line and wireless technologies such as coax and CAT6.

It is common for the residential gateway to be permanently installed in a central location in each home. IP traffic from this gateway is then routed to each STB located inside the subscriber's home. In many systems, connections on this gateway are also provided for the customer's telephone and PC.

In addition to being used in homes by the cable television industry, coaxial cabling can be used for supporting computer networks, including Ethernet. Because it carries more data and a clearer signal, it has often been considered worth the added expense over regular telephone wire and is a legacy in many homes today.

CAT6 (Category6), composed of copper wire pairs, is a higher performance—and higher priced—cable that supports GigE at bit rates of up to 1000 Mbps at a maximum length of 90 meters. Considered a little bit of overkill for current data flow in the home, many experts maintain that CAT6 is the right future-proofing choice for the long haul.

Home Phoneline Networking Alliance

The *Home Phoneline Networking Alliance* (HPNA), with technology members such as AT&T, HP, IBM, and Intel, is an industry organization that explores ways to establish home networking standards that drive innovation and interoperability between telecom and IT data, device, and service providers. HPNA's stated goal is to "develop triple-play home networking solutions for distributing entertainment data over both existing coax cable and phone lines."

Their 3.0 technical specification had the mission of enabling devices to "simultaneously communicate at their native speed" in networks without degrading the QoS. Its aim is optimizing for "broadband entertainment, voice, data file, peripheral and Internet sharing applications throughout the home without affecting standard telephone service."[6] This goal is exemplified in its promotion of initiatives such as the International Telecommunication Union's (ITU) all-wire G.hn 1 Gbps home networking standard.[7] Other organizations promoting cross-device compatibility and connectivity important to watch include BroadbandForum, Digital Entertainment Content Ecosystem, and Open IPTV Forum.

Home Networking Growth

Home networking is anticipated to grow significantly, with the number of enabled households increasing worldwide from around 172 million in 2008 to nearly 280 million by 2013.[8] Momentum will likely build from home networking advantages such as shared Internet and printer access and home entertainment distribution into areas such as home device control, security, and telecommuting benefits. Furthermore, this is just the beginning, as we start to connect not just living room, home office, and bedroom, but also the utility room, kitchen, and beyond.

Multiple Televisions

"It's what I call the dirty little secret of IPTV," says Entone Technologies CEO Steve McKay. "The huge issue today is that it's one thing to get the signal to one TV, but what if you have four or five TVs in the home?"[9] In conventional TV broadcast scenarios such as terrestrial, cable, and satellite, there is no overhead or impact when adding additional televisions to the household, except possibly the addition of an STB for certain services.

Not so with IPTV. Each IPTV destination device requires its own bandwidth allocation, taking an additive toll on IP packet delivery. Thus, stringing new TVs into bedrooms, dens, and kitchens requires greater bandwidth, which is a challenge for IPTV to scale as gracefully as its multicast broadcast counterpart. But consumers want this flexibility, and services such as AT&T's U-Verse IPTV now enable customers to play back recorded programs from a single DVR to any connected television in the house.

How to Calculate Bandwidth

Today, some approaches to bandwidth calculation must cover current implications to planning for IPTV deployment such as MPEG-4, H.264. There are two different incentives, or forces, acting on IPTV service providers when they determine the bandwidths that will be used for new DSL networks.

---

[6]From Home Networking MR-002. http://www.broadband-forum.org/marketing/download/mktgdocs/ABCs_home_networking_final.pdf
[7]http://www.homepna.org/imwp/idms/popups/pop_download.asp?contentID=15414
[8]Home Networks for Consumer Electronics, Parks Associates, 2008.
[9]From *Light Reading*. www.lightreading.com/document.asp?doc_id573558&site5lightreading

- One force is to offer as many different services as possible, thereby giving subscribers the widest variety of offerings to choose from. However, as each additional service requires room on the DSL circuit, this approach tends to increase the amount of bandwidth used.
- Another force is to maximize the number of subscribers that can be served from each DSLAM location. Since there is a trade-off between distance and speed, higher data rates mean that shorter distances are covered, and therefore fewer homes are reached. This force tends to reduce the amount of bandwidth used.

Because video signals are typically the largest users of bandwidth on an IPTV system, calculating the amount of bandwidth required for video and audio streams on an IPTV system is extremely important. Here is how one supplier of video compression equipment does the calculations for a standard television feed with two audio channels and some associated data.

A Bandwidth Calculation Example

Calculating the amount of actual bandwidth consumed by an MPEG stream is very important. It is also somewhat tricky. Let's look at how one manufacturer (HaiVision Systems of Montreal, Quebec) does this for one H.264 product (the hai200 TASMAN video encoder).

As in most MPEG devices, the hai200 user is given control over the rate of the raw MPEG stream. For this device, the video bit rate can be set anywhere from 150 kbps to 2 Mbps. The user can also set the audio stream rates over a range from 64 to 256 kbps. For the purposes of our example, we will use a video bandwidth of 2 Mbps and an audio bandwidth of 128 kbps.

Because we are going to be transporting these raw streams over a network, the first thing we want to do is convert the raw MPEG streams (in MPEG-2 these are known as *elementary streams*; in H.264 these are known as NAL units) into a transport stream (TS). Since fractional TS packets aren't allowed, each video frame will occupy 46 TS packets and each audio frame will occupy 2 TS packets. For audio, this adds 9.3% overhead to the raw bandwidth and 3.8% to the raw video bandwidth. So our original audio stream is now a 140-kbps TS, and our video TS now occupies 2.076 Mbps. We also need to add 46.5 kbps to these streams to provide room for the program map table and the program clock reference, which are used for MPEG stream management. Figure 9.3 illustrates this example.

The next step is to calculate the IP and Ethernet overhead. Since the hai200 TASMAN uses RTP over UDP, we must allow for a 12-byte RTP header and an 8-byte UDP header. Then we must add a 20-byte IP header and a 26-byte Ethernet header. (The Ethernet frame structure consists of a 7-byte preamble, a 1-byte start frame delimiter, a 6-byte destination MAC address, a 6-byte source MAC address, a 2-byte length/type identifier, and a 4-byte frame check sequence in addition to the payload.)

This brings the total of all the headers to 66 bytes. We can accommodate anywhere from two to seven TS packets (which are always 188 bytes long) in each

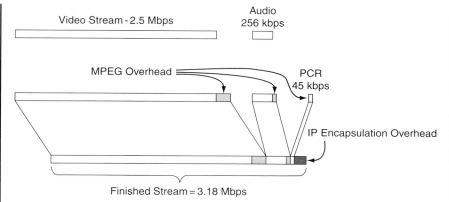

Figure 9.3 *Sample total bandwidth calculation for an MPEG stream.*

Ethernet frame. For our example, let's use seven TS packets (or 1316 bytes) per Ethernet frame, as this gives us the highest ratio of data to headers. With 66 bytes of header for 1316 bytes of data, we have an overhead of approximately 5% so our total bandwidth for both audio and video streams comes out to 2.376 Mbps. This calculates to 11.6% overhead on the original raw streams (2 Mbps plus 128 kbps). In terms of packets, this equates to roughly 215 packets per second.

This example clearly shows the importance of viewing an IPTV system as an integrated whole. Video bandwidth decisions can affect network bandwidth decisions, which in turn can affect network geography and DSLAM deployment decisions. All of these factors can affect the IPTV system business model and need to be considered when technology decisions are made.

Channel Changing

Channel changing is a very important issue for IPTV networks. It's important to grasp why many consider this part of the technical Holy Grail for attaining viable, scalable IPTV deployment. As one industry Web site reports it,

> *Simultaneous delivery of channels is necessary to keep IPTV competitive with cable. Obviously, multiple streams are needed to support picture-in-picture, but they're also needed by DVRs, which can record one show while a user is watching another. For IPTV to become a viable whole-house solution, it will also need to support enough simultaneous channels to allow televisions in different rooms to display different content, and juggling resulting bandwidth issues is one of the trickiest parts of implementing an IPTV network that will be attractive to consumers.[10]*

[10]From "An Introduction to IPTV," by Nate Anderson, March 12, 2006. http://arstechnica.com/guides/other/iptv.ars

On conventional television, changing channels is relatively straightforward. The television simply tunes to another already existing radio frequency and then displays it through hardware and monitor to the viewer. There is usually little latency, and no significant technical issues stand between viewer and clicker—not even for the fervent channel surfer.

In an IPTV system, that is not the case. Instead of merely switching between an existing flow of content being delivered over satellite or cable, IPTV system programming control must first traverse a series of data flows, or digital transport points and processes, to complete the cutover from one channel to another. Some of those points along the way from viewer to IPTV channel change include the STB, DSLAM, routers, servers, and source broadcast feed itself.

Here is a breakdown of the basic steps entailed in the IPTV channel changing process.

1. The customer presses a button on the remote control.
2. The STB recognizes that the user has requested a different stream from the one it is currently sending.
3. The STB sends an IP Multicast Join command upstream to the service provider.
4. When the DSLAM receives this command, it determines whether the stream requested is available.
5. If the stream is available, DSLAM initiates, making copies of packets that are, in turn, sent to the user.

Another challenge in IPTV channel change is that the system must determine if the requested stream is currently in the middle of a long, inaccessible play-back segment. If so, the system will have to compensate for that.

Another way to analyze the hurdle of IPTV channel change is to consider the sequence of steps and elapsed *zapping* time that accrues from STB to display. Hosts and local routers use Internet Group Management Protocol (IGMP) to communicate with each other during channel change. The STB must first send IGMP commands instructing the DSLAM to switch streams (change channels) being sent back to the STB. Each of these steps plus any DSL latency can require 10 to 200 milliseconds. Add to that additional dejitter and decode buffering steps that can be equal or longer in duration, and the challenge is on to beat the clock at each point along the way so that the viewer won't experience lag time in switching from one channel to another.

Among the factors affecting channel cutover and streaming performance, the television itself and EPG are usually not the culprits. Because the real bottlenecks are more likely to occur in server, encryption, and middleware processes,[11] encoding, encryption, STBs, and network design must all be coordinated. Other technical certainty includes ensuring consistent sound quality, solving networking issues (such as the *jitter buffer*), and accommodating other data traffic, such as triple-play content, that strains network performance.

In IPTV channel changing, there are many latency issues. The purpose of this book as an executive briefing would not be well served by dwelling there in too

---

[11]"Managing Delay in IP Video Networks," Cisco Systems.

much detail. Nonetheless, the parsing of MPEG streams is important to understand in a little more depth. Content in an MPEG stream or file is structured into Groups of Pictures (GOPs). Long GOPs can present a challenge in channel changing. As described in Chapter 6, the configuration of GOPs can cause serious delays for IPTV MPEG decoding when a channel is changed.

Upon attempting a channel change to a new stream, the system must determine "where in the stream" the video is currently playing. It's possible that the decoder could have no idea at that point in time what's going on in the image and require 10 to 40 frames before the right information (from what's called an I frame) puts the system back on track, instructing it correctly for display.

The über issue is scalability: if thousands of viewers are simultaneously watching a major sporting event or popular television drama, will there be a crunch? Namely, how well can the systems retain low-latency and high-user satisfaction when there are thousands of deployments per community in district after district?

IPTV is still relatively new. Its digital packet-based service model is still being refined. Nonetheless, its performance must match or exceed the prime-time standard because the whole world is watching—for results. While IPTV innovation continues, troubleshooting will be part of the landscape. New tests for monitoring that performance will keep the pressure on providers to meet or beat broadcast TV quality. Technologies from QoS testing vendors, such as IneoQuest's Cricket,[12] Mirifice's MiriMON, Mariner Partners' xVu, and others will report on quality until the day customers experience no QoS issues when they switch channels or interact with their IPTV programming.

Bandwidth for a Triple-Play, HD Future

Bandwidth is key to the future of IP environments. Some industry observers project that IPTV will flourish to full potential only after video bandwidth becomes a commodity—low cost and ubiquitous. And as we have discussed, as if raising the bar for broadcast-quality video over DSL weren't daunting enough, other serious developments pose an even higher standard, creating what some analysts refer to as a bandwidth crunch.

One of those developments is an increasingly common triple-play service offering that demands ever more voluminous data over existing pipes. The other is the increasing expectation, and prevalence, of an HDTV future: "Consumers lust for the new big, flat TV sets ... as HDTV penetration grows past 50 million homes ... ," according to Forrester Research, adding that "telcos should make the breadth of HDTV choices a selling point as they roll out TV over IP."[13]

Without adequate bandwidth, dropout, flicker, and frozen frames mean a lost market window through the failure to deliver prime-time quality that audiences have

---

[12]http://www.ineoquest.com/cricket-family
[13]"HDTV and the Coming Bandwidth Crunch," Forrester Research, February 17, 2005, http://www.forrester.com/Research/Document/Excerpt/0,7211,35146,00.html

come to count on. Your network either has the right capacity video flows or it doesn't—there's no in-between.

Despite the long, winding technical path to TV programming over IP, from broadcast head end to the residential viewer, high-speed networks have arrived. Channel changing response times are improving, and advanced technologies will continue to drive increased price performance. In conjunction with slick, efficient EPG interface design and increasing prime-time and niche content, users are responding favorably.

Reality Check

This chapter's Reality Checks focus on two issues at the front line of bandwidth provisioning and change. The first, describing *passive optical networks* (PONs), is the emergence of high-powered fiber network technologies that tackle the bandwidth question head on. The second is the problematic side of PONs that entail system powering requirements that sometimes must sit with the customer. Traditional telephone services don't have batteries that require customer intervention when they need replacement. Will this be tolerated as part of the new residential responsibility fiber optic deployment sites?

Fiber-Based Future

Technology does not stand still, and competing fiber technologies are fast on the heels of DSL's popularity. Fiber communication technology is fast and has high bandwidth with low power and maintenance requirements. Recent work on PONs has created a new method for delivering video services to the subscriber. PON terminal revenues reached $568 million in 2008, and PON manufacturer revenue is expected to maintain a CAGR of 23% from 2008 and 2013.[14]

In essence, a PON is an all-optical network with no active components between the service provider and the customer. The network is optical because the path from the service provider to the customer is entirely made up of fiber optic and optical components. The network is passive because there are no active elements (such as electronics, lasers, optical detectors, or optical amplifiers) between the service provider and the customer.

One key feature of a PON network is use of an optical splitter near the customer premises, which improves the economics of the system greatly. In the case of one popular standard, up to 32 customers can be served by one fiber from the service provider. A second key feature of a PON network is that the optical fibers and the optical splitter are configured to handle a wide range of laser wavelengths.

The promises of PONs are in providing GigE capacity for business applications, as well as "supporting the multiple simultaneous streams of high definition time-shifted IPTV—crucial for future residential deployments," as one executive says.[15]

---

[14]http://www.infonetics.com/pr/2009/4q08-PON-FTTH-market-research-highlights.asp
[15]Shane Eleniak, vice-president of marketing and business development for Alloptic, a PON provider.

At the physical level, PONs have virtually unlimited bandwidth potential—their speed depends primarily on the speeds of the devices at each end. Thus, PON-based networks can be upgraded to reach even higher speeds as new technologies come onto the market. This is in contrast to DSL technology, which has begun reaching the point of diminishing returns.

Installation and Power Issues

Passive optical networks offer numerous features and advantages that exceed previous-generation copper cable, but they do not come without their price. One major drawback of PON technology is that it requires the service provider to install a fiber optic connection to each PON customer. Replacing a large installed base of copper cabling with optical fiber and supplying each user with an ONT can be a very large investment for existing customers. Also, because each customer must have an ONT, which typically operates using power supplied by the customer using normal commercial power, the ONT must have a method to power itself (i.e., a battery) in the event of a power outage if it is required to support emergency communication. This is a big step for consumers, as the risks of battery fluid leakage, fire, and depletion over a multi-year horizon need to be factored into any cost estimates for a PON deployment.

Summary

In this chapter, we learned about the amount of bandwidth needed for various services, including Internet access, VoIP, and SD video, and the implications of HD video, as well as competitive triple-play service. We talked about current and emerging varieties of DSL and improvements in capacity and throughput steadily bringing the pieces together for quality end-to-end video delivery. The chapter also discussed the important role of DSLAM and IP switching in the twisted-pair architecture that once ran over POTS.

With that in mind, we saw how some of the contention and latency issues can be caused by adding multiple televisions and by the channel change process itself. We took a look at how home gateways and networks facilitate DSL data flow and the internal home wiring technologies of coax and CAT6 and how the HPNA and other organizations are driving adoption.

Finally, some examples showed how to calculate bandwidth before discussing an increasing demand for throughput that will lay the groundwork for faster digital IP video offerings.

10 Set-Top Boxes

Navigation is almost the crux of the future of television; not everyone has figured it out yet, but they will.

Tim Hanlon, vice-president, Starcom MediaVest

Probably the most visible physical component of an IPTV network to most consumers is the *set-top box* (STB) that usually resides in close vicinity (or even on top of, hence the name) their television sets. This box provides a number of significant functions and can have a huge impact on the customers' viewing experiences. The STB also produces essentially all of the information shown on a user's display that is not actual video and audio programming.

Because STBs can represent a significant portion of a service provider's total investment per subscriber, selecting the correct set of functions is critical. In fact, the portion of overall IPTV system capital cost absorbed by STBs can approach 60%. In addition, maintenance practices and procedures need to be developed to resolve STB issues. Because they are located inside viewer homes, STBs may be more failure-prone than other devices that make up an IPTV network.

This chapter reviews the key functions of the STB, including internal features and external connections. User controls are discussed briefly. It also discusses the middleware that supports a variety of software applications on the STB, which can be a crucial part of the viewing experience. The chapter concludes with a look at some of the business and economic issues that can influence the STB selection process.

The Corner Office View

So it's not just software for the PC or software for the phone or software for the videogame, it's software for the user. . . . As I move between devices, the people I've chosen to share my presence with becomes available to them. A friend can see, if I want, what game I'm playing and say they might want to play with me. . . . Even watching TV, the ability to chat with your friends while you're watching the same show or different shows, should be something that's very straightforward.

So this cross-device approach is a very, very important approach. In fact, that's complemented by the fact that there will be what we call Live services, where a lot of your files, your information will actually be stored out in the Internet, and even if you pick somebody else's device up, once you authenticate, all that information becomes available to you. So moving between different PCs can be a very, very easy thing.

There's a lot of themes there, themes of personalization, themes of empowerment, themes of everything moving to the Internet. What is telephony moving to the Internet? That's voice. What is TV moving to the Internet? That's Internet TV or IPTV. People have to have confidence in these things, automatically backed up, security built-in, very reliable systems that use the cloud storage for those kinds of guarantees, and easy connections, connecting to people, connecting up to devices, a very strong way of driving through all these different scenarios and making them very simple.

—*Bill Gates, chairman and chief software architect, Microsoft*[1]

Basic Functions

The main job of the STB is to receive the incoming IPTV signal and convert it to a video signal that can be displayed on the viewer's television. In addition, the STB provides the user interface that enables viewers to select the video programming to be viewed. To accomplish these tasks, the STB must contain the following functional elements.

- Network interface, to receive the IPTV signals and transmit user commands
- Video and audio outputs, which are connected to the viewer's video display and speaker system
- User interface, both on the front panel of the STB and by way of an on-screen display and remote control

The following features are often also provided in STBs.

- *Conditional access* hardware/software, to support secure viewing of valuable content
- Hard disk drive, for recording video programs

The following sections discuss each of these elements in more detail.

Network Interface

The network interface on the STB is normally a bidirectional Ethernet interface that enables IP traffic to flow into and out of the STB. IP packets flow through this interface, containing data such as encoded video information, user commands, device status information, and other useful information. Typically, these flows are highly asymmetrical, with lots of data flowing into the STB and very few packets in the return direction.

Often, the STB interface is not connected directly to a DSL or other type of line circuits, but rather to the home gateway that takes DSL data and converts them into Ethernet. While this might seem somewhat wasteful, it provides several benefits. First, this removes the need to make different versions of the STB for different types of DSL or other data circuits—with a standard Ethernet interface, all STB connections

---

[1]Keynote remarks by Bill Gates, Microsoft Corporation 2006 International Consumer Electronics Show.

can be the same. Also, from a safety and reliability standpoint, it is better to have the home gateway connected directly to the DSL or other circuit in a permanent, out-of-the-way location instead of being part of a customer's furniture that may be moved from time to time.

Several new types of network interfaces are being considered for use in STBs. Wireless connections have a certain attraction because they can eliminate the headache of connecting network cables; however, basic Wi-Fi technology does not have the performance required for reliable IPTV operation. Other technologies, such as *ultrawide band* (UWB), have shown promise in this area, but more development work is required before widespread deployment can occur. Four of the five largest carriers in the United States and Canada are using *Home Phoneline Networking Alliance* (HPNA) connections.[2] HPNA utilizes existing home telephone wiring, only at much higher data speeds (100 megabits and up). This scheme has the advantage of eliminating the need for rewiring a home, but relatively few devices have been equipped to handle HPNA interfaces directly. Another alterative is power line networking; as this technology matures it may become interesting for use in video delivery around a house.

Video and Audio Outputs

As consumer home theater systems continue to grow in popularity and complexity, the demands placed on the STB will grow apace. In addition to supplying clean, noise-free signals in a variety of formats and connectors, these connections can be the weak link in the content security chain unless they are constructed appropriately. A number of popular choices for these interfaces are illustrated in Figure 10.1.

Analog RCA Jacks

A composite video signal contains all of the information required to form a full-motion, full-color image on an SD television screen. A composite signal is normally sent on a single coaxial cable between devices such as a DVR and a television set. Standard RCA jacks, which are slide-on coaxial connectors, are often used in threes—a yellow connector for video, a red connector for right audio, and a white connector for left audio.

S-Video

S-video signals are similar to composite video signals, with one crucial difference. In S-video, picture luminance and color information are carried on different wires. This is why an S-video cable has four pins: one pair for the chroma signal and another pair for the luma (plus an outer shield). Particularly for the digital STBs used in IPTV applications, S-video can deliver a higher quality SD image to the display by avoiding the step of combining the luminance and color information in the STB output and the step of separating those two signals again when they enter the display.

---

[2]http://www.fiercetelecom.com/story/current-state-home-networking-technology/2009-04-06

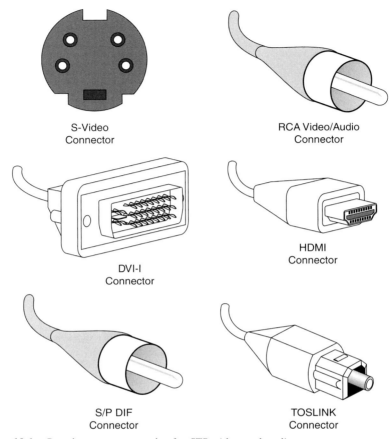

S-Video
Connector

RCA Video/Audio
Connector

DVI-I
Connector

HDMI
Connector

S/P DIF
Connector

TOSLINK
Connector

Figure 10.1 *Popular connector styles for STB video and audio outputs.*

Component Video

Component analog video offers benefits over composite and S-video. Because different color signals are carried on different sets of conductors, processing of the signals is kept to a minimum. YUV or YPbPr (also known as Y R-Y B-Y) component video signals use three signal paths: one for a luminance signal (Y) and one for each of two color difference signals (U and V or Pb and Pr). Component video can be used for both SD and HD applications.

Component Colors

The Y signal in YUV contains information from all three color channels (red, green, and blue) and is formed by combining different amounts of each color. The two color difference signals have the advantage of requiring less bandwidth than the Y signal, which is useful for reducing the signal bandwidths needed in digital video signals. RGB is another component video standard that uses one conductor for each of the three main video component signals: red, green, and blue. Each signal carries a full-resolution image, with data for every pixel. Many consumer video devices such as DVD players, projectors, and LCD and plasma displays can use YUV interfaces.

Digital Visual Interface

The *Digital Visual Interface* (DVI) connector can be used to carry digital or analog video signals and audio signals. DVI connectors are found on many computer monitors and video graphics cards, and for a while were used on some brands of STBs. This connector has been largely replaced with the HDMI connector for home video applications, so DVI tends to be found more often in computer applications.

High-Definition Multimedia Interface

The *High-Definition Multimedia Interface* (HDMI) connector format can be used to carry digital video and audio signals. The specification has been adopted by more than 850 consumer electronics and PC manufacturers and builds on the DVI spec by adding digital audio capability to the same cable. However, it retains electrical compatibility to the DVI-Digital spec, so the possibility of changeover cables exists. HDMI has been widely adopted for newer consumer HD televisions and is forecast to surpass DVI shipments. In fact, HDMI-enabled devices are expected to increase by 23% annually between 2007 and 2012.[3]

High-Bandwidth Digital Content Protection Security

High-bandwidth Digital Content Protection (HDCP) can be used on both DVI and HDMI interfaces to prevent unauthorized copying of HD digital video signals by encrypting data for each pixel. This encryption happens on-the-fly in many types of devices that can generate HD content, including STBs, Blu-Ray disc players, and other sources. At the display device, pixel data are decrypted and used to generate an image on a digital display, such as plasma, LCD, and DLP projectors.

High-bandwidth digital content protection is normally implemented inside specialized chips in both the source and the display (Intel was one of the early developers of this technology). This makes it very difficult to remove or bypass this technology for making perfect copies of digital HD content. When an HDCP source is connected to an HDCP display, a handshake process takes place, resulting in an encryption key that can be used to encode the content in the source and decode it in the destination.

Broadcasters, Blu-Ray disc suppliers, and other content owners have the ability to require that HDCP be in place in an operation before any true HD signals are

---

[3]http://www.tmcnet.com/ce/articles/50380-in-stat-predicts-increase-hdmi-enabled-product-shipments.htm

delivered. If HDCP is not in place, then the source hardware may be restricted to only providing a degraded HD or even an SD output in place of the full-performance HD signal.

Sony/Philips Digital Interface Format Audio

Sony/Philips Digital Interface Format (S/PDIF) is a widely used interface for carrying digital audio signals between different system components, such as from an STB to a home theater sound system. Because this interface has been standardized internationally (IEC 60958-3), it can be found on a huge number of devices, including many STBs. This interface is used to carry uncompressed audio signals and can be physically implemented with either an RCA jack or a BNC.

Fiber Optic Audio

A variation of the S/PDIF interface is an optical version that carries the same data, also known as a TOSLINK, which is a registered trademark of Toshiba. This connection, while not as common as electrical S/PDIF interfaces, can be found on a significant number of high-performance audio devices.

User Interface

Beyond the physical presence of the STB exists the combination of software and hardware that provides the user interface, literally where the human is able to communicate with the machine. When this is poorly done, it can be a great annoyance to viewers; when created with skill and style, it can become so much a part of a viewer's experience that it becomes invisible. On a business level, an effective STB user interface increases customer satisfaction and average revenue per user while reducing call center requirements and subscriber churn. Physically, the STB user interface consists of three main elements. First, the front of the STB may have a display and/or status lights that give basic information to the user, such as channel selection, time of day, and power on/off status. These indicators may be the only means of communicating with a user if the video display is not available; as such, they can be very important during the installation and setup process.

Second, some form of infrared remote control is used to allow the user to sit a comfortable distance away from the STB and issue commands to interact with the information being shown on the display.

Third is the software that resides inside the STB and creates the menus and displays that support viewer interactions. Because the bulk of the user experience is focused on the latter two elements, we will focus our discussion on them.

Many different functions need to be supported by the user remote and on-screen display. Here is a list of some of the basic functions that need to be provided.

- Device control, such as power, sound volume, and input selection
- Channel selection and changing
- *Electronic Program Guide* display and navigation

- Access control, including parental control and secret PINs used to secure payment for some types of programming
- Basic interactivity, such as pause, rewind, and fast-forward, for on-demand content viewing
- Advanced interactivity, such as on-screen shopping or audience participation

In some cases, users can program the STB infrared remote device to control other devices in the audio/video setup, such as audio systems, DVD players, and video displays. Care needs to be taken to balance the benefits of consolidating many functions into a single device against the need to add more buttons (and thereby complexity) to the remote control device.

Conditional Access Hardware/Software

As discussed in Chapter 7, *conditional access* and *digital rights management* are very important to IPTV system operators. Without an effective CA/DRM system in place, it would be hard for operators to ensure that viewers are paying for the content they are viewing. It might even be impossible to obtain some types of content (Hollywood movies, for example) unless the owners of the content had confidence that their properties would be protected from unauthorized copying and distribution. The STB is one of the most important links in the CA/DRM system for IPTV operators.

Any security system depends on the capability to uniquely identify a user. In a system to verify the identity of a human, secret passwords, personal identification numbers, and responses to security questions are often used. In the case of an IPTV system, the STB needs to play a similar role—the STB must be able to uniquely identify itself to the content delivery system and must also be in a position to safeguard the security of any content streamed through or stored within the device. Both hardware- and software-based technologies have been used successfully for this purpose.

One traditional hardware-based technology is the smart card. These cards are called "smart" because they incorporate a processor and memory that can be used by a variety of applications. Each device that uses smart cards must be equipped with a smart card reader, usually in the form of a slot in one side of the STB into which the smart card is inserted. Of course, some system needs to be set up to distribute the cards to consumers, deactivate them when services are cancelled, and so forth.

Software-based technologies are also available that can provide the same (or higher) level of security as hardware-based systems. This consists of a specialized module or software code located in each STB that offers many of the same security capabilities as smart cards without requiring the management of physical smart cards and associated reader hardware.

Software-based CA/DRM techniques are becoming much more common for new IPTV service providers. This is due to the major logistics problems associated with hardware-based systems. Every smart card needs to be kept physically secure to prevent unauthorized parties from using stolen cards to obtain unauthorized services. In addition, if a smart card technology became compromised due to hackers, the service provider would be faced with the task of distributing thousands or even millions of new smart cards in order to resecure their networks. In contrast, with a software-based system, a new code could be downloaded from the central servers to each STB in the event of a security breach. Of course, no CA/DRM system is deployable unless content owners are satisfied with the level of security provided, so any discussions of hardware versus software technology security need to include these parties.

Hard Disk Drive

As in desktop and laptop computers, hard disk drives can be installed inside STBs to provide large amounts of digital storage. Of course, in an STB, this storage is going to be used for digital video content. With current compression technology, it is possible to store 1360 hours of standard definition or 150 hours of high-definition video content on a single disk drive.[4] Also, as disk technology continues to progress, even larger storage capacities will soon be available.

When it comes to deciding how the content gets recorded into this vast pool of storage, there are two schools of thought. The first school leaves it entirely up to the user to select programming to record, thereby making the disk a *DVR* (also known as a personal video recorder, or PVR). The second school uses the disk drive as a storage location for content that has been downloaded by the service provider to make it available to viewers, a service that has been called *push VOD*. Both of these concepts deserve a little more discussion.

Digital Video Recorders

Digital video recorders (DVR) have become a very popular new device for consumers. Popularized in the United States under the brand name "TiVo," but now offered by many programming providers, these devices record television programs in compressed digital form on hard disk drives for later viewing. Users program the units to record certain programs; an important function of the DVR is to provide a user-friendly way to select the programs to be recorded. Basic services simply show a list of upcoming programs and enable the user to choose the ones to record on a one-time or repetitive basis. More advanced services help viewers select programs by displaying recommendations similar to other programs that have been recorded previously by the viewer.

DVRs give viewers the ability to select when they want to watch each of their recorded items. Viewers are given VCR-like controls so that they can pause, rewind, fast-forward, and skip commercials when they are playing the video back. This latter feature has caused a great deal of concern for advertisers, who not only fear commercial *zapping* but also worry about viewers not being exposed to their advertisements at the correct time (say, ads for a movie the night before a big release). How these issues impact broadcasters in the long run is a subject of much current concern and analysis.

[4]http://www.thetechherald.com/article.php/200836/1957/Get-a-terabyte-of-TiVo-with-the-new-TiVo-HD-XL-DVR

Push VOD

Push VOD uses idle network bandwidth to deliver content to STBs that can be played back in the future by a viewer. This content can be free to viewers, distributed as part of a paid service funded by viewer subscriptions, or used to deliver content that viewers can purchase on a title-by-title basis. Since the service provider selects the programming to be pushed to the STBs, push VOD content is often restricted to the most popular titles, although these may be distributed without inserted commercials.

Push VOD has typically been used by service providers with very restricted two-way capability in their networks, such as in the case of satellite and (potentially) terrestrial over-the-air broadcasters. In IPTV applications, these types of network restrictions tend to be less prevalent, but push VOD can be used to help ease the burden on network bandwidth and centralized video servers for extremely popular VOD offerings or highly interactive content such as games.

Middleware

Trying to define the term *middleware* is like trying to define the term *beauty*—it is truly in the eye of the beholder. However, for our purposes, we define middleware as software functions or services that link specific components (such as application servers, VOD servers, and STBs) and application software (such as conditional access control, billing systems, and interactive services).

Middleware also links client and server systems used for CA and DRM purposes. Because part of the function for these technologies is implemented on the STB while another part is implemented on a centralized server, a secure means of communication is needed between end points. This is an excellent role for middleware because it is often designed to operate in the middle ground between STBs and central servers.

"Now that IPTV is maturing as an industry, operators are revisiting their middleware platform decisions," says Steve Hawley, industry analyst and author of *IPTV Middleware and Beyond*. "While some platforms stop at basic TV services, others accommodate multiscreen and over-the-top content. Because middleware has a direct impact on other IPTV infrastructure, from security to set-tops, it's a hugely strategic decision and the operator must be well informed."[5]

Middleware can be thought of as a form of operating system for both an STB and an IPTV system. In particular, a couple of standards have been designed specifically to enable third-party developers to write applications for a generic STB, without having to adapt the code for each different type and manufacturer of STB in the marketplace. Two significant examples of a standard are *MhP* and *true2way* (formerly OCAP), both of which will be the subject of a Reality Check at the end of this chapter.

[5]http://www.iptv-news.com/iptv_news/march_3/new_iptv_middleware_report_predicts_latest_advances_will_propel_telcos_beyond_me_too_stage

Understanding Middleware

Middleware is the glue that holds IPTV systems together. It provides mechanisms to accomplish many of the key tasks that must be performed to give users the ability to select and view programming and to support payment systems that drive revenue to the IPTV system operator. Here are some of the key functions often provided by middleware.

User Identification

Keeping track of exactly which users are connected to which portions of the network is crucial for a number of reasons. First and foremost, the middleware system must be able to deliver video and audio content to the user who requested it. To accomplish this, the middleware system must be able to track which IP network connections are associated with each user.

Screen Navigation Functions

Moving a cursor and issuing commands in real time on the screen involve close coordination among the user's remote control, the STB's operating system, and the application software driving the displayed image.

Text and Menu Generation

Middleware will typically support mechanisms for managing a variety of different fonts and type styles that can, in turn, be used by other applications that interface with the middleware.

Electronic Program Guide Primitives and Utilities

Creating a program guide can be quite complex for an IPTV system. Gathering all required data from broadcast sources, formatting it into a readable grid that the viewer can scroll through, and taking action once the desired content has been selected all require a significant amount of work. Middleware can provide support for some or all of these tasks and remove the need for the system operator to develop a different version of the program guide software for each different STB deployed in their network.

Channel Changing

With IPTV, each time a new television channel is selected by a viewer, new and different data need to be sent to the viewer's STB. This can require a whole sequence of events, such as leaving one multicast group and joining another at the DSLAM or passing instructions through the DSLAM to the video serving office upstream of the DSLAM. Managing this process in a speedy and efficient manner is a sign of well-designed middleware.

Back Office Integration

Middleware can also provide the link between different applications and the back office systems used by a service provider. Back office systems can include subscriber billing and management systems, installation and repair crew scheduling and tracking, VOD systems, and more. Without a good middleware system to act as a translator between these devices, it would be uneconomical to offer many advanced services that IPTV providers are using as market entry strategies.

Interactivity

Middleware can be heavily involved with interactivity at all levels. Virtually any time a viewer presses a button on the remote control for an IPTV STB, middleware can take over. Even basic interactivity, such as channel changing, involves middleware. More sophisticated forms of interactivity also involve middleware, such as playback control (rewind, pause, and fast-forward). Even content interactivity, such as voting on a talent contest, requires middleware to accept user votes from remote controls and change that data into a form that can be forwarded to the program provider to tally the votes.

Video-on-Demand Middleware Example

The following example considers the process that must take place when a viewer decides to order a pay-per-view movie.

First, the user must decide which content to view. This is normally achieved through the use of an EPG. The guide application needs to obtain data from the VOD server that indicates the titles available on the server, along with related data. These data might include the price, the length (in minutes) of the title, a synopsis, a list of the cast, and possibly reviews or recommendations from either professional reviewers or other subscribers. All these data need to come from somewhere, and there is a significant chance that data coming from different sources are in different formats. Middleware can help by providing conversion filters from different data formats into a common format that can be displayed on the screen. In addition, middleware can provide the proper protocols and handshakes to the other data sources to get the required information.

Next, the user needs to navigate through the EPG and choose a program to watch. These tasks are supported by middleware in several ways. First, the middleware can take care of distributing program guide data to all of the STBs in the service provider's network. Second, the middleware provides a clean interface for the software to create display elements needed to show the guide information.

Once the viewer starts to interact with the EPG, the middleware really gets a workout. Any information that flows between the central systems and the STBs will pass through the middleware, which will help ensure that the information is delivered securely and reliably.

When the user makes a selection of VOD content, the middleware plays an important role in the financial transaction. A query is made to the subscriber information database to determine if the viewer is permitted to order VOD content of the type selected. Once the reply is affirmative, the middleware system will send the appropriate information to the VOD server so playback to the proper IP address can begin. Also, a message must be sent to the billing system to record the transaction details to enable the proper fees to be collected from the viewer.

Set-Top Box Selection Issues

There are many different STBs on the market today offering a wide variety of features and functions. Here is a checklist of some of the items that service providers need to consider when selecting STB technology.

- Supported video output types: analog or digital? SD or HD? Component or composite? Will HDMI and HDCP be required for some content?
- Audio types: analog or digital? Electrical or optical? Stereo or surround sound?
- Video compression standards: MPEG-2, MPEG-4, H.264, or VC-1?
- DRM system: hardware based (smart card) or software based?
- Network interface: Ethernet, HPNA, Coax, or Wi-Fi?
- Hard disk drive: present or not? DVR, push VOD, or both?
- Middleware platform: MhP, true2way, or proprietary?

The STB of the Future

Future STB capabilities will be influenced or determined by a range of emerging technologies and standards, as well as competitive market forces and customer preferences. However, regardless of those variables, expect to see a more versatile, feature-rich device.

Advanced STB capabilities include MPEG-4 and HD support and will increasingly consist of greater processing power and memory, as well as PC and broadband connectivity for over-the-top programming and content. As Table 10.1 highlights,

Table 10.1 Comparing the STB Hardware of Today and Tomorrow[6]

STB of Today	STB of Tomorrow
H.264 HD	Ultra-HD, 3DTV, increased frame rates
Thin RTOS	Feature-rich OS
Stand-alone STB	Home networking
Watch anytime	Watch anywhere
VOD, gaming, gambling	Personalized content
Upgradeable middleware	Dynamic application environment

[6]"The Myth of the Future Proof STB," Paul Kavanagh, General Manager, S3 North America, 2009.

features on the horizon will enable new applications, home network connectivity, and interactive viewing habits.

Reality Check

The reality check for this chapter focuses on two very important standards for middleware. Both have been developed for applications other than IPTV, but because of their popularity and widespread adoption in the STB market, it is prudent to study these examples as they are likely to affect set-top middleware development.

MhP and true2way

Both MhP and true2way (formerly OCAP) standards have been developed by industry groups for STB middleware. The benefit of these standards is that they enable applications developers to write programs that will run on any STBs that support the MhP standard, thereby increasing their target market greatly. Similarly, system operators who deploy STBs that support MhP or true2way gain access to a large selection of compatible applications.

Both MhP and true2way require a fair amount of processing capacity in each STB. In particular, MhP requires a JAVA Virtual Machine on each STB, which requires a reasonable amount of processing power and memory. As a result, some of the older STBs with limited functionality may not be capable of supporting this technology.

Keep in mind that neither of these specifications is targeted directly at IPTV, but STBs with both technologies have been used in IPTV deployments. MhP was developed for the *Digital Video Broadcasting* (DVB) project, which focused primarily on terrestrial broadcasting and, to some extent, satellite broadcasting. MhP was developed with the European broadcast market in mind. true2way was based on MhP, but was developed to meet the needs of digital cable TV providers in the United States. Fortunately, many of the functions of the STB are the same regardless of the type of digital data link used to receive programming.

The work to develop MhP formally began in Europe in 1993 and was provided under the auspices of the DVB. Membership consists of companies involved in manufacturing, broadcasting, regulating, and serving the television broadcast market. The aim of the group is to produce a series of standards that enable different devices to interoperate smoothly across national boundaries. In December 1997, the DVB formally approved the functional requirements for MhP, upon which subsequent standards were based. In May 2000, the MhP standards were approved and formally launched to the world that same year.

The path toward developing the true2way standard was significantly quicker. In October 2001, CableLabs, a group based in the United States that develops standards and practices for the cable TV industry, adopted MhP as the basis for true2way. Today, true2way licensees include Cisco, Echostar, LG Electronics, Motorola, Sony, Texas Instruments, and many others. true2way offers an open source reference implementation that allows developers "to work with a wider community of technology contributors," says Craig Smithpeters, Cox director of interactive services engineering, which will enable them to "more rapidly implement additions or updates to the specification modeled after the example implement."[7]

Summary

This chapter focused on a crucial component of any IPTV network—the STB. The STB is responsible for accepting IP packets that contain the video, audio, and related digital content and producing signals that can be displayed on television sets and played through audio loudspeakers. The STB is also responsible for receiving and processing user commands and sending messages back to the central systems when action is required (say, for a channel change command).

Middleware also plays a key role in IPTV deployments. By enabling many of the key functions of an IPTV network, middleware can greatly simplify the deployment of a variety of advanced, integrated services. With the right platform combined with one or more compatible STB choices, service providers can readily offer the innovative, consumer-friendly services that consumers will be willing to pay for.

[7]http://www.cablelabs.com/news/pr/2009/09_pr_tru2way_RI_040209.html

11 Internet Video Technologies

> *I see streaming media as the building blocks ... whether it's to deliver content to a cell phone wirelessly or to a set top box via IPTV.*
> **Dan Rayburn, The Business of Streaming Media**

Throughout this book we have discussed the deployment of IPTV and explored various technical and business implications of broadband video in general. This chapter reviews the ways that video is being delivered over the Web, including basic concepts and technology building blocks. It looks at various forms of delivery that are used for IP VOD, Internet TV, and Internet video. It also takes a look at the production workflow process running from capture to playout.

Increasingly, viewers in the United States are using the Internet to get access to a variety of content that was unimaginable a few short years ago. Due to the proliferation of Web sites hosting professionally produced content, more current programming is becoming available online than ever before. It is even becoming conceivable that some viewers will now choose to abandon their cable TV or satellite subscriptions and do most of their television viewing via the Internet, which bodes well for those networks willing to put their content online.

The Corner Office View

Notable findings from February 2009 include:

- 75.5% of the total U.S. Internet audience viewed online video
- The average online video viewer watched 312 minutes of video (more than 5 hours)
- 98.8 million viewers watched 5.3 billion videos on YouTube.com (53.8 videos per viewer)
- 41.2 million viewers watched 384 million videos on MySpace.com (8.5 videos per viewer)
- The duration of the average online video was 3.5 minutes[1]

Users encounter video streaming more and more while surfing popular Web sites, such as YouTube and MySpace, for personalized clips and references to mainstream media. Other sites include CNN.com for news stories; sonypictures.com, warnerbros.com, and Disney.com for trailers of upcoming movies; and mtv.com or music.yahoo.com for music videos. In addition, a growing number of Web destinations offer actual television programming over the Internet, including researchchannel.com, Hulu.com, and Bloomberg television (at www.bloomberg.com/streams/

[1] http://www.comscore.com/press/release.asp?press=2756

video/LiveBTV200.asxx), as well as most of the television network sites (NBC.com, CBS.com, etc.). These sites all provide users with full-motion video and synchronized audio that can be played on a normal PC equipped with a suitable-speed Internet connection and the software necessary to receive, decode, and display the video streams. The quality and variety of available Internet video just keep improving.

Web video streams are used increasingly for marketing, entertainment, training, and communications. Its powerful visual capacity to engage new business audiences, to educate and train, and also to provide multimedia social networking environments is riveting. Let's look at some of the tools for deployment, and some of the practices for integrating video into Web sites.

Types of Internet Streaming

There are several forms of video streaming, as summarized in Table 11.1. First, there is *true streaming*, in which the video signal arrives in real time and is displayed to the viewer immediately. With true streaming, a two-minute video takes two minutes to deliver to the viewer—not more, not less.

In *download and play*, a file containing compressed video/audio data is downloaded onto the user's device before playback begins. With download and play, a two-minute video could take 10 seconds to download on a fast network or 10 minutes to download on a slow network.

Table 11.1 Streaming Summary Advantages and Disadvantages

	Advantages	Disadvantages
True streaming	Low delay; can support live content and doesn't require storage in display device. Supports true interactivity with server.	Trouble getting through firewalls, hard to do fast-forward and rewind (requires sophisticated interaction between client and server). Must remain connected to network for full duration of stream.
Download and play	With a fast network, expedient way to obtain content; will work with most firewalls and standard settings (because video data appear as a file).	Doesn't support true interactivity with server; need to wait for all content to be delivered before you can start watching. Need enough storage to hold entire file. Can take a while for all content to arrive before playing. Content must be resident on user device before playback— potential security concern.

Table 11.1 (*continued*)

	Advantages	Disadvantages
Progressive download	Playback starts more quickly. Avoids firewall problems (TCP/IP). Video file cached on user's PC for greater user control and management (fast-forward, rewind, etc.).	Content segmentation may not be supported by all media players. Can take up significant storage on end-user device.
Podcasting	Reaches mobile audience. Enables content to be played on device not connected to network. Doesn't require PC for playback. Excellent audio quality; can be delivered automatically upon subscription.	Limited screen size. Cannot interact with Web or PC content.

Finally, *progressive download and play* is a hybrid of the two preceding technologies that tries to capture the benefits of both. Using this technique, the video program is broken up into small files, each of which is downloaded to the user's device during playback. With progressive download and play, a two-minute video might be broken up into 20 files, each six seconds long, that would be successively downloaded to the viewer's device before each file is scheduled to play.

We'll look further at some of the respective advantages and disadvantages of these streaming techniques later in this chapter.

Streaming and Downloading

Another industry observer compares the uses of Internet streaming and downloading:

Streaming offers an instant experience to consumers used to immediate gratification and is ideal for promotional material. But because some broadband networks are not yet fast enough to stream full-screen quality video without periodic buffering and dropped connections, all content can't be delivered in this way.

Downloading content means that operators need to deploy software to users' PCs to manage the download process. These download managers also offer other useful functionality such as the ability to prebook content for download or be able to view content when the user is off-line.

All the platforms will emerge with a hybrid combination of streaming for shorts and promotional materials and live and simulcast, scheduled ahead of transmission; download for news programming and series; and download for high-quality movies and other high value content.[2]

---

[2]Fearghal Kelly, IBC Daily, October, 2006.

To understand the principles better, consider a simple analogy for true streaming versus download and play: the two options available for the supply of fuel used for home heating. One alternative is natural gas, which is piped by means of a distribution network that runs into each customer's home. Another alternative is fuel oil, which is delivered on a periodic basis to each customer's home.

A true streaming system is somewhat like the natural gas system—the fuel (content) is delivered at exactly the rate in which it is consumed and no storage is present inside the consumer's home. A download and play system is like the fuel oil delivery system, as each user must own and operate a large tank (disk drive) in which the fuel (content) is loaded periodically by a fuel supplier. If the natural gas supply becomes inadequate, the rate of gas delivery to each consumer can slow down, possibly causing difficulty in heating some customers' homes. With the fuel oil tank, once the delivery has taken place, customers have control over that fuel oil and can use it however they wish.

One technology issue that can arise in attempting to deliver streaming video to a mass Internet audience is ensuring that nothing impedes or blocks stream transmission between the provider and the user. The many advantages and disadvantages of technical transport trade-offs that systems architects grapple with are important for executives and decision makers on the business side because they highlight the terrain in setting up a content business for prime time or Web time.

For instance, true streaming often uses *User Datagram Protocol* (UDP), a standard IP protocol, for sending a sequence of data packets. However, firewalls tend to block UDP because it has security risks (because packet sequences are not numbered, packets can be inserted maliciously). Many network administrators therefore block UDP on their firewalls, which makes it difficult to get UDP streams consistently.

Transmission Control Protocol (TCP), which is utilized in most day-to-day Web surfing, makes it extremely difficult to insert malicious data into a stream. However, even TCP has some built-in behaviors that, while very effective for data transfer, are not well suited for real-time video transport.

Another important protocol designed for real-time multimedia applications, *Real-time Transport Protocol* (RTP), monitors packet delivery rates and critical thresholds and contains time-stamping and synchronization features. RTP operates in conjunction with UDP and can have similar problems with firewalls and system administrators.

Webcasting: Going Live or Real Time

During Webcasting, an entire audience accesses a linear stream at the same time, which may be live or may come from a previously produced and stored file. That viewing audience can consist of a handful of people or thousands. Often used in sports, entertainment, and marketing, Webcasting can also play a central role in a training or Webinar event.

Highly viewed Webcast events that are streamed or simulcast live over the Web, such as Apple Computer's annual meetings, have always been the acid test for how well streaming video scales. User demand for a particular event has crashed the servers more than once. In the very early days of Internet video, a Victoria's Secret's live Webcast (1.5 million viewers in 1999) became a legendary case study because viewer demand overwhelmed the capacity of the servers that were set up to generate the video streams. Such a spike in simultaneous Webcast viewers online and streams required exposes whether the server's stream replication is robust enough to serve everyone. By 2008, the situation had improved remarkably—NBC's Olympics coverage for the United States alone delivered 75.5 million streams with a peak of 130,000 simultaneous streams[3]; this was in addition to the coverage that was available for free on broadcast television.

Streaming service providers distinguish themselves in their ability to foresee and overcome these obstacles, providing server load balancing, as well as security and live broadcast simulation to customers before the event.[4] We'll delve deeper into the dynamics of live Webcasting in the content workflow section later in this chapter.

Streaming System Architecture

Streaming technologies have specific objectives, one of which is to deliver video over the Internet to a viewer through their Web browser, media player application, or Internet video appliance. Producing and deploying direct Internet streaming require an infrastructure that includes a media server, network, and media player application, as well as a content preparation process (see Figure 11.1). We'll look at the key elements that are unique to streaming systems.

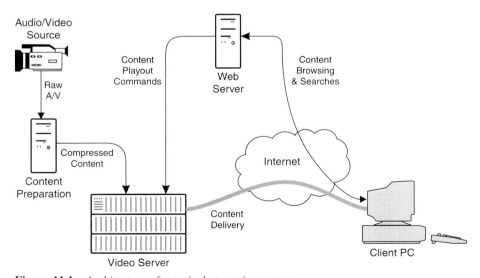

Figure 11.1   *Architecture of a typical streaming system.*

[3]http://news.softpedia.com/news/Silverlight-to-Stream-the-Next-Olympics-Fully-in-HD-107265.shtml
[4]Grateful acknowledgment to Rick Kolow, audiovideoWeb.com, November 2006.

The Streaming Server

The streaming server is responsible for distributing media streams to viewers. It takes media content that has been stored internally and creates a stream for each viewer request. This stream can be either *unicast* or *multicast* and can be controlled by a variety of mechanisms. Content storage and retrieval are main functions of a streaming server. As mentioned before, when content is prepared, it is normally produced in a variety of compression ratios so that users with different network connection speeds can select the video rate that they require.

For example, on many Web sites, multiple video stream bit rates are available, which can be switched automatically to viewers depending on their connection speed. Each of these different playback speeds requires a different version of the content file to be created during the compression process. This means that one piece of content may be contained in many different files inside the server—one for each of the playback speed choices, and often others to handle different media player formats, which we'll discuss later in the chapter.

Other responsibilities of the server are to encrypt the packets in the outgoing stream, if required, and create well-behaved streams, meaning that the pace of the packets should be consistent. Finally, the server must be capable of accepting media player commands and changing the outbound stream appropriately, as well as be able to support hundreds or thousands of users by being part of a matrix of multiple load-balanced servers placed at different physical locations around the Internet. Needless to say, the ultimate maintenance and operational costs of the server networks and bandwidth charges are charged back to the content provider.

Transport Network

Next there is the transport network between the server and the viewing device. Without delving extensively into network architecture, a few key points are good to keep in mind. Streaming servers supplying a number of simultaneous viewers require high-speed storage and network connections. For instance, a 3.2-GHz multicore Pentium server could easily source enough simultaneous video streams to overwhelm a 1.5-Mbps T1 line several times over or a 10BaseT Ethernet link. For large servers handling broadband streams, Gigabit Ethernet network interfaces are becoming common.

Typically, a streaming system will function better if some of the key IP network performance variables are controlled. One of the main parameters that affects streaming is the packet loss ratio because streaming performance will suffer if too many packets are lost. Another example includes delays such as packet delay variation—critical because if a packet arrives too late, it can't be used in the playback, and end-to-end delay, mostly important to ensure reliability in two-way conversation links.

As stated, the final key pieces are the media player application and content preparation, or workflow, which we'll look at further in a later section of this chapter.

Streaming Applications: Media Players

What is a media player and why do we always have to be downloading some new software application or version update simply to play streaming media over the Web? Is it really that important? One historical answer to that question is the European Union's (EU) decision to levy a 500-million Euro fine on Microsoft in 2004. The European Union's issue was with the company's "near monopoly" in bundling the media player with its ubiquitous operating system. An 899-million Euro fine was also issued in 2008 when the EU deemed that Microsoft was failing to comply with its 2004 ruling.

Why such a big deal about a commonplace PC application? First, the controversy stems from the media player application being the de facto interface to video and audio content at the junction of the three powerful, merging commercial domains of the PC, Internet, and broadcast. Then there is the money factor: People are increasingly making credit card and PayPal purchases of music subscriptions, downloadable videos, and other e-commerce transactions through a media player interface or influence.

In a sense, the media player provider gains a measure of control over future commercial choices of the user (e.g., downloading music, subscribing to video services) by being the first to grab the user's attention with a rich interface displaying a myriad of content guides and subscription options. Media players are an important part of the user experience and gain commercial influence through first mover influence over the user's choice of Internet content. The following applications are the dominant gatekeepers of Web surfer media content access.

Player Software

Player software is responsible for accepting the incoming stream and converting it into an image that can be shown on the viewer's display. The performance of this software can have a major influence on how satisfied the user is with the streaming system overall.

Before streaming can begin, the user must select the content. This can be a complex process because maintaining an accurate, up-to-date list of the available content can be a dynamic, daunting task. Unlike commercial broadcast networks, for most private streaming applications, the content supplier must maintain this list. Typically, the list is presented to the user inside a Web page, and the user simply clicks the appropriate link to begin content playback.

If the streaming server has encrypted the content, the player software needs to decrypt the incoming packets. This is a fairly simple process once the key is known. The keys can be obtained by communicating with the server or by connecting to a third-party authentication service.

The player software is also responsible for managing correct packet timing and a buffer that receives the incoming packets. Because buffer underflows (too little data) and overflows (too much data) can severely impact the display of the stream, the buffers need to be sized appropriately for the application. Overall, careful buffer design is a key factor in player success.

Because some streaming protocols, such as RTP, separate the audio and the video signals into two different streams, the player software is responsible for resynchronizing the incoming streams. This is accomplished by looking at time-stamp data contained in each stream and comparing it to time-stamp data contained in the associated RTP overhead packets.

One of the most intensive jobs of the player software is to decompress the incoming signal and create an image for display. The amount of processing required varies depending on the size of the image and on the compression method. Older compression systems (such as MPEG-1) are easier to decode than newer systems (such as H.264) and therefore place less of a burden on the decoding device. Smaller images, with fewer pixels to process, are also easier to decode. Stand-alone devices, such as STBs, traditionally had hardware-based decoders that were restricted to a limited range of compression methods (primarily in the MPEG family). Current technologies using flexible architecture chips are becoming more common; these devices permit new decoder functionality to be downloaded.

Most recent-vintage PCs are also capable of running player software. This category includes desktop and laptop machines, as well as Windows-, Macintosh-, and Linux-based systems. It is also increasingly common to purchase handheld devices capable of running player software.

Internet Video Appliances

Internet video appliances are closely related to STBs because they provide a network interface for receiving content and video outputs that can be connected directly to television displays. Many of these devices can be used to stream live video directly from an Internet source to a television. Some of these devices can also store video content that has been downloaded to them from a locally connected PC or from an online source.

Control of an Internet video appliance is an interesting conundrum for software designers. On the one hand, most of these devices come with a handheld remote control with a small number of controls, such as fast-forward, rewind, and up/down. This forces the software interface on the appliance to work with a limited set of commands. On the other hand, full access to the rich variety of content that is available on the Internet requires the use of text for searches and so on.

One solution to this issue has been to pair each appliance with an online user account. This approach has been followed both by Apple TV by pairing their device with a viewer's YouTube account and by Netflix with a user's Netflix account. In this setup, viewers use a PC to log into their account and selects a variety of content that they place into a group of favorites or into a playout queue. Then, while viewing the appliance, they merely need to use the remote control to scroll through the list of content that they have preselected and choose what they want to watch. This also has the benefit of ensuring that an account is set up for each appliance.

Another solution is to provide a software keyboard inside the appliance's user interface. Patient users can manipulate the cursor using their remote control to select each letter in a keyword and then launch a search.

Home Streaming Devices

An interesting niche has developed for road warriors and other travelers who wish to take their home video services with them: the home streaming device (HSD). Sling-box provides one well-known version of this technology. In its simplest form, the HSD takes video content from a variety of sources, compresses it, and converts it into a stream that can be sent out of a private network to the Internet. To view this (unicast) stream, a PC with a software decoder receives the stream and displays it to a viewer.

Several logistical problems need to be solved in order for this system to work. First of all, the HSD needs to be able to connect with the software player. This can be slightly complicated if the unit is located on a home network with a firewall; the way around this is to open up some required TCP ports on the firewall and to utilize a server provided by the HSD vendor that allows both the streaming device and the software utility to locate each other's IP address and establish a connection.

Another logistical problem is allowing the remote user to control the home video equipment. For example, the remote user may want to watch a program recorded on a DVR and then switch to watching the local news broadcast later. This control function can be accomplished through the use of a software module on the remote PC that captures the user commands coupled with an infrared output port on the HSD to transmit the appropriate commands to the devices located in the viewer's home. One drawback to this arrangement is that only one person can control the home devices at any given time so that when the remote user is controlling the cable TV STB, a user at home cannot also be controlling the same device.

Commercial Players for PCs

A number of companies have developed video and audio player software that oper-ates on personal computer platforms. All the major players will play content that has been encoded using standards such as MPEG video and MP3 audio, along with a variety of other proprietary and nonproprietary formats.

The following sections discuss the three most popular players supplied by Apple Computer, Microsoft, and Adobe and how their technology works.

Apple Computer

Apple Computer has been very active in developing a number of industry standards for streaming media and has made significant contributions to the realm of intellec-tual property in streaming standards. Many of these innovations center on *Quick-Time*, which is Apple's name for its media streaming system. Apple provides free movie editing software (iMovie) as part of some software releases and sells a highly respected professional tool for editing movies called Final Cut Pro. The company has also actively embraced international standards, including H.264.

QuickTime was originally created to support video clips that were stored on CDs and played back on personal computers. It has become a widely used format, with hundreds of millions of copies downloaded for both Windows and Macintosh PCs. Some of the best uses of QuickTime combine video, audio, animation, and still images into a virtually seamless presentation to the viewer. A great many computer games and multimedia titles have been produced using QuickTime tools.

As in the other cases described previously, several different pieces of technology are used together to support QuickTime streaming. There are components for content preparation, streaming server management, and various versions of player software. Like some of the other systems, content can be prepared and streamed on the same physical device, although system performance needs to be watched carefully to ensure that users will have their streams delivered smoothly.

For content owners and creators, Apple's use of standards can be a big positive. The QuickTime file format is the foundation for the MPEG-4 file format, which handles both MPEG-4 part 2 and H.264 compression formats. The latest versions of QuickTime also use H.264 compression technology. Apple provides players that work on both Windows and Macintosh PCs, and a version has even been designed for some Linux installations.

Microsoft

Microsoft developed Windows Media Player to enable playback of video and audio files on PCs running Microsoft operating systems. Movie Maker is a free utility that enables users to capture video from camcorders and other devices and create finished movies that can be viewed with Windows Media Player. In addition, Microsoft has developed a number of file formats specifically to support streaming.

Several different file formats are commonly used for Windows Media content, including the following.

- Windows Advanced Systems Format File (.asf): A file format designed specifically for the transport and storage of content intended for streaming applications.
- Windows Media Audio File (.wma): A file that contains audio signals encoded using the Windows Media Audio compression system and is in the ASF file format.
- Windows Media Video File (.wmv): A file that contains video and audio signals encoded using the Windows Media Video and Windows Media Audio compression system and is in the ASF file format.

Let's take a closer look at the ASF file format. Microsoft developed ASF and controls its destiny, in part due to patents on the fundamental stream format. ASF files can contain video, audio, text, Web pages, and other types of data. Both live and prerecorded streaming signals are supported. ASF can support image streams, which are still images intended to be presented at a specific time during play. ASF provides support for industry-standard time stamps and enables streams to be played beginning at times other than the start of the media file. Non-Microsoft encoders and decoders are supported inside ASF files; however, their data are treated as pure data and are not supported by some of the nifty features that allow skipping forward and back in a stream—this task needs to be handled by specific user applications.

Adobe

Adobe has developed a large following in the streaming media market for two different but related media formats.

- SWF (ShockWave Flash): Container format for multimedia files. Supports raster and vector graphics, audio, and embedded FLV video files.
- FLV (Flash Video): Video compression format designed specifically for Web streaming and download applications. Used by many popular video-hosting Web sites.

Adobe Flash encoders and decoders employ sophisticated encoding techniques that are targeted specifically for Web applications. They are typically not employed for IPTV or other broadcast formats, unlike other compression schemes such as H.264 and Microsoft's Windows Media. Some specifications have been issued from time to time for these technologies, but this information has not been adequate to make them into open standards.

The fact that Adobe's compression algorithms are private delivers both benefits and drawbacks to users. One benefit is the rapid pace of innovation for these products. While standards bodies serve an extremely critical function for the network as a whole, the due process rules can extend approval times for new compression methods into periods lasting several years. Adobe can develop and deploy new encoder/decoder technology more rapidly because standards bodies are not involved. This also drives another benefit, in that one company is responsible for both encoder (producer) and decoder (player) functions so that compatibility is assured.

One drawback of Adobe's proprietary stance is that the algorithms the company deploys are not directly accessible to third parties so users are restricted to using software tools and plug-ins supplied by Adobe. Also, since a single company has to bear all of the development costs, the resources available for innovation may be smaller than what would be available if multiple firms were all developing products. Finally, users with large libraries of content to encode may have some concerns about relying on a single company for all future support.

Selecting a Streaming Format

All three of the streaming solutions discussed in this chapter (Adobe, Windows Media, and QuickTime) deliver high-quality video and audio streams to the desktop. Because the market is competitive, these different formats are constantly being updated and upgraded to deliver more pleasing visual and audio results that require fewer and fewer bits.

When selecting a streaming format, popularity and previous adoption are important. It makes business sense to prepare content for a platform that the target audience will have available. This does not necessarily mean the player that came with the operating system for the PC; all the three leading players have versions that work on both Windows and Macintosh PCs. The players are not interchangeable; an FLV video stream needs to be played using an Adobe player or plug-in, a WMV stream needs to be played with a Windows Media player, and so on.

Another important consideration is the version of the player that viewers will be using. If the video stream is created using the latest version of an encoder, but the viewer's player has not been upgraded, the video stream may not play. (This is true for some upgrades, but not all.) Of course, this can be remedied by having a user download and install a new version of the player. However, this may not be acceptable to many corporate installations, which require regression testing before updates can be rolled out to large user communities.

Many third-party, content-processing solutions will produce output in multiple formats and at multiple stream speeds. These tools, including offerings from Adobe, Discreet, Avid, and others, enable the creation of a group of output files from a single source stream. One tool can be used to produce content simultaneously for, say, QuickTime, WMV, and many others, such as MPEG. This capability can provide a lot of benefit to Web video production workflows.

When you consider the number of different stream rates that might be required, it is easy to see a dozen or more different output files being created, each with a different combination of stream rate and player format. Many Web sites will provide several combinations of stream format and bit rate, allowing users to obtain one that is compatible with their installed viewer software and network connection speed.

Alternative Players and Plug-ins

At first glance, the difference between players and plug-ins seems straightforward enough. Whereas the media player is a separate application residing on the viewer's PC (as discussed in Chapter 4), plug-ins are software stored on the viewer's PC that give additional functionality to their Web browser. Plug-ins enable the user to interact with more content types and perform transactions that the browser or HTML feature set does not inherently support. For example, an Adobe Acrobat Reader plug-in enables reading of PDF files within a browser. Software vendors supply plug-ins to enable users to access multimedia on the Web over their browser.

The twist is that media players themselves support their own plug-ins. For instance, WinAmp and MediaPlayer plug-ins can add local language menu support, sound effects, alarm clocks, and other functions to a media player. Other important media player features include DRM to combat piracy and a tiered licensing model (free version with basic play/display and a premium version with additional features such as QuickTime Pro's full-screen display, editing, and export capabilities.)

If most of the player software market to date has been dominated by the entrenched providers, there are alternatives. One example is WinAmp, freeware with a large user base. Many users develop new features for the product that are, in turn, made available to other WinAmp users.

Other media players are constantly being developed. For example, SongBird is a free, multiplatform application built by Pioneers of the Inevitable. One advantage of open-source developments is that they benefit from large developer community contributions. As one open community enthusiast gushes, "It's like taking iTunes, ripping out the music store, and replacing it with the rest of the Internet."[5]

---

[5]Ross Karchner, http://rossnotes.com/archives/2006/10/01/playing-with-songbird-2006

Content Creation Workflows

Whether it's the summer family reunion at the coast, a European rugby match, or a prime-time nature series, as the producer, what do you need to do to get content ready for Internet playout?

You've got to compress it, tag it so people can find it, and get it hosted on a server. You might also need to prepare the file for different formats, media players, and download/resolution qualities. However, the more complete answer is that many different steps go into successful deployment. Although there is a difference between the types of video services that can be deployed over IP, there is a similarity in how most content must be created, managed, and deployed for successful technical and commercial results.

Raw video generated by a camera or video recorded to tape is generally not well suited for streaming applications. Normally, the content needs to be processed to make it ready for streaming. To be utilized in a network production setting, the video content must be digitized and compressed in various formats, indexed, tagged, and distributed to meet various technical standards and performance requirements. There are benefits to getting this process right: (1) valuable, time-sensitive content is more available to internal and external audiences and (2) the content life cycle is likely extended.

Scenarios for capturing and preparing content for viewing can be simple or intensive, depending on the goals of the users, their time constraints, and budget allocations. The first step of this process involves aggregating the video from a contribution network, which may consist of satellite, tape, live feed, VPN, or Internet, and then ingesting, or digitizing, video that may include segmentation, metadata, and storyboarding for later editing or preview. Figure 11.2 shows the content development process.

Along the way, storage, security, and disaster recovery functions are implemented, after which a systems operator assigns user group access permissions to various internal production, marketing, or advertising teams, as well as to the public. After any appropriate editing and formatting, the content is pushed to a server for download, streaming, or playout.

As time goes by, production processes are increasingly influenced by new online video techniques and viewer expectations. Likewise, in addition to bandwidth aspects discussed in Chapter 9, content must be protected at each stage, from source to market, and tailored to evolving channels and distribution forms. Moreover, many telcos and ISPs will need to build a network operations culture.

Perhaps the most demanding instance of streaming is live Webcasting where media production and distribution must be fully reliable and fault-tolerant. Webcasting in real time exposes the nitty-gritty audio-visual production issues, as discussed in *Webcasting* by Steve Mack and Dan Rayburn (Focal Press, 2006):

> *Producing a Webcast is basically the same process as creating an on-demand streaming media file. Webcasting, however, is a little trickier because there is no room for error. Webcasts are produced in real time; this affects each stage of the streaming media process. But with a little forethought and a lot of planning, a successful Webcast is well within your reach.*

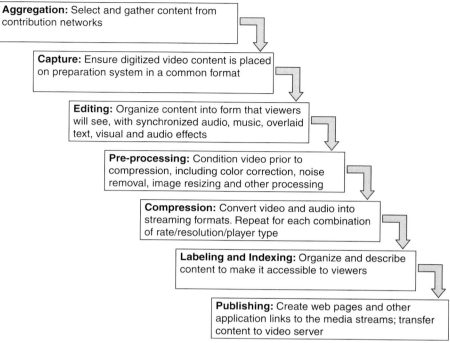

Figure 11.2 *Streaming content creation workflows.*

The Webcasting process is the same as creating on-demand streaming media files, with the important addition of a planning phase:

- *Planning:* Justifying the costs, securing the location, tools, and crew
- *Production:* Capturing the raw audio and video feeds, any other data types
- *Encoding:* Converting raw media into formats that can be streamed
- *Authoring:* Connecting the audience to the Webcast via a link on a Web page
- *Distribution:* Securing the infrastructure to distribute the streams

Each phase has unique requirements during a Webcast. The most important thing to remember is that you only get one shot at a Webcast. If something goes wrong, the Webcast may grind to a halt if you haven't planned appropriately. Bearing this in mind, the planning phase becomes paramount, and the key to all other phases can be summed up in a single word: redundancy.

User Scenarios: Turning Streams into Dollars and Influence

After analyzing the workflow, successfully applying the technology to the real world is what really counts. Whereas IPTV, as we have described it, pertains to professional broadcasting channels with a budget and an infrastructure to rival commercial television broadcasting, the versatility and effectiveness of streaming to niche audiences offer great advantages to smaller organizations. Some application examples are considered in the following section.

Video streaming is an ideal way to leverage the global reach of the Internet to *narrowcast*, that is, to broadcast to a specialized audience. These may be fly fishermen, digital signage point-of-purchase shoppers, or clients of the new restaurant in town. Narrowcasting can potentially reach these specific audiences more easily, affordably, and thoroughly. Let's take a brief look at some of the ways in which streaming video is being used today.

Entertainment

Video over the Internet got a jump-start in the late 1990s with the availability of Hollywood movie previews on Web sites. No longer constrained to showing their wares on expensive television commercials or as coming attractions in theaters, movie studios began to reach out to the online community. At first, much of this content was set up for download and play because very few home users had access to broadband connections that were suitable for high-quality streaming. One of the classics was the *Star Wars Episode I* trailer at a hefty 10.4 MB. It was released in March 1999 and, according to a press release, was downloaded 3.5 million times in its first five days of availability, even though it could take up to an hour to download over a dial-up connection.[6]

According to the Organisation for Economic Co-operation and Development (OECD), 51% of U.S. homes had access to broadband connections by the end of 2007.[7] As a result, more and more content is available in streaming form. All types of video content is available online, including television programs, Hollywood movies, short video documentaries, user-generated video, and a host of other content. Substantial portions of these are available for free, while many require payment of subscription fees or are supported by advertising.

Corporate Video

Corporate video consists of content intended to improve the performance of an organization. We'll use the term *corporate* loosely here because we want this term to apply to all types of public and private organizations, including government agencies, not-for-profit organizations, and true private corporations.

Corporate video tends to focus on two areas: employee education and information sharing. Education can cover a wide range of topics, including training for new employees, instruction on new work procedures and equipment, job enrichment training, and personal skills development, to name a few. Corporate executives use information sharing to make employees aware of corporate or organizational performance, to improve communication with employees, and to deal with unusual

---

[6]A good source of movie information and trailers can be found at www.imdb.com, the Internet movie database.

[7]http://www.oecd.org/dataoecd/20/59/39574039.xls

challenges or opportunities. Sometimes the corporation produces this content strictly for internal consumption; other times, content is acquired from or distributed to outside parties.

Live streaming is normally used for time-critical corporate video applications, such as company news distribution or executive speeches. Before streaming video became feasible, companies had gone to the expense of renting satellite time and deploying portable satellite receivers for special events. Permanent satellite systems have become popular with retail chains that have a large number of fixed locations with heavy needs for live video transmission, but this tends to be the exception rather than the rule. High-quality streaming has made it possible to use corporate IP networks for this same function.

Many other forms of content are well suited to storage and subsequent on-demand streaming playback. For example, recorded training video material is very effective because it enables students to watch at their own pace; they can review material or skip ahead without disturbing other students.

Material can also be stored and played back at different times to meet the schedules of employees who work on different shifts or in different time zones or for those who may have missed the original presentation. The server can also keep track of the number of times that each piece of content is viewed for royalty payment tracking. Contrast this with a download and play environment, where content gets dispatched to users around the network, thereby making accurate usage accounting difficult.

Investor Relations

Due to a wave of corporate scandals in the United States after 2000, treating investors equally has become a priority. Many companies decided to give both large and small investors the ability to participate in major corporate events. An increasingly popular way of accomplishing this is by using streaming video to transmit live meetings over the Internet. The content can also be recorded and played back on demand for users who were not able to watch the original live broadcast or for those who wish to review what had transpired.

During live corporate video coverage, it is not unusual for several hundred simultaneous users or more to be connected. Multicasting (see Chapter 5) can be used to reach viewers located on properly equipped network segments. Typically, this applies only to private networks where multicasting can be enabled on the IP networking equipment. For users who are not connected to a suitable network, replicated unicasting can be used. With this technique, special servers are used to take a single incoming stream and produce multiple outgoing streams. This technology is particularly useful for investor relations uses because it can scale up as more viewers connect by adding new server capacity as needed.

Internet Radio and TV

A number of free and subscription services have appeared on the Internet to provide both audio and video content. There are literally thousands of Internet radio stations, due in part to the relatively low cost of equipment and the low bandwidth required.

Internet television stations are less common, but they are becoming more feasible as the number of users with broadband connections increases.

Video and audio streaming sites have been developed for a number of purposes, including corporate branding (free sites), advertising-supported (also free), and subscription (monthly or other periodic payment system). A huge variety of content is available, including newscasts, music, adult programming, and entertainment. Because this material is organized similarly to a traditional radio or television broadcast, users are restricted to viewing the content in the order in which it is presented. For example, the Pandora music service allows the user to select a song or an artist as a jumping-off point for creating a play list that is not under direct user control (and, interestingly, does not include the selected song, at least in the initial play list). Pandora is not a content-on-demand service, where each user can watch in any order any content he or she chooses.

Because much of this content is prerecorded, download and play technology is perfectly adequate. However, that method would be somewhat disruptive to the flow of the broadcast because each file would need to be downloaded before play can begin. (This technology is much more disruptive for video files than audio files, simply because video files are much larger and take much longer to download.) Progressive download and play greatly alleviates this problem because playback of each new file of content can begin as soon as the first segment is downloaded to the PC. Of course, for live broadcasts, only streaming will do.

Reality Check

Because there is great attention being drawn to the use and impact of podcasting and commercial sites that offer complete episodes of current television programs, we turn to those subjects for the focus of this chapter's Reality Check.

Podcasting

Content providers and audiences are being wooed in new ways. For example, podcasting has captivated listeners around the world in an on-demand audio exchange—even though there is no single formula for how it is operated or monetized. Podcasting is online media publishing that enables producers to upload their content and listeners to download or subscribe to regular feeds that retrieve new files as they become available. The technique and terminology were validated when, in response to podcasting's sudden prevalence, the *New Oxford American Dictionary* named it Word of the Year in 2005.

Podcasting's power of syndication means that you can upload your podcast with an XML Web publication file using Really Simple Syndication (RSS), which enables other Web users to subscribe to content feeds of their choice. The RSS reader in the subscriber's application (e.g., browser) looks on the Web for new publications and downloads them automatically to subscribers (Figure 11.3).

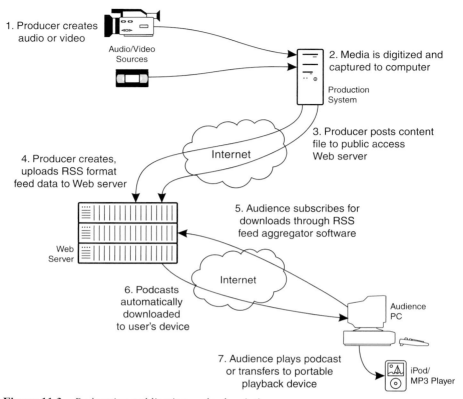

Figure 11.3 *Podcasting publication and subscription.*

Thanks to the low cost of entry of podcasting, anyone aspiring to produce and host their DJ radio talk show, broadcast garage band music demos, or issue new corporate communications can post files of their recordings and make them available to a world audience on the Web. But when the technical team presents online strategies to the CEO, eager to launch to the world over IPTV, should podcasting be included in that evaluation? The criterion should be whether it will generate results, which makes podcasting a contender. So, here are some podcasting characteristics to consider for push or pull publication of audio and video.

- Subscriber- or download-based options
- Syndication feed compliance
- Supports user interface for interaction with other Web content and e-commerce
- To date, typically audio-centric, but as portable music players and other mobile devices increasingly gain ability to support video file standards and display, also becoming a video medium

Perhaps unsurprisingly, podcasters who have a significant media profile before they begin podcasting can have significant numbers of downloads right from the beginning of their online existence. For example, when Adam Carolla left mainstream radio for a podcast-only presence, his podcast was downloaded over one million times in the first week it was available, which greatly exceeded original expectations.[8]

Commercial "Catch-Up" Television

One unfortunate side effect of many current television dramas, reality shows, and even some sit-coms that employ lengthy story arcs is the discontinuity that is created when an episode is missed. This can occur for many reasons, such as a DVR malfunction, a sudden shift in the television schedule, an unavoidable appointment with an important client or a child's teacher, or a host of other causes. Broadcasters have realized that they can keep their audiences loyal and more likely to tune in to catch the next episode of the program if viewers can be provided with a means to "catch-up" with missed episodes. Fortunately, IP video on demand provides an ideal mechanism for doing just that. For example, the BBC iPlayer enables television audiences in the United Kingdom to find and play programs from the past seven days on Windows, Macs, Linux, Nintendo Wii and iPhones-including HD content.

Here's how it works. Television networks and other content distributors sign agreements with content owners that allow them to set up Web sites with full episodes of television programs available for viewing. Contracts are made with advertisers for either long (one-to-two minute) preroll advertisements or shorter midroll ads. Viewers are solicited through Web or television advertising (such as the hilarious Hulu commercial during the 2009 Super Bowl)[9] and are encouraged to view the programs online (with a PC but not yet a TV). Program episodes may only be available for a few weeks to help avoid any obligations to pay royalties to performers and to make sure that content is removed from the market well in advance of when it becomes available in DVD format.

Apparently, this approach has been a success, according to Nielsen, with viewership up strongly for commercial television Web sites. Plus, overall television viewership is at an all-time high.

Summary

This chapter took a much closer look at the variety of Internet video technologies that offer a public universe of content delivery as an alternative to managed, billable, broadcast-quality IPTV networks being deployed around the world. In addition to discussing varying views on the contrasts between IPTV and Internet video streaming, we looked at the basic end-to-end topology of streaming architectures that can be developed and deployed by enterprises or individuals that don't have the budget, staff, or motivation to launch a full-scale, broadcast-quality channel.

Of the many ways to stream over the Internet, there are significant variations in the respective benefits to true streaming, download, and progressive download and

[8]http://www.podcastingnews.com/2009/03/01/adam-carolla-podcast-makes-radio-irrelevant
[9]http://bits.blogs.nytimes.com/2009/02/02/hulu-unveils-evil-intentions-with-free-super-bowl-ad

play. Although this book is designed as an executive briefing, it has taken the initiative to delve into some of the technology layers, such as RTP, TCP, and UDP transport to expose why the investment of time and resources in streaming applications requires skillful planning by technical and marketing teams to ensure the best end results.

We have also looked at media players offered by the mainstream industry software vendors and alternatives from the open-source community, as well as detailed the primary elements or steps in the capture and preparation of video content for audiences. Finally, we examined some of the main application domains where Internet video is being applied and some of the experiences of organizations seeking to exploit the power of visual interactive narrowcasting to their respective constituencies.

12 The Future of IP Video

In 5 years, people will laugh at the TV we've had up to now.

Bill Gates, Microsoft

We just want to get to the point where you will put video on your Web site as a default behavior.

Peter Chane, Google Video

Communications networks continue to evolve rapidly. This final chapter highlights important trends for managers and business leaders navigating the emerging environment. The focus will be on an array of global technical and business developments forging a path for video transport over IP. We begin by reviewing advanced technologies that are steadily becoming mainstream offerings.

Throughout this book, we have examined technical and business drivers behind IPTV and Internet video that are sparking new service delivery models around the world. Perhaps this chapter is best titled after an IBM report whose title proclaimed it's "The End of TV as We Know It."[1] Whatever the outcome, the changing IP landscape will continue to offer a more versatile framework for TV programming over the public Internet as well as privately managed networks.

The Corner Office View

By late 2008, ABC reported over 400 million total episodes and one billion ads served since it began delivering its programming over ABC.com. Anne Sweeney, President, Disney-ABC Television Group, comments on the future of television and turning content into revenue:

- Quadruple-Play Ahead: " . . . technology is additive. It allows content to follow you. This additive technology is changing the landscape of our industry. To find our way through the unfamiliar terrain, we'll have to stop navigating by old landmarks. . . ."
- Change and Risk: " . . . The music industry is a sobering example of what happens when you ignore this particular threat. We have to understand that we are competing with piracy for consumers. . . ."
- New Models: " . . . We can't cling to old models or old ways of thinking. We have to actively look for opportunities to make our content available in convenient ways at reasonable prices. . . ."

---

[1] www-935.ibm.com/services/us/index.wss/ibvstudy/imc/a1023172?cntxt5a1000062

IP is an enabler. Its powerful abilities to control packets and manage services over so many types of networks, as explored in Chapter 5, are why it serves as the foundation for so many streams, channels, and devices that evolve into end-to-end businesses. Examining the mechanics of video transport in earlier chapters, we have seen how the union of adequate bandwidth to the consumer, advanced server middleware technology, and STB functionality is combining to stream video to viewers in a manner that could not be achieved until this time.

By 2012, 32 million U.S. homes are expected to have 10 Mbps or higher broadband connections, mostly used for carrying video content.[2] Like the social, collaborative Web 2.0 environment, other breakthroughs in compression, security, and server scalability are contributing to next-generation video. This so-called *Video 2.0* combines traditional TV, movie, and Internet video into a single consumer product often delivered through quadruple play services that offer ubiquitous access and interactivity.

Today your computer helps you search for content while your TV, until recently, just displayed existing channels. But video consumers operate increasingly at the heart of their own content kingdom, with new set-top and streaming devices offering advanced EPGs and bountiful DVR storage access on its way. "Our new form of search really does Google-ize television in a way that you can get to exactly what you're interested in quickly," says TiVo CEO Tom Rogers. "And this is the way people are going to use television to get to what they want to watch when they want to watch it."[3] But sweeping change doesn't automatically generate winning products and market traction. "Early adopters may want to play around with new services," as one analyst puts it, "but most users just want to turn on the TV and sit back and be entertained." Will they ultimately pay more for lean back or lean forward modes of consumption?[4]

Ultimately, it will require creativity to combine the new online and traditional on-air broadcast models, and there will be risk and experimentation along the way as broadcast networks, cable and satellite companies, telcos, and ISPs seek to convert customers to new services while reducing churn. The winners and losers of these new multibillion-dollar markets will only be apparent after the next several years of competition and industry shakeouts. We next look at this and other business drivers behind these expectations.

Business Drivers

The impact of IPTV technology advances on new service offerings shows no signs of slowing down. Exhilarating and challenging at the same time, the myriad of new features, devices, standards, and initiatives is not easy to track. Adding to the complexity as discussed earlier in this book, the overlap between IPTV and Internet video is increasing as the choices of delivery platforms proliferate. This

[2]Parks Associates, October 2008.
[3]Tom Rogers, CEO, TiVo, on their new search capability. TV news interview, 1/8/09.
[4]Deepa Iyer from "IPTV Promise Meets Reality," C/NET, 2006.

proliferation of technical choice entails experimentation to get the formula for mass audience appeal and monetization right.

We spoke about business models in Chapter 3. Now, distinguishing the money-makers from the attention grabbers is key to commercial success. In other words, as TV executive Terry Mackin once remarked: "It may be cool, but is it a business? The test becomes how do I turn this into a complete business, and what is the revenue strategy?" Turning content into cash presents challenges such as:

- Settling licensing and distribution rights
- Delivering a user interface with broad appeal
- Offering excellent quality of service
- Monetizing new, unproven services
- Solving piracy and copyright infringement

Analysts and trend watchers focus on a few of key data points when it comes to estimating products and revenue. Two chief indicators are infrastructure commitment (investment) by operators and large, strategic acquisitions.

One proof that IP video business transformation is gaining momentum is the massive multibillion-dollar investment by telcos worldwide in new networks and infrastructure. For years, business headlines reflected the change—and the risk/reward ahead. "Phone Carriers Set Sights on Cable Television's Turf," reads the *Los Angeles Times*. "The competitive landscape is shifting," according to one cable industry analyst. "That's why folks are cautious about telephone, cable and satellite stocks. If you look at them, Wall Street is saying there isn't going to be a winner." Economic dynamics continue to be a key determining factor in what types of services we'll see from this competition.[5]

In addition to the financial investment telcos have poured into DSL and fiber networks to the home, there are many signs of growth ahead, including acquisitions and mergers. Among them, several industry mergers and acquisitions in recent years come to mind, also referenced briefly in previous chapters. The first, eBay's $2.6 billion acquisition of VoIP leader Skype, was a wake-up call to telcos declaring change afoot: cash cow phone line and long distance revenues are going into decline. (The fact that this deal later proved to be a burden on eBay was more due to a lack of synergy and poor monetization than an issue with Skype's core business.) This transaction, and several to follow, set the stage for a new alignment of previously entrenched broadcast, media, and telecommunications sectors.

Other mergers and acquisitions in recent years' events have signaled a changing of the guard.

- News Corp's purchase of Intermix Media for $580 million, which included social media networking icon MySpace, was a giant step for old guard broadcast into next wave Internet business.
- Adobe Systems' acquisition of Web development giant Macromedia in 2005 for $3.6 billion may have seemed like a software play. However, as an IP video business driver, bringing star products Flash, Dreamweaver, and Adobe production under one

[5]http://articles.latimes.com/2005/dec/10/business/fi-cable10

roof, the merger created further critical mass development focus on new HTML, video, and animation production tools that cross the traditional boundary between broadcast and data networks. Winner of the 2006 Technical and Engineering Emmy Award from the National Academy of Television Arts and Sciences for its Flash video technology, the company emphasized their role in how broadcasters deliver content and reach new audiences.[6]

- The highly observed acquisition of user-generated video portal YouTube may have sounded "like heresy for Google," said Google cofounder Sergey Brin, explaining $1.65 billion outlay to gain higher ground in online video portals, "but search isn't always the best way to learn things. If you want to learn a sport or learn how to build a house, video is the best way to do that."[7]

More recently, CBS's $1.8 billion cash acquisition of CNET instantly made CBS one of the top ten Internet properties in popularity with an international audience of around 200 million. Also, in 2007, a joint venture between NBC, News Corp and Providence Equity Partners invested $100 million in a Web site, now known as Hulu, designed to stream prime-time network programming over the Web.

To some, a new media market is opening up, while to others, this new generation of video technology is merely the new wrapper for existing products and services. But as leading analysts and integrators do the math the talk is bullish about the momentum ahead. Is the IP market a trillion-dollar sector? Consider some trends, starting with the fact that over 1.5 billion people are already connected to the Internet worldwide.[8]

In the 2007 edition of this book, we reported that in the United States alone, one-third of all households were online, with that number expected to double by 2010. Today, more than 14 billion online videos are viewed each month according to Comscore, who estimated that nearly 150 million U.S. Internet users watched 96 videos per viewer in December 2008.[9] In the United Kingdom, that same online video audience grew 10% within the past year to 30 million users[10] and in France 16% to 27 million users.[11] Online video streaming advertising will exceed $6 billion by 2012.[12] Likewise, today's 20 million broadband TV services subscribers will nearly triple by 2012 according to Gartner.[13] By mid-June 2008, Apple Computer had reported more than 5 billion legal iTunes downloads and 50,000 movies per day, bringing in an estimated $527 million per quarter.[14] In the meantime, mobile advertising spending is forecast to grow by 42% from 2008 to 2013 revenues reaching $2.79 billion by 2012.[15]

---

[6]Adobe Systems, www.adobe.com/aboutadobe/pressroom/pressreleases/200611/110206Emmy.html

[7]http://www.lightreading.com/document.asp?doc_id=107860

[8]http://www.internetworldstats.com/stats.htm

[9]http://www.comscore.com/press/release.asp?press=2714

[10]http://www.comscore.com/press/release.asp?press=2753

[11]http://www.comscore.com/press/release.asp?press=2747

[12]Parks Associates.

[13]http://informitv.com/articles/2008/09/25/iptvmarketgrows/

[14]http://www.businessinsider.com/2008/6/what-apples-5-billion-songs-mean

[15]http://www.fiercemobilecontent.com/story/forecast-mobile-ad-revs-to-reach-2.79b-by-2012/2008-04-29

By most accounts, these statistics reflect a high-growth outlook. Other business drivers already discussed include increasingly commonplace time-shifting DVRs that make custom content more widely available and attractive. Viewers get their video when they want and can also have portable media to go, as examined later in this chapter.

The future of television is about participation, as many of today's broadcast executives are beginning to understand and tout. Programming is becoming increasingly controllable through links to Web content—sport stats, cooking tips, election analyses, and so on. But are we there yet? Monetization of IPTV and Internet video is a work in progress. Commercializing online video through advertising is still a work in progress with some, like Google CEO Eric Schmidt, even calling it the "Holy Grail" of a new broadband entertainment medium. As one blogger recently put it, "There is no doubt in my mind that IPTV will prevail. I just hope it follows a shorter, faster path than VoIP to my living room."[16]

Advanced Technology

It would be hard to point to hotter technology media growth categories than IPTV and Internet video. We may not have yet achieved final standards and scale, but industry executives around the world recognize that we have embarked on one of the most creative, exciting periods for the industry. "When you move into the wired phase, the on-demand phase, what actually happens?" asks John Varney, former BBC chief technical officer. "We're not seeing a set of established behaviors that would suggest we truly understand this yet. That said, we are starting to see the first signs of a coming together of social networks, user creation and video distribution. If this is sustained, then the democratizing effects will make this the most fascinating phase in broadcasting history."[17]

But delivering the next breakthrough will mean experimenting with interface and delivery design, benchmarking network speed and market coverage, and working out everything from device compatibility to quality of service. Part project management, part futurology, it involves a combination of calculated risk and smart investment of resources. As *Crossing the Chasm* author and Mohr Davidow venture capital partner Geoff Moore says about digital media and tomorrow's 2.0 technology innovation, when it comes to determining what comes next in this market, "It's not about making decisions, it's about making bets."

Only a few years ago, with some notable exceptions such as France, Italy, and parts of Asia, IPTV seemed stalled by a combination of slow-to-arrive chipsets and STBs and delays to Microsoft's IPTV solution at several of the biggest telcos, including AT&T, BT, and Swisscom. However, IPTV subscribers continue to grow as we've pointed out with compelling examples such as AT&T and PCCW surpassing the 1 million subscriber barrier. During 2008, IPTV subscribers grew from around 13 million (Q4 2007) to nearly 22 million (Q4 2008).[18]

---

[16]TekTidbits, www.tektidbits.com/2006/11/iptv_the_future.html, November 2006.

[17]"Broadcast's New Media Course," TVB-Europe, July 2005, Greenfield.

[18]http://www.tvover.net/2009/03/25/IPTV+Growth+Doubles+In+North+America+In+2008.aspx

Pressure on operators to increase DSL performance to the consumer will continue. Increasing network capacity and reducing channel change time to emulate conventional TV will push providers to hit performance targets and eliminate latency. Some companies are already looking beyond ADSL2+ for added bandwidth to provide more services to each customer. There's no magic solution yet for HD to multiple televisions in a home, but VDSL2 is one promising standard, and compression innovation will also continue in this area.

Today's operators seek the most advanced network that combines TV, PC, and STB-based IPTV with zero latency access to everything: on-demand, prime-time programming; user-generated Internet video; DIY channels; interactive services; and portable, wireless access.

Will tomorrow's winning network architecture be hybrid IP, TV, and wireless? The building blocks are improving: real-time H.264 encoding, RTP and RTSP protocol, STB on a chip, CPU+ DSP decoding, and 802.11g Wi-Fi. But are these sufficient to meet performance requirements and deliver economies of scale? Let's consider some of the anticipation surrounding what's ahead.

Great Expectations

New ways to navigate, collaborate, and interact with content are the hallmarks of tomorrow's television. That is the expectation we've touched on throughout this book. However, to become established, interactive video services will likely evolve and integrate little by little with today's conventions and viewing habits.

Everything on Demand: Free and Billable

As discussed earlier, one vision of the future is everything-on-demand (EOD) oriented, delivered via VOD, DVRs, online access, DVDs, mobile devices, and more. "Appointment-based television is dead,"[19] as William Randolph Hearst III and others put it, as TV becomes a when-you-want-it experience.

The consumer's history of getting free programming from broadcast TV, and, perhaps even more so, free content from the Web, has created great expectations for whatever they want, whenever they want it, and, eventually, wherever they want it. We looked at payment methods in Chapter 3 and some of the economics of the programming business. The effect of time-shifting, ad-zapping DVRs has not eluded the advertising industry anxious to protect a multibillion dollar TV advertising revenue stream.

But "advertising change happens at the speed of molasses," says Rory Sutherland, vice-chairman of OgilvyOne, who believes essentially nothing in advertising changed between the 1950s and the advent of the Internet. However, new media make possible a new kind of brand and require a 21st-century business model, according to Sutherland and other colleagues.[20] As harbingers we have seen advertising on the

---

[19]William Randolph Hearst III, partner, Kleiner Perkins Caufield & Byers, *New York Times*, January 2, 2006.
[20]Rory Sutherland, vice-chairman, OgilvyOne, BT Global Summit, September 2006.

Web masquerading as entertainment in recent years, such as Smirnoff's Tea Party ad campaign, Taco Bell's top model online photo shoot, and, more recently, the Pepsi MacGruber parody commercial short, which debuted on *Saturday Night Live* and was a Superbowl 43 favorite. A new generation of online video advertising monetization start-ups that go beyond midroll, overlay, and banner ads are delivering more engaging, less intrusive interactive ad content.

Internet TV ad spending is on an upward arc, with the online video market poised for steady growth over the next few years when spending is expected to more than double. Media companies are reorganizing themselves around the concept of multiplatform content because video now reaches across television, computers, cell phones, and iPods. This, according to others at Ogilvy, means "media companies must worry about how to monetize this content on multiple screens, while agencies only need ensure that our marketing messages reach consumers on these platforms."[21] The way forward therefore unites advertisers and content providers in a common cause: create new content that spans platforms and devices and reaches all audiences.

DVD mail rental services such as Netflix and Blockbuster (which have provided movie watchers with unprecedented access and variety) are being superseded by another type of Internet video delivery. Innovations such as the $99 Roku box discussed earlier offer unlimited views of thousands of TV programs and movies on demand for under $10 a month. In the traditional continuum of "rent, buy, subscribe" payment methods, watch for flexibility ahead: multitiered payment options, a broader range of niche content, and interactive incentives (such as "buy this," "vote on that," or "get a free sample"). The Rhapsody and Pandora "all you can listen to" audio subscription paradigms that have worked for music libraries are also being applied to video such as the Netflix "Watch Instantly" service.

Demographically targeted advertising is also the future. Custom advertising by new ad scientists will train its sights on fragmenting age, culture, economic, and geographic subgroups and on viewing constituencies. Why? To learn more of what they want and to customize ads through the feedback loop: "On the Internet, marketers love their dashboards, their control panels, the ability to see results and to make changes based on those results," according to Seth Haberman, CEO of Visible World. "When you look at off-line advertising research, it's like going to the morgue," says Haberman. "They cut the guy open and tell you why he died. But that's worthless unless you can make a change. The real opportunity is in coordination and feedback."[22]

Channels for All

> The next big thing is small.
> **Seth Godin, author**

Is tomorrow's economy based on mass audiences or many niche markets? Because the Internet often surpasses the reach and effectiveness of traditional broadcast and marketing campaigns, aspiring content providers have spotted a new online

---

[21]Maria Mandel, OgilvyInteractive, August 2006
[22]*Wired Magazine*, February 2006.

TV opportunity to get their message out. Maybe you're an independent music video production company, a regional tourist board, or a budding news and entertainment broadcaster trying to grow your audience without depleting next year's operating budget. More and more IP video solutions enable you to create your own channel without breaking the bank.

In the good old days, television channels carried a succession of linear programming that viewers could watch each hour. Today, TV programming is available online from the likes of Hulu, Veoh, and BBC iPlayer. "Channels" are being redefined as always-on Web video destinations. For instance, according to Ustream CEO John Ham, their live channels are not just for watching: they're for connecting. The interaction between broadcaster and audience is key. "Ustream is not a destination," says Ham, "it's a platform for 'live moments.'" The power of live Web channels will only increase, according to Ham, who says that live, Web-based video interactivity will be a common social networking foundation in the future.

Streaming providers enable any size company to do what previously was only within the reach of large corporate marketing budgets by providing the technical talent and infrastructure to produce and deploy programming over the Web. Streaming media providers offer the following advantages.

- Global audience reach
- Live Internet program delivery
- Ability to create pay-per-view content options
- Podcast replication capability
- Load-balanced delivery for surges in audience size
- Archiving and DRM
- Advice on effective, commercial Webcasting

This approach enables commercial companies and nonprofits alike to operate in a new mode: "thinking vertically and interacting globally with people that really need to get the information."[23]

Although more and more companies can host their own video portal, uploading content for ad hoc streaming, most are not expert at video and multimedia Web production and may lack the time, skills, and talent to be successful. This is especially true as some seek improved broadcast quality by way of their own Internet TV channel. IPTV channel services will let smaller enterprises or new product developers broadcast to the world.

This approach replicates what the consumer would experience at home using their remote control and TV—with similar quality to what you would expect from a satellite or cable provider. These end-to-end service providers run fully managed Internet TV channels with compression technologies that display on a television. Other services include billing and customer relationship management. Content companies reach a target audience and reach the world. Different from traditional cable services, users can plug their STB into the Internet from anywhere in the world and access their content.[24]

[23]Dave Gardy, www.tvworldwide.com.
[24]www.neulion.com-example custom IPTV provider.

These and other broadband channel solutions continue to create new options for communicating through this medium. YouTube, Yahoo!, and others offer even more user-friendly ways to click and upload videos for universal access. What, then, is a channel? ABC, BBC, MTV? Maybe it's just simpler to say that "a channel is a series of videos from the same source or user."[25]

Portable Media: IPTV to Mobile Devices

More than a billion mobile phones are sold each year. Although they have small viewing screens, they are becoming smarter and more capable all the time. Sharp 184-pixel-per-inch resolution screens can support hundreds of millions of mobile applications and programs being sold and downloaded. Over 500 million mobile TV viewers are expected to be watching by 2013 as the medium becomes "positioned in a more proper role as an extension of traditional broadcast TV services," according to senior ABI research analyst Jeff Orr.[26]

But is portable streaming finally ready for prime time? The social debate continues over people's interest in watching TV on two-inch screens. But with more than two billion cell phones in use worldwide, hundreds of millions already equipped with 3G and other technologies enabling video playback, a continuing adoption trend is likely.

The world's leading broadcasters are entering the fray while mobile phone and PDA providers ready new video-enabled handheld devices. Start-ups are springing up to deliver a variety of mobile video programming, search, audio, radio, and advertising models. MobiTV, which supports the iPhone and more than 350 other mobile platforms, delivers content from the likes of HBO and can work with Wi-Fi, Edge, and 3G Internet connections. When *CNBC On The Money* asked the CEO of MobiTV what is attracting an audience to the small screen, there's little hesitation that it's across the board interest: "We're seeing broad usage across entertainment content, the 'time fillers,' as well as the breaking news events and sports scores. So, really there's something for everybody."

The attraction of portable media is individual access to watch or listen to your choice of content when and where you want to. "You may be on the east coast and want to watch the [San Francisco] Giants game that's not available to you when you're out and about," says Matt Crowley, senior manager multimedia products, Palm, Inc. "It's really about getting access to the content you care about when and where you want to."[27]

Valuation of a New Network

Networks have a reputation for becoming increasingly valuable as more customers join the service. This is particularly true for wireless services where the more customers on the network, the more people there are to talk to and reach for business,

[25]video.yahoo.com/video
[26]http://www.abiresearch.com/press/1366-Half+a+Billion+Mobile+TV+Viewers+and+Subscribers+in+2013
[27]Streaming Media 2006, San Jose, California.

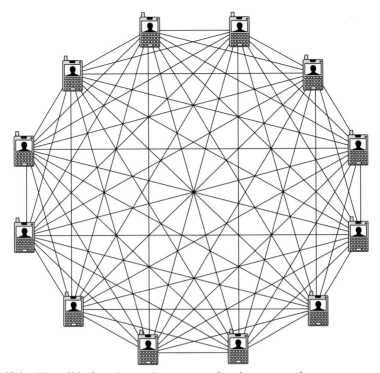

Figure 12.1 *Metcalfe's law: increasing returns of scale as networks grow.*

personal, medical, educational purposes, etc. The Metcalfe law of increasing returns to scale captures this very well (Figure 12.1). It posits that the value of a network increases exponentially with the number of nodes. Just as fax machines became a business necessity once most companies used them, broadcast networks are more valuable to broadcasters when there are more viewers: advertisers will pay more to sponsor highly viewed content. The same holds for portable video devices, but issues remain for creating a viable service.

Mobile: Crossing the Technical Chasm

To date, monetizing small-screen, walk-about video has been slow to go mainstream because of technical issues such as rights-management, billing, and interactivity (such as sharing videos and collaboration). Then there are human factor design issues in creating a new user interface, EPG, input–output control, and so on. Finally, custom creation of effective miniscreen content, real-time, and multiplatform version production requirements must also be tackled.

Some of the technology issues are:

- Finding the most viable model for content consumption (e.g., incentives to adopting a new medium and interface, and "downloads or streams?")
- Trade-offs among 4G, WiMAX, and Wi-Fi network deployments
- Standards such as DVB-H (Digital Video Broadcasting-Handheld)
- Integration with GPS and with Bluetooth for control of home security, services, devices, etc.
- Battery life (screen display, potential WiMAX demands)

Another technical issue that will be key to mobile media profitability is finding intelligent ways to provide and manage adequate broadcast bandwidth—and pricing services attractively enough to attract consumers.

The mobile chasm is not just a technical one. "We're still learning how people are consuming [small screen mobile] video," says Kai Johansson, CTO, MobiTV. The biggest industry mistake could be the belief that it's possible to simply move video from a standard home display to a small screen mobile device and that people will watch. "That's just not the case," says Johansson. "Everyone has a different idea of what the mobile killer application will be, but I don't think anyone really knows ... but it's coming!"[28] That time is drawing closer as handheld video devices such as the iTouch become more affordable, and by 2013 smart phones will account for 23% of the mobile phone market.[29]

2021: Having It All in Your Laptop

The trail to mass market for mobile media may be led by a new millennial generation born after 2000 that is more likely to embrace the convenience of a new breed of mobile device and functionality.[30] Another way to understand this group's media adoption, writes *IPTVi Magazine* publisher Nick Snow, is that "success will rest on the outcome of that other never-ending debate: is successful TV a passive pursuit or an active engagement? I'm guessing it's a generation thing."[31]

In addition to providing handheld sports, news, and dramatic mobile video episodes, the fruits of data storage will also be driven by an extraordinary continued price/performance improvement arc. Like a *Dick Tracy* déjà vu all over again, we will soon have visual content and communications wherever we go. We wrote in 2007 that with disk drive storage capacity doubling approximately every year and a half, a 3.5-inch drive capacity would reach a terabyte by 2009. In fact, by 2008, Hitachi, Samsung, Seagate, and Western Digital *all* attained 1 TB, and we may be seeing 3 TB by 2012 according to IDC.[32] It has even been projected that, by 2015, drive capacity will grow to 16 TB (enough to hold all the music that was ever recorded) and by

[28]Streaming Media 2006, San Jose, California.
[29]http://www.mobiletechnews.com/info/2009/03/09/185536.html
[30]Anne Sweeney, Disney-ABC, "Monetizing New Distribution Platforms," April 2006.
[31]*IPTVi Magazine*, September 2006.
[32]"IDC Predicts 3 TB Hard Drives By 2012," http://www.tomshardware.com/news/IDC-HDD-SSD,5527
.html

2021 to 256 TB (640,000 hours of video, or all the video and audio ever created up until now for movies and television—73 years of continuous viewing).

The business potential is very attractive. Will there be time for a strategy, given the speed of product and market change? In typical "ready, fire, aim" fashion, the industry continues to experiment its way into the future. "We're basically 'trying everything,'" says Larry Kramer, former president of CBS Digital Media. "We're trying to put all our entertainment content on as many platforms as we can, to see how consumers accept it."[33]

Voices from the Industry

For our final reflections on IPTV and Internet video, we will consider how the myth of the blind men and the elephant provides an analogy for how today's business thought leaders and technical experts envision a world influenced by IPTV and Internet video technologies. The tale is of three blind men who had heard of, but had never seen, an elephant. When an elephant passed through their village one day, each man felt it. Upon inspection, the first blind man determined it was like a wall, the second man said it was a spear, and the third was sure it was a rope. The men had respectively felt the elephant's side, its tusk, and its tail. Each man called the other a fool.

Whether your pulse on the industry originates from news feeds, analyst reports, or the buzz at the office, most agree that today's IPTV deployments are steadily gaining game-changing momentum. From development through adoption, we are on our way to places only seen in part by the early visionaries.

The post-analog era is driving wider Internet video consumption. We continue to witness the emergence of a new online marketplace for video distribution. Studios and video bloggers alike will have a bigger and better platform for TV-grade, full-screen delivery to consumers—often without the financial, geographical, or regulatory limitations imposed by conventional broadcast systems. This "democratization of television broadcasting" is as profound as the arrival of the Internet itself. As video propagates in all directions, the transition might be parsed into old and new media characteristics something like Table 12.1.

As armchair futurists, we all speculate about the IPTV space, but here's what some of the most qualified people are telling us about the elephant.

Table 12.1 Media Empire Building Blocks

Old Media	New Media
20th century	21st century
Analog broadcast	Digital/IP format
Centralized	Distributed: personal/portable
Daily–weekly, appointment based	On-demand 24/7
Secure, authorized installments	Time-shifted, with piracy issues

[33]"Turning Content into Revenue," NAB, April 2006.

What the Business Leaders Say

Whether it's new broadband sites offering prime-time television, movies, or user-generated video content, the power of Internet video portals is a growing force this year, next year, and beyond. Also, as social media and networking spreads, a whole new way to put video to work for your business is developing.

For many, the broadcast era is over and it is distribution, not content, that is now king. "Maybe that's a temporary situation," says Chuck Vaughn, VP of Business Development at MMAX Enterprises, "but the fragmentation has shifted everything on its head, which is why everyone in Hollywood is nervous. We want to be positioned for the unplugging of the cable box when the Web supplies all the content to the three screens—PC/TV/mobile." Vaughn continues, "We want to break into the back door guerrilla style but also be positioned for distribution and monetization in the future . . . . social media is a huge part of that strategy. It's the winning model: a sense of community that supports the 'long tail' infinite storage for content. This shared experience puts user first and content second."

Many business executives have long foreseen IPTV prevailing commercially as it evolves and improves. "To me, it's more about ergonomic user experience and uniqueness of the service; this is the real challenge in the IPTV space," says Mario Mariani, former CEO of Italian alternative telecommunications provider Tiscali.[34] Companies transitioning to new IPTV service offerings seek to protect and increase revenue per user (RPU) by filling their end-to-end network.

So, filling the network with several services to increase RPU is an important goal. "Another IPTV/PC-TV challenge is the content availability," says Mariani. "The content industry is used to working with television broadcasters and is not yet well enough organized to have relationships, at least not in Europe, with ISPs and telco providers."

Can IPTV truly compete with cable? Can Internet video provide a compelling enough alternative to traditional broadcast? Nielsen research in a Q1 2009 study says that the viewers watch 153 hours video on their TV compared to 3 hours of Internet video, But even that analysis is changing as televisions have begun to ship with integrated Internet on board. One example is Yahoo! software on LG, Samsung, and Sony televisions. Yahoo! *widgets* "bring the Internet directly to the TV screen" says Patrick Barry, Yahoo! VP ConnectedTV who sees an improvement in television through a merger with Internet media and the winners ahead based on "survival of the most popular."

One of the assumptions by IPTV business leaders in Europe is that "the European customer wants a better TV experience, which means a better TV environment with HD content using an IPTV environment," says Carl Rijsbrack, former Alcatel Bell vice-president, marketing and communications. Because you can use the platform to create individual TV environments that connect subscribers together in buddy lists and consume at any time, "IPTV is here and happening—the train has already pulled out of the station," believes Rijsbrack. "TV becomes way better TV. It becomes personalized and it's a true triple-play experience."[35]

[34]Interview with Greenfield, August 2006.
[35]September 11, 2006, IBC.

For others, there will be a variety of devices that will keep consumers in touch with an expanding media experience. "The near-term is about additive media" on home, office, and mobile devices, says Disney-ABC Television president Anne Sweeney, adding that "Disney's bet is that the new technology allows content to follow you—and your money."[36]

When Showtime first announced its 3G content portal, it knew mobile broadcasting was "increasingly important . . . offering an excellent subscriber acquisition and program sampling opportunity," according to Robert Hayes, Showtime's general manager of digital media.[37] Today, many content providers have moved into high gear, such as CBS, whose free TV.com mobile application provides full episodes of programs over Wi-Fi and 3G networks, including CBS News, Sports, and Showtime.

The ability to become a producer is falling into the hands of amateurs everywhere. Some industry veterans maintain that this type of video has a long way to go before really competing with television. Ricky Gervais, co-creator of "The Office" television comedy series, argues that "you can't [create] an episode of *The Sopranos* or *24* on a little handheld digital camera."[38] However, other insiders maintain that we need to take a serious look at best practices and reconsider where it's all headed. "This is a fascinating new production and sharing of stuff, a phenomenon I find truly astounding," says Nick De Martino, director of the American Film Institute (AFI) New Media Ventures. "With a $500 computer, a $500 camera, and a $300-a-year broadband connection, you're in business. You have the pieces in place for phenomenal change in what an individual voice can become," believes De Martino. "It's epic-making change in what the Internet can do."

The advent of people's video is a new force influencing things to come. Sites such as ManiaTV Network and Blip.tv are the harbingers of online broadcasting models that are reshaping audience content. User-generated content sites have made everyone a producer. "Initially there was a lot of viral growth in terms of people sharing links and embedding videos," explains YouTube CEO Chad Hurley about his Web site's growing popularity. "There's still a lot of that going on, but we've primarily become a destination zone on video," says Hurley. "Our idea is that everyone exists on the same level; we're just creating a stage. Even with NBC [U.S. network broadcaster], we're not pushing NBC on our users. They just exist on our system like everyone else."

According to former NAB President and CEO David K. Rehr, we finally have built a strong foundation for digital TV and "are about to reinvent our industry." Rehr says, "We are about to ride a new wave of technology that will take us places that we have never been before."

What the Analysts Say

Adding to the momentum of new technologies and business models, the most influential industry players are voting with their feet. "AOL, Google, Yahoo!, MSN, Apple, major broadcast TV networks, pay-TV services, and local TV stations are

---

[36]Anne Sweeney, Disney-ABC, "Monetizing New Distribution Platforms," April 2006.
[37]www.prwebdirect.com/releases/2006/10/prweb448357.htm
[38]Interview with Greenfield, November 2006, London.

all working on ways to blend their video assets with personalized TV services," says Gerry Kaufhold, In-Stat principal analyst. He adds, "The future of television is slowly being defined online, where the big Internet portals are finding ways to blend professional video with their high-touch services that follow consumers from screen to screen during the course of a typical day."

So how do we get to this seamless new experience of tomorrow from here? IPTV is already making waves in the broadcast sector, but according to many industry analysts, it will accelerate only after a few more pieces of the puzzle fall into place.

- Web and TV programming must be better and joined together more seamlessly through a more singular format
- In many countries, including the United States, higher speed broadband is needed to distribute a competitive, scalable IPTV offering, particularly when it comes to broadcast DTV bandwidth requirements
- There must be a more uniform architecture uniting PC, STB, cable, and telcos

Another issue is service assurance. "If something goes wrong or it doesn't work, how is it reported and who's going to fix it?" asks Mark Weiss, formerly IBM's IPTV/Triple Play Solutions executive. To be successful, it will be essential to synchronize back office systems to log, monitor, and respond cohesively. "If somebody says they didn't get a movie," says Weiss, "you've got the ability to verify it."

Some would call it a new TV culture. The next-generation video combination of social networking, buddy lists, and community DVRs shared between viewers is a market driver, as is user-generated video, such as the YouTube portal where you can share video, as well as interact with friends in real time through instant messaging (IM), which delivers user-controlled content.

Whether it's a BBC documentary or political debate, ABC running the latest episode of *Lost*, or a Chinese broadcaster covering the Beijing Olympics, IPTV and communications layers are interweaving. You may be watching at the same time with a friend in your community—or on another continent—and commenting to one another through IM, or another video interface layer, just as if you were together in the same place watching the same show.

Dedicated IPTV and Web streaming both confront the same user-interface challenge in the transition from browse to search. The PC filters Internet content with increasing efficiency, but the same cannot be said for TV's ability to glean what viewers seek. "Where today you browse through channel grids and you channel surf, in the future you're going to interact with your TV set like you do with Google," according to Craig Moffett, vice-president and senior analyst at Bernstein Research. Moffett believes that "at least some of the time, you will be actively searching for what you want to watch and you'll be searching through content libraries of movies, old shows, and entertainment from the Web."[39]

---

[39]"Streaming vs. IPTV," Greenfield, Advanced Television, 2005.

What the Geeks Say

We all stand on the shoulders of giants, the forerunners who have dreamed big and then delivered the technologies that make a huge impact. We respectfully salute the geeks—counting ourselves among them—and turn to them next for an outlook on what is moving the IPTV and Internet video culture forward.

In Chapter 9, we talked about the vital role that bandwidth plays in any practical service provider offering, especially as viewers will not tolerate picture jitters or sluggish channel surfing. Imagine a world where throughput is no longer an issue, where there is enough speed and volume for all. Advances between now and 2020 are so inevitable that, by then, we'll likely look back at today's devices and interfaces and laugh at how primitive they were. Some even assert that broadband speeds will exceed 1 Gbps by 2020. While we think this is hardly likely, there will definitely be the continuing ramp in speed alluded to earlier with an expected 32 million plus broadband households with 10 Mbps or greater by 2012.[40] In addition to the rising performance and subscriber base, global IP traffic will reach 44 exabytes per month by 2012 (over six times the total traffic in 2007) with video traffic expected to reach almost 90% of consumer IP traffic.[41]

Another observer, veteran *New York Times* Silicon Valley correspondent, John Markoff, interprets tomorrow's multimedia developments and IPTV in *Coming Soon to TV Land: The Internet, Actually*:

> *At the onset of the dot-com era, large online service companies like AOL, Compuserve, and MSN tried to lock customers into electronic walled gardens of digital information.*
>
> *But it quickly became apparent that no single company could compete with the vast variety of information and entertainment sources provided on the Web.*
>
> *The same phenomenon may well overtake traditional TV providers. Potentially, IPTV could replace the 100- or 500-channel world of the cable and satellite companies with millions of hybrid combinations that increasingly blend video, text from the Web and even video-game-style interactivity.[42]*

As Google VP Bradley Horowitz (then Yahoo director of media search) once told us: "Convergence is not about smashing the TV and PC together, it's more about . . . making it 'my media' as opposed to 'mass media.'" That vision is steadily coming to pass as television continues to mature into a fully personalized, interactive "viewable-anywhere" medium. These changes facing TV "will dwarf the changes to the Internet referred to as Web 2.0," according to Forbes Magazine.

IPTV: Convergence of the Old or Something New?

The ground floor of a global 21st-century broadband network is now in place, bandwidth is increasing, and more and more content is being accessed on new hybrid

---

[40]Parks Associates.
[41]http://www.cisco.com/en/US/netsol/ns827/networking_solutions_sub_solution.html
[42]"Coming Soon to TV Land: The Internet, Actually," John Markoff, *New York Times*, January 7, 2006.

broadcast–broadband platforms. Like Metcalfe's law of networks discussed earlier in this chapter, the result of these factors will be greater than the sum of its parts. Just as the fax machine or connecting of the railroad in the 19th-century created new forms of commerce and communication and grew over subsequent decades, emerging media convergence innovations comprise a golden spike of the future.

Although new network technologies continue to appear, the business drivers are what determine success. For instance, VDSL is useful for areas with very dense pockets of population (because the useful distances are quite short), but most telecoms deployments today are leaning toward ADSL2+.

Last but not least, don't underestimate the impact of consumer design innovators—companies pushing forward on the buzz and revenues of multimedia devices and service markets. Of the many examples of additional new products and services being developed and perfected, several come to mind—disruptors that will create a place for themselves in this emerging marketplace.

From Babelgum to Blinx, Hulu to Vudu, Yahoo! to Zattoo, broadband video is coming into its own. Other compelling examples include BBC's on-demand iPlayer "catch-up" service for the Internet, Xbox games console IPTV integration, and any other hybrid solutions mentioned earlier in this book that bridge the broadcast and broadband domains.

Simply put, IPTV and online video are in their infancy. Online content providers such as Veoh, Vuze, and Joost are forerunners. The first movies merely pointed a camera at the proscenium arch stage. True cinematographic technique, special effects, and great movies came later after decades of experimentation.

Whereas TiVo lets you time shift video to watch whenever you wanted, place shifting sounded like sci-fi jargon until the Slingbox (acquired by Echostar in 2007 for $380 million) delivered your home TV or TiVo to you whether you are in Singapore or St. Louis. Slingbox brings the TV signal from the user's home TV, cable, and DVR devices to them via the Internet anywhere in the world. With the broadcast DTV and mobile compatibilities (including 3G) to deliver content over PDA and smart phones, an improved value proposition for portable media is providing access to personal media anywhere any time.

Slingbox uses a Texas Instruments DSP to digitally encode video in real time from component sources (480i to 480p, 720p and 1080i) and transmits it as a protected Windows Media Video (WMV) format for streaming at resolutions up to 640×480. Each Slingbox has a unique 32 digit alphanumeric ID and customers assign passwords to their device. Because only one SlingPlayer software client can connect to a Slingbox at a given time, the content remains personalized. Yet the practice of allowing video "retransmission" over the Internet—even though it's only to yourself—is creating waves in the entertainment business.

But it's not about the technology. "You can't underestimate the importance of delivering great experiences to the consumer," says former Slingbox CEO Blake Krikorian. "In the past the consumer didn't have as much power so things could be force fed. In this day and age, the consumer has to have a say in things and has to be delighted, but also the business models need to make sense."

Will Apple, Inc. continue to be the proactive force that brings the Mac or PC to the center of content distribution? In Apple's model, content flows into the PC and the Mac integrates "Web-based interactivity through the IPTV layer, with traditional cable, telco, and satellite as a secondary layer," says Tim Bajarin, principal analyst with Creative Strategies. "And in the short term, that may be the way that all these guys are gonna have to deal with it." According to Bajarin, their industry influence has set the standard for best user interface look and feel and "to make it much simpler to move the content from the TV to the PC—whether in the living room or upstairs." ("Den, living room, car, pocket," as Jobs puts it.)

Another increasingly popular approach is *social media*: combining online video sharing with social networking. The Joost Internet TV service, for example, attempted this by partnering with Netlog, the pan-European pageview market leader (four billion views per month). Founded by the creators of Kazaa and Skype and VC backers of Yahoo, Google, and YouTube, Sequoia Capital, they are "fixing TV," according to founder Niklas Zennström, by "removing artificial limits such as the number of channels that your cable or the airwaves can carry, and then bringing it into the Internet age, adding community features, interactivity, etc." It is designed to take the best from the new Web 2.0 culture of sharing and collaboration and combine it with legitimate rights and professional broadcast culture, like many other new services.

Software and hardware vendors are also inventing ever more powerful, cost-effective tools and are facilitating content production, storage, and distribution at a new level. Crowd-pleasing benefits of storage, compression, ingest, and playout advances are carrying us toward a "fully connected tomorrow," as former Thomson Chairman & CEO Frank Dangeard once put it, "where the consumer is in charge of the content they watch." We will no doubt continue to see greater proficiencies for collaborative content creation and rolling out on-demand services, new mobile platforms, and a commonplace broadcast DTV presence.

Some viewpoints included in this final chapter emphasize disruption. We, however, envision remarkable opportunity in change. The fully connected tomorrow may still be somewhere over the rainbow, continuing to keep us guessing about its final features. But the next phase belongs to those organizations—large or small, start-up or incumbent—willing to embrace the future by mastering the processes and markets that emerge with any new technology. We leave it for you to exploit these viewpoints and fuel the next period in this extraordinary series of events that will continue to evolve and impact the industry for years to come.

Summary

During this book's journey through the high-growth world of IPTV and Internet video we have seen that new services, business practices, and economic models are springing up. As an executive briefing, we have endeavored to provide a sound perspective on the state of the industry, inspecting technology more deeply when it seemed valuable and appropriate for the reader.

This chapter revisited the IPTV story so far and then explored the business drivers and advanced technology on the horizon that are shaping this emerging world of interactive media. It then considered the expectations surrounding these new, often overhyped developments. It considered the increasing availability of more and more types of content and programming in an everything-on-demand media universe.

We also took stock of services enabling personal and enterprise producers to create their own custom channels or programming networks. In the world of portable media, we saw how all content is going mobile, as consumers continue to hold more and more information in the palm of their hands and as devices get smaller, smarter, and more connected.

In our final reflections on IP video, we looked at how the myth of the blind men and the elephant provides an analogy for how today's thought leaders, soothsayers, and technical wizards envision the world influenced by IPTV and Internet video technologies.

Glossary

3G Third-generation mobile communications technology. Technology provides increased bandwidth, up to 128 Kbps in a moving automobile, up to 384 Kbps when a device is moving at less than walking speed, and up to 2 Mbps in stationary locations. Subject of a multibillion dollar radio spectrum auction at the dawn of the 21st century.

AAC (Advance Audio Coding) Audio coding system for MPEG-2 and MPEG-4 signals that provides up to 48 channels of audio. Frequently used at 192 kbps for 5.1 surround sound.

ADSL (Asymmetric Digital Subscriber Line) Technology that enables a standard telephone line to carry high-speed data in addition to normal voice telephony. Operates by using very high frequencies to carry data; requires DSL modem devices to be installed at customer premises and in provider facilities. Technology is termed "asymmetric" because the data rate from the service provider to the end user is higher than the data rate from the user back to the provider.

Aggregator Software designed to periodically check for, collect, and consolidate new content from remote Web sites based on a list of sites that have been "subscribed" to by the user. Many Web browsers and e-mail programs have built-in aggregator functions, as well as a number of portal Web sites.

AP (access points) Device used to provide connections for wireless PCs and other devices to a wired network, often providing some means to send and receive data from the Internet.

ATM (Asynchronous Transfer Mode) Digital multiplexing and networking standard that transports information in uniform size packets called "cells." Each cell contains 48 bytes of user data and a 5-byte header. Popularized in the 1990s for video and data transport.

ATSC (Advanced Television Systems Committee) Industry consortium originally formed in 1982 to coordinate television standards across different media. ATSC was instrumental in developing standards for digital and high-definition television broadcasts in the United States. Current standards cover many areas of digital broadcasting, including compression profiles, radio frequency modulation techniques, and other areas needed to ensure compatibility between broadcaster and viewer equipment.

Avail Time slot in linear programming feed available to a system operator for local advertisement insertion.

AVC (Advanced Video Coding) Video compression system standardized in 2003 that provides significant improvement in coding efficiency over earlier algorithms. Also known as H.264 and MPEG-4 Part 10.

Bandwidth Measurement of the network capacity or throughput, usually expressed in Mbps or kbps.

B Frame The most highly compressed type of MPEG-2 video frame; uses data of the preceding and following I or P frames.

Blu-Ray Industry standard optical disc format designed to enable record, rewrite, and play back of high-definition video.

Broadband Term used to describe signals or systems that carry a high bandwidth signal, at a speed of at least 256 kbps.

CA (Conditional Access) Policies for controlling access to video, audio, or other data files. User access, such as viewing or recording of video files, can be limited to specific categories of viewers that meet specific conditions, such as only those viewers who subscribe to a premium movie service.

Cache Short-term, temporary storage location. Commonly used in conjunction with disk drives and microprocessors to speed up data transfer by allowing larger blocks of data to be transferred in each read or write operation. Can also be used to simplify the connection between high-speed devices and low-speed networks.

Capture Process of converting raw audio and video content into files that can be manipulated by computer-based editing, production, and streaming systems.

CAS (Conditional Access System) Hardware and/or software system that enforces conditional access policies. Typically includes a mechanism for scrambling or encrypting content prior to transmission, a mechanism to permit authorized user devices to descramble or decrypt content at the user's location, and a mechanism to securely distribute the required descrambling or decryption keys to authorized users.

CAT5 (Category 5 Unshielded Twisted Pair Cable) Type of data communication cable certified for use in 10BaseT and 100BaseT (Ethernet) network connections.

CAT6 (Category 6 Unshielded Twisted Pair Cable) Type of data communication cable certified for use in 1000BaseT (Gigabit Ethernet) network connections.

CATV (Cable Television or Community Antenna Television) System that distributes video programming to subscribers through the use of broadband fiber and coaxial cables. Modern systems offer several hundred channels of broadcast and on-demand video programming, as well as data and voice services.

CDN (Content Delivery Network) Network of distributed servers used to deliver content such as Web pages or video/audio files to users in multiple geographic areas. Can also be used for streaming applications.

Closed Captioning Process that adds text captions to video images that can be displayed on suitably equipped televisions. These captions are called "closed" because they are not visible on-screen unless the viewer chooses to display them. In many cases these captions will include descriptions of sound effects in addition to a text rendition of any spoken dialog.

CO (Central Office) Facility used by a telephone company or other service provider to deliver signals to subscribers. Normally, a telephone CO will contain equipment that is used to process user telephone calls; it may also contain data or video transport and processing equipment.

Coaxial Cable or connector that contains two conductors, one in the center of the cable and another that surrounds it completely, separated by an insulating layer. Coaxial cables are used frequently for video applications because of their superior performance with both analog and digital video signals.

Codec Device or software that encodes (compresses) and decodes (decompresses) digital stream or data.

CSS (Content Scramble System) Method used to scramble the content of DVDs, intended to prevent them from being duplicated or played on unauthorized playback devices.

Decoder Device used to convert compressed audio and/or video content into original form, using technologies such as MPEG and JPEG.

Digital Turnaround Process of taking video and audio signals that are encoded in one format and converting them into another format. This normally occurs under the control of a service provider to help standardize the operation of a multi-channel system and is a widespread practice in IPTV systems.

DOCSIS (Data Over Cable Interface Specification) Industry standard that specifies how cable modems communicate over cable television lines.

Domain Name System Translation system that takes easy-to-remember names (i.e., "elsevier.com") and converts them into IP addresses required for Internet communication.

Download and Play Content delivery method wherein a file containing compressed video/audio data is downloaded onto the user's device before playback begins. With download and play, a two-minute video could take 10 seconds to download on a fast network, or 10 minutes to download on a slow network.

DRM (Digital Rights Management) Generic term used to describe various mechanisms for controlling users' access to digital content. This can include a variety of functions, including encryption, scrambling, and copy protection, which are commonly applied to copyrighted or other proprietary works.

DSL (Digital Subscriber Line) Popular mechanism for providing high-speed data connections to users over existing telephone wiring. Several different generations of technology have come to market, with varying combinations of speed and useful distance.

DSLAM (Digital Subscriber Line Access Multiplexer) Provides a high-speed data conduit between multiple DSLs and the high bandwidth network backbone.

DTH (Direct-To-Home) Satellite television broadcasting system in which programming is transmitted directly to antennas mounted on subscribers' premises. Differs from other satellite-based services that deliver programming to Cable TV, IPTV, and terrestrial service providers who then distribute programming to viewers.

DTV (Digital Television) System for broadcasting video using compressed digital signals. Can be either standard-definition or high-definition video images. Employs an analog 6-MHz television channel that has been converted into a digital transmission channel capable of carrying 19 Mbps or more of data traffic.

DVB (Digital Video Broadcasting) Organization formed in Europe to create standards for broadcasting digital television signals. Includes a variety of distribution methods (see DVB-H) and formats that can be used in the content–creation process.

DVB-H (Digital Video Broadcasting–Handheld) One standard for delivering live television to handheld devices competing with other standards such as DMB/DAB and FLO (Forward Link Only).

DVD (Digital Versatile Disc) High-density, removable storage medium commonly used for recording high-quality digital video and audio signals. Widely used for movie and other video content sales/rentals to consumers; has displaced VHS tapes as most popular format for new consumer purchases.

DVI (Digital Visual Interface) Connector used to carry digital video signals between signal sources (PCs, DVD players, STBs) and displays of various types. Supports High-bandwidth Digital Content Protection protocol that can be used to ensure that content is distributed only to proper display devices and not to recording equipment that could be used to pirate video content. This 24-pin connector can now be found on many high-performance video displays.

DVR (Digital Video Recorder) Device that allows the recording and playback of content under the control of an end user; normally based on video compression and hard disk technology. TiVo was one of the first brand names for this technology.

EAS (Emergency Alert System) Government-mandated system for broadcasters in the United States used for transmitting emergency alerts to the public in the event of a natural or man-made disaster or other emergency.

Encoder Device used to convert raw audio and/or video content into compressed form, using technologies such as MPEG and JPEG.

Encryption Technique used to make data unreadable to parties other than the sender and intended recipients. Normally accomplished through the use of a mathematical operation performed on raw data in conjunction with a key known only to the sender and the recipients. Encryption algorithms are considered strong when third parties that do not have access to the key are unable to recover original data.

EOD (Everything On Demand) Potential future video content delivery concept where all content is delivered to users at the time of their choosing; the complete elimination of linear programming and scheduling.

EPG (Electronic Program Guide) An on-screen display that allows viewer navigation of television programs scheduled for broadcast and available for VOD playback.

ES (Elementary Stream) Term used in MPEG systems to describe raw compressed data fed into a video or an audio decoder. These streams can also be converted into other forms for recording (see PS, Program Stream) or transport (see TS, Transport Stream).

Feeder Plant Portion of a telephone network that transports signals between local central offices and remote terminals. Remote terminals are in turn connected by means of local loops to individual houses over twisted pair copper or other technology.

Firewall Device used at junction point between two networks to ensure that certain types of data on one network do not get transmitted to another network. Commonly used when connecting private LANs to the Internet to protect local users from harmful data or unwanted probes.

Flash Popular multimedia platform available from Adobe Systems that is one of the most widely used methods of adding animation, video, and interactivity to a Web site.

Forward Error Correction (FEC) Technology used to identify and correct transmission errors in digital network feeds. Adds variable amount of overhead to content streams.

FTTH (Fiber To The Home) System for distributing high-speed data and video services directly to customer premises using optical fiber for the entire link. Also known as Fiber To The Premises (FTTP). Contrast with DSL and HFC networks, both of which typically employ fiber in portions of the network but use electrical cables for connection to customers.

GB (Gigabyte) Storage capacity equal to 1024 Megabytes of computer memory. Also defined as 1 billion bytes on a hard disk drive.

Gbps (Gigabit per second) Data transmission speed of 1 billion bits per second.

GigE (Gigabit Ethernet) LAN data transmission standard operating at 1 Gbps, standardized in IEEE 802.3.

Group of Pictures (GOP) A series of frames in an MPEG system consisting of a single I frame and zero or more P and B frames.

HD (High Definition) Video image with resolution greater than standard definition. Typical formats include 720-line progressively scanned images, 1080-line interlaced images, among many others. Many HD signals have an aspect ratio of 16:9.

HDCP (High-Bandwidth Digital Content Protection) DRM technology used between HD receivers and digital displays to prevent unauthorized copying of digital content files.

HDMI (High-Definition Multimedia Interface) High-performance digital audio and video connector system used to connect STB, Blu-Ray Disc players, and HD displays.

HDTV (High-Definition Television) Broadcast version of HD signal, typically compressed to 18 Mbps or lower to fit into a single DTV broadcast channel.

Head End In a Cable TV or IPTV system, the source of video and other programming distributed to numerous subscribers.

HFC (Hybrid Fiber Coax) Architecture used commonly in Cable TV distribution systems in which fiber optic cable is used for long-distance connections from the head end into local areas and coaxial cables are used to distribute the signals into subscriber premises. This has the benefit of providing high-bandwidth, low-loss fiber optic transport for analog and digital signals over long distances without the expense of having to install fiber optic receivers in every customer's location.

Home Gateway Device that provides connectivity between an in-home network and an external network such as DSL, Cable TV or FTTH. May provide storage or other functions for HPNA or similar networks.

Homes passed Number of residences where a network is physically present and available for connection to any residences that want to become subscribers.

HPNA (Home Phoneline Networking Alliance) An industry organization with technology members such as AT&T, HP, IBM, and Intel that explores ways to establish home networking standards that drive innovation and interoperability between telecom and IT data, device, and service providers.

HTTP (HyperText Transfer Protocol) Primary protocol used on the World Wide Web to provide communications between clients and servers. Much of the information transported by HTTP consists of Web pages and related data. HTTP is stateless, meaning that each transaction is self-contained and that there is no built-in mechanism to associate a server with a particular client. To get around this limitation, many servers issue "cookies" to clients to enable the server to keep track of the status of different clients.

Hub Data communications device used in twisted pair Ethernet networks to connect multiple circuits within the same domain.

Hulu A commercial streaming video Web site started as a $100 million joint venture between NBC Universal and Fox (News Corp), with funding by Providence Equity Partners to bring prime-time video programming to Internet users.

IETF (Internet Engineering Task Force) Group of engineers that develop solutions and specifications needed to provide a common framework for operation of the Internet. The IETF is responsible for creating the technical content of RFCs that make up the standards that govern operation of the Internet.

I Frame Type of MPEG frame that is intracoded, that is, a frame that does not depend on data from any other frames. I frames typically require the most amount of data to encode, and are used by the decoder whenever a new stream is presented, such as during a channel change.

Impulse PPV Method used by consumers to order Video on Demand (VOD) services offered on a pay-per-view (PPV) basis. With Impulse PPV, subscribers can simply use their remote control to order VOD content, with the charges normally being deducted from a prearranged account. This contrasts with the method used on many traditional PPV systems in which viewers call a telephone number displayed on their screen to order VOD content by speaking with a customer service agent.

Interactive TV Video programming style that allows viewers to participate in various ways through a user interface with video content they are receiving.

Internet Global network that provides interconnection among a large community of data providers and users. The Internet is used on a daily basis by millions of users for communication, reference, and entertainment; it provides a common medium for a diverse set of applications that support many modern business, government, and personal activities.

Internet Video Video content delivered in discrete segments selected by individual Web viewers for viewing on a display connected to a personal computer or other Internet-enabled device.

IP (Internet Protocol) Standard set of rules for formatting and transporting data across the Internet and other networks that use packetized datagrams for communication. These rules include a standard format for headers that appear on each packet and a mechanism for addressing packets so that they can be sent from a source to a destination. The standard that we call IP today was defined in RFC 791 in September 1981 for the Defense Advanced Research Projects Agency of the U.S. government; it is now part of the set of standards maintained by the IETF.

IP Address A 32-bit number that provides unique identification of each data transmitter and receiver on an IP network. Often represented in dotted decimal form, such as 129.35.76.177.

IPTV A two-way digital broadcast signal over broadband that uses STBs and is delivered over switched telephone or cable networks. Similar to traditional Cable TV, satellite, and broadcast television, where continuous channels of programming are delivered to consumers for viewing on television sets.

IRD (Integrated Receiver/Decoder) Device used in satellite television systems to receive an incoming signal and decode it into a video signal. Often includes circuits necessary to descramble protected content and to convert digital satellite signals into analog or digital video signals that are compatible with video displays and other processing devices.

ISO (International Organization for Standardization) International body made up of member organizations from around the world that defines and establishes international standards in a wide variety of areas.

ISO/IEC The International Organization for Standardization and the International Electrotechnical Commission have a joint committee for developing standards on information and communications technology. Many of the MPEG standards have been approved by this committee and so carry the designation ISO/IEC before their number.

ISP (Internet Service Provider) Company or group that provides network access to the Internet for business and individuals, generally on a fee-for-service basis.

Jitter buffer A bank of memory in a video or audio receiver used to temporarily store packets prior to processing, allowing the receiver to use a smoothed clock rate to extract the packets for decoding.

JPEG A standard method of compression for digital images established by the Joint Photographic Experts Group.

kbps (kilobit per second) Data transmission rate equal to 1000 bits per second.

kbyte (kilobyte) 1024 bytes of data.

Key (Encryption Key) Secret digital value that is manipulated along with user data by an encryption algorithm to produce an encoded message. Because only the sender and the receiver possess the key to an encoded message, other parties cannot understand the message, provided the encryption algorithm has not been compromised.

LAN (Local Area Network) Data communications network that covers a local area, such as a house, a business office, or a small building. Most LAN technologies are limited to transmission distances on the order of hundreds of meters.

LEO (Local End Office) Portion of an IPTV network closest to viewer where video signals are converted into the form that will be delivered to each individual household.

Lip-sync Property of video and audio signals in which both are aligned in time so that on-screen images of lip motions match the voice sounds. When lip-sync is not present, video programming can be annoying to watch.

Macroblock Fundamental working unit of the MPEG compression system that contains a 16×16 pixel portion of one frame or field of a video sequence. Often used to describe a deteriorated MPEG image in which portions of the image have been replaced with single color blocks that occupy a 16×16 pixel portion of the displayed image; this is normally caused by missing or corrupt data in a compressed video stream that is being processed by an MPEG decoder.

MB (Megabyte) Storage capacity equal to 1024 kilobytes of computer memory.

Mbps (Megabit per second) Data transmission rate equal to 1 million bits per second.

Metadata Literally, "data about data." Metadata is used to describe the contents of digital files, with the goal of making the files easier to identify and work with. Metadata about video content may include information such as the title of the work, the duration, the format, and other useful information. Often, some metadata is inserted into the video stream itself to allow automatic identification of the content of the video. An analogy for metadata would be a label on the outside of a videotape cassette, which allows a person to find a specific piece of material without needing to view the actual content of each tape.

Metcalfe's Law States that a network's value is related to the square of the number of users of the system. Robert Metcalfe formulated the axiom in regard to Ethernet; it helps explain the additive effects and value of Internet and wireless communication networks.

MhP (Multimedia Home Platform) Middleware standard developed by DVB that defines the interfaces between operating system software and user applications on set top boxes. Used to simplify the tasks of software developers and STB designers and to provide a common platform for development and deployment.

Middleware Series of software functions or services that link specific components (such as application servers, VOD servers, and STBs) and application software (such as conditional access control, billing systems, and interactive services).

Mid-roll Advertising displayed to viewers during content playout, thereby temporarily interrupting the selected video and audio program. Contrast with Pre-roll and Post-roll.

Moore's Law A prediction about transistor density as applied to processors that has come to apply to a doubling of information technology price–performance every 18 months.

Motion Estimation A key part of the compression process used in MPEG. Successive frames of video are analyzed and compared to determine if any portions of the image have moved. If so, the MPEG decoder can be instructed to simply move one or more macroblocks from one location in the image to another location in the following frame.

Motion Vectors These describe the motion of a macroblock from one position to another between two successive frames of a video image, including both direction and magnitude of the motion.

MPEG (Moving Pictures Experts Group) A committee first formed in 1988 to develop international standards for video and encoding for digital storage. Numerous standards have been produced by this group and given international approval by ISO/IEC. Today, the MPEG acronym is used to describe a wide range of compression formats.

MPEG LA (MPEG Licensing Authority) Providers of consolidated patent licenses for MPEG technology.

MPLS (Multi-Protocol Label Switching) Technology used in a variety of pocket transport networks to simplify the functions performed by core routers and improve the flow of many different types of data.

Multicast Data transmission from a single source to multiple, simultaneous destinations. Contrast with unicast.

Musicam Another name for MPEG Layer 2 audio. This is used in DAB (Digital Audio Broadcasting) and DVB (Digital Video Broadcasting) systems in Europe.

Narrowcast A content distribution method that efficiently delivers programming to a small audience dispersed throughout a large population. Contrast with "broadcast," which distributes content to a large audience within a large population.

NTSC (National Television System Committee) Committee that in the early 1950s selected the color television broadcast standard for the United States. NTSC is often used as an abbreviation for the 525-line, 29.97 frames per second, interlaced video standard used in North America, Japan, and a number of other countries.

NVOD (Near Video On Demand) Video delivery system that simulates some of the attributes of a video-on-demand system without the individual video stream control capabilities. One common form of NVOD is sometimes called staggercasting, in which multiple copies of a program are played starting at five-minute intervals, thereby limiting any individual viewer to no more than a five-minute wait before his or her program begins to play.

OCAP (OpenCable Application Platform) Middleware interface standard developed by CableLabs to permit portability of software applications and STBs for cable operators in the United States. Based in part on MhP standards.

OTA (Over the Air) Television broadcast technique that uses standard radio frequency transmission to aerials on receiving televisions, also called terrestrial broadcast.

Packet A variable length data container that can be transported over an IP network.

PAL (Phase Alternating Line) Color video signal that is commonly used in Europe, where the individual lines alternate in phase from one line to the next. Also used as shorthand for the 625-line, 25 frames per second interlaced video standard used extensively in Europe and other countries around the world.

PC (Personal Computer) Generic term used to describe desktop and portable computers, often those based on Intel/AMD processors and running an operating system supplied by Microsoft. Can also be used to describe Macintosh- and Linux-based computers in some contexts.

Peer-to-Peer File distribution system that relies on computers to act as "peers" instead of as clients and servers; each device can act simultaneously as both a receiver of files and a sender of files. Commonly used for both legal and illegal sharing of large content files; also used in some live video distribution systems.

PES (Packetized Elementary Stream) Term used in MPEG to describe an elementary stream that has been divided into packets, prior to further processing. Because PES packets can be hundreds of kilobytes long, they typically need further processing into transport stream packets before they are sent over an IP network.

P Frame Type of MPEG video frame that uses data from a prior I frame. Typically contains more data than a B frame but less than an I frame.

PID (Packet Identifier) Method used to identify each of the different video and audio content streams contained in an MPEG transport stream. Each packet contained in a transport stream can have data from only one elementary stream, such as a video or an audio ES, and each packet has a single PID. A demultiplexer can easily locate the streams it desires by sorting the incoming packets by their PID.

Placeshifting Transporting video programming from a source such as a user's home TV, cable STB, DVR, and so on to a destination such as a user's PC or wireless device over the Internet.

Podcasting Online media publishing that enables producers to upload content files and audience to download or subscribe to regular feeds that retrieve new files as they become available.

PONs (passive optical networks) A last-mile networking technology entirely made up of optical fibers and passive optical components between the service provider and the customer. No active elements (such as electronics, lasers, optical detectors, or optical amplifiers) are present between the service provider and the customer.

Portable Media General term referring to the growing mobility of audio, video, and image content files that can be accessed wirelessly and carried compactly on ever more powerful, streamlined devices with greater disk drive capacity. These content files are typically downloaded or streamed by way of a high-speed network.

Post Office Protocol–Version 3 (pop3) The most recent version of a client/server protocol for receiving and storing email by an Internet service provider. Used for receiving incoming mail by most PCs.

Post-roll Advertising displayed to viewers after content playout has ended; contrast with Pre-roll and Mid-roll. Generally not terribly effective in environments where the user is allowed to select other content streams at any time.

PPV (Pay-Per-View) Method for charging viewers for the right to watch or listen to a specific piece of content for a specific time. Rights may be limited to a single showing of the content or may expire after a designated period of time (such as 24 hours).

Pre-roll Advertising displayed to viewers before content playout begins; contrast with Mid-roll and Post-roll.

Progressive Download and Play Internet video delivery technique where the video content is broken up into a series of small files, each of which is downloaded in turn to the user's device during playback. Contrast with streaming and download and play.

PS (Program Stream) An MPEG stream that contains one or more packetized elementary streams that have a common clock source. These streams can be different types (such as video and audio) and can be played in synchronization. Program streams are not well suited for transport, but do work well for recording purposes and disk storage, including DVDs.

Push VOD (Push Video on Demand) Technique for storing VOD content in user STBs for playback under user control. Removes need for high-speed video data connection to central servers used in normal VOD systems.

PVR (Personal Video Recorder) See DVR.

QoS (Quality of Service) Mechanism in IP and other data networks that allows some data flows to have higher priority over other flows that share the same communications line or device.

Quadruple play A combined telecommunications service offering that consists of Internet access, television, telephone, and wireless services.

QuickTime A software framework developed by Apple Computer to integrate a set of multimedia applications and functionality that handle video, audio, image, animation, music, and text.

Remote Terminal Portion of traditional telephone network where digital telephony signals are converted into standard two-wire analog telephony signals. Often used to provide physical space, power, and so on for installing DSLAM devices.

Return Path Communications channel flowing in the opposite direction to the principal flow of information. Term popularized in cable television applications in which many networks were originally constructed to operate in one direction only (from cable TV provider to subscriber homes). A return path is required for two-way applications such as data or voice communication.

RF (Radio Frequency) High-frequency electrical signals capable of radiating from or being received by an antenna. A huge variety of devices use RF signals, including AM/FM radios, televisions, cellular phones, satellite receivers, and all modern computing devices. The typical frequency range is between 3 kHz and 30 GHz.

RJ-45 Standard connector for 10BaseT and subsequent data communication standards used commonly for Ethernet communication. The RJ-45 connector is a small plastic clip with up to eight wires that is very similar in appearance to the four- or six-wire connectors that are widely used for connecting telephone sets to wall plugs. "RJ" stands for "Registered Jack."

Router (1) In IP networks, a device responsible for processing the headers on IP packets and forwarding them toward their ultimate destination. (2) In video networks, a device that provides switching of connections between video sources and their destinations.

RTCP (Real Time Control Protocol) Data transport control protocol that works in conjunction with RTP for transporting real-time media streams. Includes functions to support synchronization between different media types (e.g., audio and video) and to provide information to streaming applications about network quality, number of viewers, identity of viewers, etc.

RTP (Real Time Protocol or Real-time Transport Protocol) Data transport protocol specifically designed for transporting real-time signals such as streaming video and audio. RTP is often used in conjunction with UDP and provides important functions such as packet sequence numbering and packet time stamping. RTP is used in conjunction with RTCP.

RTSP (Real Time Streaming Protocol) Protocol used to set up and control real-time streams. Commonly used to create links on Web sites that point to streaming media files.

SAP (Session Announcement Protocol) Broadcast IP packets used to send out information about each of the multicast streams available on a network, along with information that devices need in order to connect to a multicast.

SD (Standard Definition) Video image with a resolution defined in standards popularized in the 1950s and widely used for television around the world. For 60-Hz NTSC systems, the video image is composed of 525 interlaced horizontal lines, of which 485 represent the actual image. For 50-Hz PAL systems, the video image is composed of 625 interlaced horizontal lines, of which 576 represent the actual image. Both of these standards use a 4:3 aspect ratio.

SHE (Super Head End) In a cable TV or large IPTV system, a SHE is used commonly to receive signals from various sources and distribute them to head ends or VSOs located within the territory of an MSO. It is not uncommon for one SHE to provide service to several hundred thousand subscribers.

Simple Mail Transfer Protocol (smtp) An Internet standard for electronic mail (e-mail) transmission across Internet Protocol networks. Used for outbound mail delivery by most PCs.

SLA (Service Level Agreement) A contractual agreement between a carrier and a customer that specifies the level of network performance that the carrier will deliver to the customer. This often includes a set of network performance guarantees (minimum availability, maximum error rate, etc.) and a set of remedies (such as billing credits) if these minimums are not met.

Slingbox Brand name for one of the first commercially successful TV devices that delivers a TV signal from the user's home TV, cable, and DVR devices to the user over the Internet anywhere in the world. See placeshifting.

Smart Card Small plastic card or chip that contains a microprocessor and memory. Often used for storing and transporting decryption and authorization codes for devices such as set top boxes or mobile phones.

SMPTE (Society of Motion Picture and Television Engineers) U.S.-based organization that, among other things, develops standards for movie and video technology. For more information, go to www.smpte.org.

Social Networking Web interaction between users facilitated by voice, chat (IM), Web pages, sharing of videos, buddy lists in a collaborative manner; often described as a characteristic of Web 2.0.

Soft Real Time Video transport application in which video signals are transported in the same amount of time as it takes to display them. Video signals may be live or prerecorded for soft real time; significant end-to-end delays are acceptable.

S/PDIF (Sony/Philips Digital Interface Format) Digital audio format used commonly in consumer audio playback equipment.

Staggercast One common form of near video on demand content delivery in which multiple copies of a program are played starting every few minutes, thereby limiting any individual viewer to no more than a few minutes wait before the selected program begins to play.

STB (Set Top Box) Device used in conjunction with video delivery systems that performs a variety of tasks, including signal processing, demodulation, decryption, and digital-to-analog conversion. STBs are normally required for DSL-based IPTV and DTH satellite television systems and are frequently required on Cable TV systems.

Streaming Method for delivering video or other content over a network in a continuous flow at a rate that matches the speed at which data are consumed by the display device.

Streaming engine Software package that resides on a video server that is optimized for producing live or real-time video streams to the viewer.

Subtitles Text added to motion picture and television content for many purposes, including content display in another language. When content is subtitled, the text becomes part of the video image and is displayed to all viewers. Contrast this with closed captioning in the United States, which can be displayed or hidden upon viewer command.

Supertrunk High-performance link used commonly in Cable TV applications to transmit multichannel signals from one head end to another. These signals can be either analog or digital, depending on the distances and the application.

S-video Analog video signal in which the chroma and luma signals are carried over separate signal paths. This can improve video quality in comparison to a composite signal by eliminating the need to separate the chroma and luma signals in the television display.

Switch In Ethernet networks, a device that provides multiple ports, each having a separate logical and physical network interface. This function eliminates the possibility of packet collisions between devices on separate ports of the switch, thereby improving overall system performance.

Tagging The assignment of short (one or two word) descriptions to content files to assist text-based search engines in identifying and locating nontextual data files. Can be assigned by the content owner/original poster or by other users, depending on the features provided by the host Web site.

TB (Terabyte) Storage capacity equal to 1024 GB.

TCP (Transmission Control Protocol) Reliable data transfer protocol used in IP networks that offers connection-oriented data transport, along with automatic data transfer rate control and retransmission of corrupted packets. One of the most widely used data transport protocols, TCP is used throughout the public Internet. However, for live or streaming media signals, RTP over UDP is often a better choice.

Telepresence Advanced form of videoconferencing where audio, video, and room furnishings are optimized to give a strong impression to users that they are in the same room as the other parties of the conference.

Timeshifting Practice of recording a broadcast television program at one time using a DVR or other device and viewing the program at a later, more convenient time.

TiVo Brand name for one of the pioneering types of DVR (see DVR).

Transcoding Process of converting a video signal that is encoded in one technology (say MPEG-2) into another technology (say MPEG-4).

Transrating Process of changing the bit rate of a compressed video stream.

Triple Play A combined telecommunications service offering that consists of Internet, television, and telephone services.

tru2way Industry standard developed by CableLabs to support interactive television applications for cable TV systems based on Java. One particular advantage over previous systems is that much of the software, including portions of the conditional access system, is downloadable to simplify software updates and improve security.

True Streaming Internet video delivery technique where a video signal is delivered to a viewing device in real time and is displayed to the viewer immediately. Contrast with download and play.

TS (Transport Stream) Standard method used in MPEG for converting PES streams into a stream of packets that can easily be transported, say, over an IP network, a satellite link, or a digital television broadcast to a home. Each TS packet is a fixed 188 bytes long, although FEC data can be added, bringing the TS packet size up to 204 or 208 bytes. Note that IP packets for MPEG signals generally contain multiple transport stream packets.

TV 2.0 Reference to the next generation of interactivity, on-demand, and personalization of video programming delivered over traditional broadcast or broadband networks much like the advances referred to in the related term Web 2.0.

UDP (User Datagram Protocol) Data transfer protocol used on IP networks that offers connectionless, stateless data transport. It is often used in video transport applications (along with RTP) because it offers low overhead and does not provide automatic rate reductions and packet retransmissions (supplied by TCP) that can interfere with video transport.

Ultrawide band (UWB) Radio technology that can be used at very low energy levels for short-range, high-bandwidth communications by using a large portion of the radio spectrum. Often proposed as a method for delivering high-definition video over wireless links within a viewer's home.

Unicast Data transmission from a single source to a single destination. Contrast with multicast.

Upconvert Video processing technique used to convert an SD signal into an HD signal.

UTP (Unshielded Twisted Pair) Form of electrical cable used to transmit data signals, including a variety of forms of Ethernet.

VC-1 Video compression technique standardized as SMPTE 421M. Formerly known as Windows Media 9.

VDSL (Very high-speed Digital Subscriber Line) Digital Subscriber Line technology capable of delivering a large amount of bandwidth. First-generation standard provides 52 Mbps up to 1000 feet (300 meters) from source. Speeds in this range are generally required to deliver multiple simultaneous HD video streams to multiple television sets over a single DSL circuit.

Video Blogging (also called vlogging) Delivery of video stories, news, or other coverage over the Web in the form of a log, report, or updated communications series from amateurs or professionals. Like podcasting, it often takes advantage of syndication, which allows other Web users to subscribe to content feeds of their choice.

VOD (Video On Demand) Process for delivering video programming to viewers when they want it. Commonly includes the ability to skip ahead (fast-forward) or rewind the video signal under user control.

VoIP (Voice over IP) Method for voice telephony that uses IP networks in place of the public switched telephone network.

VSO (Video Serving Office) Portion of a large IPTV network where local programming is processed for distribution to CO/RT equipment for distribution to IPTV viewers.

Walled Garden A Web browsing environment where user navigation is restricted to content and navigation offered by a service provider.

WAN (Wide Area Network) Network that connects two or more network segments across a significant geographic distance—across a city or around the world.

Web 2.0 Term attributed to O'Reilly Media Web 2.0 conference in 2004 that refers to the so-called second generation of Internet applications that support communications, collaboration, and communities in the form of social networking, multimedia, wikis, and blogs.

Wi-Fi Wireless local area data networking technology, also known as 802.11. Found on a wide variety of PCs, most new laptops, and a variety of handheld devices.

xDSL (Digital Subscriber Line) In this abbreviation, "x" represents any one of a selection of words, including "A" for Asymmetric DSL, "H" for High Speed DSL, and others. xDSL is a generic term intended to mean "any of a variety of forms of DSL."

(Ad) Zapping Practice of skipping ads by the viewer through controlling program playback over a DVR or VOD system.

Index

Note: page numbers followed by *f* indicates figures, *b* indicates boxes and *t* indicates tables.